Telling the Whole Story

Telling the Whole Story

Reading and Preaching Old Testament Stories

JOHN C. HOLBERT

CASCADE *Books* · Eugene, Oregon

TELLING THE WHOLE STORY
Reading and Preaching Old Testament Stories

Cascade Books
An Imprint of Wipf and Stock Publishers
199 W. 8th Ave., Suite 3
Eugene, OR 97401

www.wipfandstock.com

ISBN 13: 978-1-62032-217-8

Cataloging-in-Publication data:

Holbert, John C.

Telling the whole story : reading and preaching Old Testament stories / John C. Holbert.

xii + 206 pp. ; 23 cm. Includes bibliographical references.

ISBN 13: 978-1-62032-217-8

1. Bible. O.T.—Homiletical use. 2. Preaching. 3. Bible. O.T.—Sermons. I. Title.

BS 1191.5 H656 2013

Manufactured in the U.S.A.

Contents

Introduction

I N SPEAKING OF SOME well-known fairy tales, Frederick Buechner writes:

> In each case, a strange world opens up when it chooses to open
> up and when they enter it things happen that in the inner world
> of who they are and the outer world of where they ordinarily live
> their lives couldn't possibly happen.[1]

In this sentence one discovers the three basic reasons for the existence of
this book. First, and primarily, the Bible, like the fairy tales of Cinderella,
*The Lion, the Witch, and the Wardrobe, The Wizard of Oz, The Lord of the
Rings*, and a host of others, presents to us a strange world, an extraordinary
world, an alternative reality to the one we customarily inhabit. And, like the
fairy tales, the Bible presents to us truth, not always or necessarily historical truth, but truth that "rings true" both to our inner and outer worlds.
But more. The Bible's truth is Truth with a capital "T." Somehow, even in a
postmodern context where truth is relativized by those claiming it, where it
is said that there can be no real capital "T" truths, the Bible reaches out to
us and lures us to enter its Truth. We preachers are called to be purveyors
of that Truth above all other truths. Our vocation begins and ends in the
Bible, however we understand and define and nuance our relationship to it.

By making these claims about the Bible's truth, I do not at all imply
that we are biblicists, fundamentalists or literalists. The Bible's truth is not
always to be found in its literal details. Indeed, in some of those details
can be found much mischief for a twenty-first-century world. Surely, no
Christian person would attempt to live by *all* that the old book says. For
example, though Deuteronomy enjoins its readers not to eat "the meat of
the pig," because it has a divided hoof and does not chew cud (like a cow?)
(Deut 14:8), few Christians today (with some exceptions to be sure) would
avoid the smell and taste of morning bacon, thinking they would thereby
be closer to the will of God. The health issue of cholesterol is for most a far

---

1. Buechner, *Telling the Truth*, 78.

more important truth for bacon avoidance. And more seriously, the public murder by stoning of a rebellious son, who is a "glutton and a drunkard" who will not obey his parents, is not a practice that should be followed by any rational person today (Deut 21:18–21). Such food "truths" and punishment "truths" can be fixed in their ancient contexts, their rationales argued over by scholars of the text, but to apply them in some sort of literal way in our century would be monstrous.[2] The Bible's truth is often to be sought elsewhere than in its very specific ancient prescriptions against human behaviors. This fact is particularly important in our day when a handful of Bible verses is being used to demean and reject significant numbers of homosexual persons from full participation in society and church.[3]

The second reason for this book articulated by the Buechner quotation is that the Bible's strangeness opens up on the inner world of who we are. In the light of the Bible's alternative reality, our personal realities are illuminated, making possible our own transformations into something more like God had in mind for us from our creation. In countless ways, the biblical story calls for us to examine ourselves in the beams of its searchlight that we might more clearly see who we are and who we can become. Jeremiah calls out that there is no need for us to continue our idolatrous ways, for as we love to say "as the Lord lives," our calling on God in this fashion is nothing less than a "false swearing" (Jer 5:2). One can quickly surmise what the old prophet would say to a twenty-first-century USA that bids God to "bless America," while forty-six million of its citizens have no easy access to health care insurance, while nearly 10 percent of its children are hungry each night, and while residents of a Gulf Coast ravaged by monster storms in the late summer of 2005 still wait eagerly for assistance to rebuild their shattered lives. Perhaps two trillion dollars are spent on an unpopular war in Iraq, while an equally unpopular conflict in Afghanistan grinds on. In the face of this outright hypocrisy, Jeremiah, in full alternative mode, promises divine surgery for each of us as our hearts become the tablets on which God will write a divine covenant, a covenant so clear and so lasting that all preachers and teachers will need to look for other work, since all

---

2. See, for example, good summaries of the scholarly work on these issues in Nelson, *Deuteronomy*, 174–82 for the food laws and 260–61 for the rebellious son.

3. The issue of the full inclusion of homosexual persons in the society and in the life of the church is highly contentious. Some helpful resources are: Thornburg and Dean, editors, *Finishing the Journey*; Scanzoni and Mollenkott, *Is the Homosexual My Neighbor?*; Horner, *Jonathan Loved David*; Sapp, *Sexuality, the Bible, and Science*; Rogers, *Jesus, the Bible, and Homosexuality*.

of God's creatures without exception will at last know God completely (Jer 31:31–34).

And in a similar manner, but with a slight change of metaphor, the prophet Ezekiel announces that the God of Israel will also perform surgery, but this time will remove all those hearts of stone to be replaced by hearts of flesh, hearts that will finally enable them to follow God's statutes and ordinances, both of which they have broken with alacrity from their days in the wilderness (Ezek 36:26–28). Thus both Jeremiah and Ezekiel announce that God will transform the lives of God's people, lives that they cannot transform on their own, no matter how carefully they give attention to the Dalai Lama or Dr. Phil or Donald Trump. The very claim that we need God to transform us is a very different way to view our lives encased in a world of individualistic entrepreneurship. "When the going gets tough, the tough get going," we claim. But in the strange world of the Bible, when the going gets tough, all turn to God for healing and transformation.

The third reason for the book, as enumerated by Buechner, is that the Bible opens out on the world where we live our lives. In fact, the Bible wants to say that there are finally no easy distinctions between our inner worlds that need transformation and the worlds outside us that need transformation, too. Both inner and outer worlds are addressed by the Bible, and the Bible does not demand that either transformation must precede the other. It is often said that we must be personally changed before society can be changed, and there is a certain rationality in that claim. However, the prophet Amos, for example, spends the bulk of his angry words denouncing a society blind to its rotten institutions, blithely living their lives completely unaware of the societal cancer in their midst. His shocking words of 5:21–23 pronounce the divine abhorrence of all of the most treasured ways of worship practiced by the deeply religious Israelites at the sacred shrine of Bethel: their colorful pilgrimage festivals, their eager congregational assemblies, their sumptuous offerings, their fine singing, their choral masterpieces accompanied by well-tuned and well-played instruments. The outer world that they have created is as far from the desires of God as can be imagined. This is no call for inner transformation but a demand for societal change. To be sure, one can hardly exist without the other, but where one starts the transformation is less significant than starting. And where one must start is to listen to the voice of the transforming God.

So, this book is an attempt to offer to preachers a way for them to enter the strange world of the Bible and to help them to present to their hearers the transformational power of that world in such a way that their listeners may hear the power and thereby have an opportunity to hear the unique voice of God. Of course, I do not propose that what I present here will approach the entirety of the Bible's strange world; I have chosen merely a slice of it to examine. That slice is the Hebrew Bible's narratives. Why have I chosen just these special texts? Three reasons are apparent.

Most obviously, they are what I know. My first published book dealt quite briefly with these sorts of texts,[4] offering suggestions about how preachers may approach them for their preaching. Though that book is long out of print, I continue to receive comments from those who have read it and found its words valuable for them. In at least one sense, this book is a sequel to that earlier one, now more than twenty years old. The manuscript I turned in for that 1991 book was far longer than the book that finally appeared. It was thought by its editors that potential readers of that book would not enjoy, nor would they read, the seven detailed examples I offered there for reading and preaching specific texts. I disagreed with that judgment then and I disagree with it still. Hence, you will find in this book several examples left out of that manuscript, albeit updated, along with an example that is for me newer.

I have also chosen to address Hebrew Bible narrative texts, their reading and preaching, because they remain texts little heard in the land. This fact needs scant proof from scholarly resources; it is self-evident that the church remains primarily and overwhelmingly a New Testament one. Of course, in one sense that is as it should be; we preach Jesus Christ crucified and risen as the basic substance of the gospel. However, no preacher would dare claim that she can preach such a gospel with integrity without a rich and full appreciation for and thorough knowledge of the ancient books that serve as ground and background of the newer testament. It is fair to say that the lack of such appreciation and knowledge has lead the gospel of Jesus to be misrepresented, truncated, and widely misunderstood in the churches. And this is true despite many attempts on the part of sensitive scholars to educate Christian preachers in the dangers of a Marcionite view of the Bible, wherein the New Testament gains a near-exclusive place.[5]

4. Holbert, *Preaching Old Testament*.

5. See, for example, Allen and Holbert, *Holy Root, Holy Branches: Christian Preaching and the Old Testament*; Achtemeier, *The Old Testament and the Proclamation of the Gospel*; Bright, *The Authority of the Old Testament*; Gowan, *Reclaiming the Old Testament for the Christian Pulpit*; Goldsworthy, *Preaching the Whole Bible as Christian Scripture*; Davis, *Wondrous Depth: Preaching the Old Testament*.

The third reason I have chosen to examine Hebrew Bible narratives is that the whole discussion of "narrative" and "story" preaching remains lively, albeit perhaps a bit muted, in the literature. When one examines narrative texts, it is inevitable to wonder just how those texts ought best to be presented from the pulpit. I will devote the whole of chapter 1 to the description and evaluation of story preaching. As I will attempt to show, "story" preaching is to be distinguished from "narrative" preaching of which it is a special example. Indeed, this book will attempt to demonstrate that only a very careful narrative reading of narrative texts will yield the most effective story sermon. The book is designed to demonstrate that kind of reading and to offer examples of that kind of preaching.

Let me be clear from the very beginning. Story preaching is not the only sort of preaching that should be done. Nor is it necessarily the most effective sort of preaching that can be done, although it may be the most effective for these particular kinds of texts. No preaching ministry will be saved by story preaching, nor will a story sermon, or even a series of them, scuttle a preacher's ministry of the pulpit. However, let me be equally clear that story preaching can be a very valuable tool in the preacher's kit, the reasons for which I will try to make evident in the second chapter.

Books have authors and then they have authors. Though I, John, have written every word of this book, its real authors are many. I taught at Perkins School of Theology for thirty-three years, and have just very recently retired from full-time teaching. I have heard literally thousands of sermons, including some of my own (I do on occasion listen to my own sermons), and have had numerous valuable colleagues. That earlier book of 1991 I dedicated to my wife and children. That same wife, now a retired twenty-year veteran of local church ministry, and those same two children, now grown and gone to their own fascinating lives, remain authors in the sense that they love me, challenge me, and still speak to me even when I pursue my own nerdy ways. My Perkins colleagues are also authors, both in personal and scholarly ways. Of course, my long-time Old Testament colleague and mentor, Bill Power (to whom I dedicated two others of my books), though now retired from teaching, is still a silent inspiration for my love of the Hebrew Bible and its stories. And my colleague in preaching, Alyce McKenzie, pushes me by her hard and careful labors to be better at what I do than I would be without her. And I should mention my worship/music colleagues, Michael Hawn (he of the demented accordion and superb musicianship), Marjorie Procter-Smith, now also retired, (she of the challenging caring), and Mark Stamm (he of our shared love of the great game of baseball as well as of the worship of God), all of whom made a trip to the campus each day a blessed one. For all these authors, and many others unnamed, I am grateful. Whether any of them finally chooses to be aligned with me, or anything else I say herein, well, you will have to ask them.

ONE

Preaching and Story

Definitions

SINCE THE RISE OF so-called narrative preaching, usually seen as tied directly to the "new homiletic" of the 1970s, there has been much confusion about the definition of this kind of proclamation. And I readily admit that my 1991 book, *Preaching Old Testament*, did little to clarify the confusion. I tended there to use interchangeably the terms "narrative" and "story." Of course, in common English usage, this is quite natural; nearly every English dictionary I have consulted defines the one term by the other. For example in my very small, desk-size Webster's New World Dictionary, "narrative" is defined, first, as "story; account." And "story" is defined, again first, as "the telling of an event or series of events; account; narration." However, this common interchangeability has led to confusion and imprecision that needs address.

Eugene Lowry in his 1997 introduction to preaching helps the move toward clarity. "Technically, the term narrative means a 'story' and a 'teller.'"[1] He borrows this basic definition from the classic 1966 text of Robert Scholes and Robert Kellogg, *The Nature of Narrative*.[2] It was that definition that lead me to use story and narrative synonymously in my earlier book. However, Lowry, the leading theorist and advocate of what he calls narrative preaching, defines narrative as a series of events related to one another in such a way as to evidence a plot. In effect, for Lowry,

---

1. Lowry, *The Homiletical Plot*, 124.
2. Scholes and Kellogg, *The Nature of Narrative*, 4.

narrative is synonymous with plot. Plot, according to Scholes/Kellogg is "the dynamic, sequential element in narrative literature. Insofar as character, or any other element in narrative, becomes dynamic, it is part of the plot."[3] The content of any sermon can be plotted, and Lowry suggests how that is so in his famous Lowry loop, the five elements of a plotted sermon he first described in his 1980 book, *The Homiletical Plot*. Though in the new edition of this seminal and accessible work, Lowry rethinks his original five-element sermon plot design, sometimes reducing the elements from five to four and redefining the original terms, the basic claim remains the same. Sermons need to be "processes in time rather than constructions in space."[4] The metaphor employed is crucial; constructions are things built from pieces, nailed or tied together. Processes, or movements, in time have forward motion rather than vertical dimension.

Story sermons are subspecies of plotted sermons; all narrative sermons are not story sermons, but all story sermons are narrative sermons. If plotted sermons involve the telling of a story, the sermon should be called a story sermon. Hence, story and narrative in homiletical practice are not synonyms, but the former is an illustration of the latter. This is so, because stories by their very nature have plots, the Aristotelian beginning, middle, and ending. But narrative sermons, in this more precise sense, may or may not use stories in their plots. It is conceivable, although perhaps not too likely, that a narrative sermon may be completely devoid of stories. A plotted story sermon, on the other hand, uses a story or stories as the central content of the sermon. The four sermon examples in this book are plotted story sermons. In the subsequent discussion of the history of story sermons, more clarity will appear concerning the importance of these more precise definitions.

STORY SERMONS: A BRIEF HISTORY

The Bible

Story sermons are as old as preaching itself, and have their origins in the pages of the Bible. After King David pursued his adulterous affair with Bathsheba, had her soldier husband murdered in battle, and then married the publicly grieving widow, in a crude attempt to cover over his misdeeds,

---

3. Ibid., 207.
4. Lowry, *The Homiletical Plot*, 123.

the prophet Nathan marches into the throne room of the king and delivers to him a story sermon. He speaks of a poor man and his one tiny ewe and of a rich man who entertained a traveler by stealing the poor man's lamb for the main course, instead of taking a lamb from his own substantial flock. Thus ends the sermon. But not quite! David is enraged, and shouts that the rich man deserves death, and before his execution should restore the tiny lamb fourfold, so he could see the restoration of the poor man just before his eyes close for the final time. The story sermon here has done its work of personal engagement. Now it is quite true that Nathan goes on to clarify the point of the story, skewering his king on the story's point. "You are the man," he thunders, and it is indeed clear that David is that arrogant rich man (see 2 Sam 12:1–15). I will return to this story again, as we explore the possible reasons for preaching in just this way.

Further Hebrew Bible examples may be noted. The eighth-century prophet, Isaiah, tells the tale of the establishment of a vineyard by his "beloved," a vineyard expected to produce sweet grapes. Instead Isaiah laments that the vineyard produced "wild grapes" or perhaps better "noxious weeds" (Isa 5:4). Isaiah 5:7 offers the point of the story.

> Surely, the vineyard of YHWH of the armies is the house of Israel,
>   the Judeans are God's delightful plants.
> God expected *mishpat* (justice) but alas *mispach* (bloodshed),
>   *tsedakah* (righteousness), but alas *ts'akah* (an outcry).

One might call this use of story allegory, where each element of the tale corresponds to an element of the targeted concern, in this case an evil and recalcitrant Israel. However, extended metaphor is perhaps a better description, since not every part of the story (the dirt, the stones, the tower, etc.) has an apparent correspondent in the case against Israel. Still, it is a sermon, using story as the major element in the proclamation.

The most obvious example of a story sermon in the Hebrew Bible is the tale of Jonah.[5] I will give extended treatment to Jonah as story sermon in a later chapter. In my earlier book, I suggested that Jonah itself represents the type of story sermon I called "pure narrative."[6] I would also argue that

---

5. The literature on this very small book is really quite large. Especially helpful to the story preacher are: Trible, *Rhetorical Criticism*; Lacocque and Lacocque, *Jonah*; Magonet, *Form and Meaning*; Fretheim, *The Message of Jonah*; Holbert, "Deliverance Belongs to Yahweh," 59–81.

6. Holbert, *Preaching Old Testament*, 42.

the book of Ruth is a story sermon, albeit a rather more complex and subtle one than Jonah.[7]

There is also the so-called parable of the trees in Judges 9:8–15. The story is spoken by Jotham as an attack against Abimelech, the would-be king of Shechem and against those elders of the city who murdered Jotham's brothers in order to clear the way for Abimelech's enthronement. In the story, various trees are asked to rule over the forest. In turn, the olive, fig, and grape vines are offered the rule of the forest, and each in turn rejects the offer, claiming that the work they are already doing is more important than any work as ruler could be. When the bramble bush is offered rule, it nastily says:

> If you are really anointing me king over you,
>   then come, hide in my shade!
> But if not, let fire burst out of the bramble
>   and devour the cedars of Lebanon!

In this story sermon, Abimelech is obviously likened to the coarse bramble whose quality of shade is minimal, if not absurd, and whose only practical use is for poor firewood. Also, a fire created by brambles is good only for the most paltry heat, let alone blazing hot enough to engulf the world's mightiest trees, the fabled cedars of Lebanon. In short, the story sermon announces the serious shortcomings of the ridiculous but murderous Abimelech and warns of his dangerous kingship. In three short years, the very elders of Shechem who made Abimelech king turn against him. Soon after, Abimelech burns one thousand Shechemites, both men and women, to death in one of their own city's towers (Judg 9:46–49). Following that atrocity, Abimelech himself is killed by his own armor-bearer after a woman of Thebez crushes his skull with a well-aimed millstone (Judg 9:50–54). It turns out that Jotham's fable, his story sermon, proved ironically prescient; the bramble Abimelech did produce a devouring fire, first burning to death one thousand of his own compatriots, but finally being himself "devoured" by the power of a woman. These examples are merely a few of the many story, or story-like, sermons to be found within the pages of the Hebrew Bible.[8]

---

7. Ibid., 93–115.

8. One could name several prophetic stories: Jer 18:1–10; 32:1–25; Ezek 15:1–8; Isa 27:1–6, among others; Dan 4:10–18 among the several dream stories contained in that book; Hos 1–3; Joel 2:1–11.

But of course the Bible's most famous storyteller is Jesus of Nazareth. His many parables have been analyzed, retold, and embellished on countless occasions in sermons over the two millennia since their first utterance in the hills and valleys of first-century Palestine. They have served as well-nigh endless sources of scholarly and pastoral comment, and any attempt fruitfully to summarize such comment is ultimately impossible, given its volume.[9] Yet, especially the narrative parables are surely story sermons, often offered without explanatory comment. A brief look at two of these will make the point.

Matthew's wonderful "Laborers in the Vineyard" story is the first example (Matt 20:1–15).[10] It addresses the question: "What is the reign (kingdom) of God like?" If you want to understand something of God's rule, says Matthew, how God might reign over the world and over the lives of those who live in that world, listen to this story.[11] The owner of a vineyard needs to hire workers to pick his crop, so goes out to the place of hiring, the market square of the town, very early in the morning. He there hires workers who all agree that they will receive a denarius for their work. He then returns some hours later that morning and hires more workers, promising them not a specific wage but "whatever is right" (*dikaion*), verse 4. Three hours later, and again three hours after that, he hires more workers, but no comments are made in the story about wages for these workers. Late in the afternoon, at 5:00 p.m., he returns to the market square and finds other workers "standing around." He accuses them of being "idle all day," but they reply that "no one has hired them." He responds, "You go to the vineyard, too," and again says nothing about pay.

After the sun sets, the workers gather to receive payment for their work. The owner tells his paymaster to distribute the pay, beginning with those who were hired last. Surprisingly, these workers receive a denarius, the payment promised to the all-day workers. The story then says that those workers hired early in the morning, who worked far longer than these last-hired ones, clearly expected to "receive more." But to their surprise, and real anger, they, too, received only one denarius. Not surprisingly to the

---

9. Among the most accessible works are: Via, *The Parables*; TeSelle, *Speaking in Parables*; Crossan, *Cliffs of Fall*; Wilder, *Jesus' Parables and the War of Myths*; Breech, *The Silence of Jesus*; Bailey, *Poet & Peasant* and *Through Peasant Eyes*; Scott, *Hear Then the Parable*; Duke, *The Parables*.

10. Nearly any of the volumes in note 9 provides useful introduction and commentary on this story.

11. For examples, see Breech, *The Silence of Jesus*, 142–43; Via, *The Parables*, 148.

readers and hearers of the tale, they began to grumble to the owner that he has made the last-hired workers who had worked only one hour, "equal to us who bore the long day and the raging heat." The owner calmly replies that he had done these all-day workers no wrong, because he had paid them precisely what they had agreed to when they were hired, no more, no less. He then adds, rather bluntly, "Take what belongs to you, and go; I choose to give to them what I give to you." Then two pointed questions. "Am I not allowed to do what I choose with what I own?" Finally, "Or are you envious because I am generous?" (NRSV). The more literal Greek rendering is: "Is your eye evil, because I am good?"

Many scholars suggest that the parable itself ends there in verse 15. Verse 16 is then an editorial addition, either from Matthew or a somewhat later commentator, attempting to explain the meaning of the parable. More than a few readers, however, have found verse 16's interpretation less than illuminating, if not more than a little lame.[12] If the story does end in verse 15, the fact of last hired, first paid does seem at best a rather minor fact of the story. The more potent fact appears to be the astonishing equality of payment, despite the enormous disparity in laboring hours. And, in addition, the three amazing claims of the owner: his absolute freedom to do whatever he wants with his own money, his rejection of the all-day workers' questions about that free choice, and his accusation that their question is a result of their own evil in the face of his own good. Somehow, says the story, observing this vineyard owner closely, both his words and his actions, will reveal to us something of the nature of the rule of God. Now there is a pure story sermon! We, the hearers/readers, are left pondering just exactly what might be the insights we are to gain concerning God's reign and rule.

Those insights are hardly obvious and are less than simple to extract. Does God, like the owner, offer God's gifts equally to all, regardless of the length or quality of their work? Does God include all of God's creatures into God's rule even if some do not recognize the reality of that rule until very late in life? Is our labor then finally irrelevant as a way to follow God's commands? Is God so free as to be unconcerned with our labor? These are only a few of the questions that arise from a hearing of this story sermon whose announced subject is the rule of God. Some story sermons might leave us grasping for meaning, as this one surely does. Later in this discussion we

12. See, as useful introductions to that vast literature, the notes on the parable in Duke, *The Parables*, 124–26; also the very detailed analysis with copious notes in Bailey, *Poet and Peasant*, 158–206.

will need again to address this open-endedness of certain types of story sermons.

Our second example is the most famous of Jesus' stories, that of a man and his two sons (Luke 15:11–32). Commentary on this so-called parable of the prodigal son is staggering in volume.[13] All preachers have sermons on it; nearly all New Testament scholars have something to say about it. But it is a story sermon, told by Luke to address the "problem" raised by listening Pharisees and scribes: "This fellow welcomes sinners and eats with them" (15:1). In response, Jesus tells three stories that appear to focus on the ways one should act when things lost have been found. The third story is the fullest story sermon of the three.

A man has two sons, and the younger of the two comes to him one day and demands that he be given his share of the father's inheritance immediately rather than wait for the old man's death, the apparent appropriate time for property division. In fact, the younger son will receive nothing until that death occurs; he is tired of waiting and, in effect, treats his father as if he were dead already. Without comment, the father does precisely what his anxious son asks; he divides the inheritance and gives the boy his share.

After a very few days, the boy takes his new-found wealth and heads off to a far-away country where he scatters his property, pursuing a dissolute life style. Soon his money was gone, and he had great need. He finally found work slopping pigs, animals held in the lowest regard by Jews. He became so hungry that he would gladly have eaten the pig's food, since no one gave him a thing. But one morning he woke up and thought to himself that his father's servants back home obviously ate better than this, so he resolved to go back and get himself some decent food. But he creates a brief religious speech to assuage the anger of his father, who must still be enraged at the boy's cruel and foolish actions. The speech focuses on the boy's admittance of sin against heaven and his father and his request that he be treated as a slave rather than a son. Whether this speech is made in genuine contrition or whether it is a clever ploy to wheedle his way into a good meal is not made clear in the story. The meaning of the central verse 17, "when he came to himself," is deliciously ambiguous: conversion or the search for better food?

Whichever it is, when the father catches sight of his missing son "far off," he "runs" toward him in a most undignified way, grabs him in a great hug, and kisses him. The boy starts his well-rehearsed speech, but he does

---

13. I refer the reader again to the volumes mentioned in note 9.

not finish it (compare vss. 18–19 with vs. 21). The father appears not to be listening to the speech, but instead calls out for his slaves to bring the very best of his robes for his son, along with rings for his fingers and sandals for his dusty feet. "Kill the fatted calf" (the definite article implies that "the" calf is well-known, set aside for the most significant meals), and "let us celebrate" the return of the lost. Perhaps most astoundingly, the father asks not a single question of his son, about the money, his life in the far country, or why the distinct odor of pig wafts from his clothing.

The party begins, and its happy noise floats out into the field where the father's elder son is working. As he approaches the house and the sound, he asks his servant what is happening. Upon hearing that the lost brother has returned home, and the father has killed the fatted calf for him, "because he has got him back safe and sound," the older brother is furious and refuses to enter the house. The father comes out to him and pleads with him to join the party. He will not! "Look! I have been working like a slave for you, never disobeying a single one of your commands. You never gave me so much as a stringy young goat so that I might party with my friends. But when this son of yours (note: not "my brother"), who devoured your living with prostitutes (of course, he cannot know this; he merely makes up the worst thing he can think of), you kill the fatted calf for him!" The father calmly replies, "Son, you are always with me, and all that I have is yours. But it is necessary that we celebrate and rejoice, because this brother of yours (the father restores the relationship of his sons) was dead and has come to life; he was lost and has been found."

As in the story of the vineyard owner and his workers, this story of a father and his two sons can be heard in several ways. Because the Lukan context claims that the story is a response to the anger of the Pharisees and scribes over Jesus's choice of dinner companions, the story may be heard as one that announces that those who in the eyes of the world are lost are always welcome at the table, no questions asked. On the other hand, the story has often focused on a reading of 15:17 that assumes when the boy "comes to himself" he has a kind of religious conversion, and goes back to his father *repentant* in genuine contrition. Thus, we could conclude that Jesus is always ready to receive the repentant sinner.

The differences between these two readings are theologically very important. In the former, the reception of the father is offered without strings; whether or not the speech of the lost boy is genuine is quite irrelevant to him. The fact that he has returned to him is all that counts. But in the latter reading, repentance must be performed before full reception and acceptance are possible. On these differences rest enormous practical, pastoral consequences.

But stories do that. They yield multiple meanings by their very nature as stories. The Bible's stories are far from propaganda. Propaganda is designed to spread specific ideas or doctrines as opposed to any other ideas or doctrines. In propaganda there is only one way to hear. I hope the biblical examples I have chosen suggest clearly and forcefully that these stories are not univocal; they are rich and complex, the source of ongoing reflection and proclamation. And because that is so, the sermons that arise from them can take several focuses and still be faithful witnesses to the story itself. The trick is in the telling. My reading and telling Jonah, for example, is hardly the only way that great tale may be told. Likewise, my reading and telling of Ruth in my earlier book is one telling only. Many more possibilities await the attentive reader. But much more of that later.

Stories in Post-Biblical Preaching through the Reformation[14]

Given the rich narrative traditions of the Bible, it would be no surprise to imagine that many preachers from the very beginning of the histories of church and synagogue used story material to illuminate the Bible's meaning for their hearers. Though we cannot understand fully the memorable scene described for us in Nehemiah 8, where Ezra, the scribe, stands above the people of a rebuilding Jerusalem, and reads to them the Torah of God from early morning until noon, what occurs there has been repeated in gathered assemblies for over 2,500 years. When it is said, "So they proclaimed the book, the law of God, with interpretation; they gave the sense, so that they (the people) understood the proclamation" (Neh 8:8), ever since preachers have tried to do the same, namely, "proclaim with interpretation" in such a way that "the people may understand the proclamation." And a part of those attempts at interpretation was the use of stories. From Tertullian to Augustine to Gregory the Great, from the second to the sixth century, stories, analogies, and other forms of practical illustrations make up a significant part of the preachers' arsenal. O. C. Edwards, for example, offers a brief appraisal of a sermon of Augustine's based on Psalm 31 in which the preacher says that bad Christians are worse than pagans since "something

14. For many of the references that follow, I am much in debt to the wonderful two volumes by Edwards, Jr., *A History of Preaching*.

may still be made out of the them (the pagans), just as something can be made from the logs in the carpenter's yard, in spite of all the knots and the twists and the bark . . . But from the twigs and trimmings he cleans off the carpenter can make nothing, they are only fit for firewood."[15] Though this is an illustration from the world of the preacher and his hearers, and not formally a story, one can see the kernel of a story here, as the congregation is asked to imagine the carpenter at work in his shop.

Gregory the Great (ca. 540–604) is said to have been "the first great preacher who attempted, in anything like a systematic fashion, to introduce non-scriptural illustrations into his instructions, to drive a religious truth with the help of an apposite story."[16] Examples may be found in his Homily 37, based on Luke 14:16–33.[17] Gregory in this sermon uses two extended stories of faithful priests and a bishop to drive home his point of the necessity of imitating the behaviors of the pious if one is to gain the heavenly reward.

If Gregory was the first well-known preacher to use stories in his sermons, he was far from the last. The preachers of the eleventh and twelfth centuries were often characterized by their interest in stories as means to convey meaning to their hearers. Perhaps the best example is Bernard of Clairvaux (1094–1153) whose sermons and sermonic writings employed stories extensively. In his *Parabolae*, a compendium of sermon stories, the titles of these sermonic illustrations suggest the sorts of stories that were told: "the king's son, the conflict of two kings, the king's son sitting on a horse, the church that was captive in Egypt, a king's three sons, the Ethiopian woman married by the king's son, the eight beatitudes, and the king and the beloved servant."[18]

In the thirteenth and fourteenth centuries, there is what Edwards terms "an explosion of preaching."[19] And a part of the fuse that ignites the explosion is collections of sermon *exempla*, designed for preachers to add insight and interest to their preaching. Such collections were rich in content from the Bible, secular history, patristic writings, poems, prose fiction, contemporary events, small personal incidents, and stories known only to

15. Edwards, *A History of Preaching*, 114.

16. Dudder, *Gregory the Great: His Place in History and Thought*, vol 1, 255.

17. Edwards, *A History of Preaching*, 138–40.

18. Ibid., 190.

19. Ibid., 210–38.

the compiler himself.[20] One can readily see that collections of "100 Snappy Sermon Starters" and "Jokes and Stories That May Be Told from the Pulpit" have at least an eight-hundred-year history!

The Reformation did not quench the interest in stories' use in sermons. In fact, it could be said that Martin Luther brought that use to a new and exciting level. When one reads especially his many Christmas sermons, one gets very close to what might be called the origins of story preaching. Read the following portion of Luther's 1522 sermon, "The Gospel for Christmas Eve, Luke 2."[21]

> . . . nobody took pity on this young woman who was about to give birth for the first time; nobody took to heart the heaviness of her body; and nobody cared that she was in strange surroundings and did not have any of the things which a woman in childbirth needs. Rather, she was there without anything ready, without light, without fire, in the middle of the night, alone in the darkness. Nobody offered her any of the services which one naturally renders to pregnant women. Everyone was drunk and roistering in the inn, a throng of guests from everywhere, and nobody bothered about this woman.

Here Luther uses what some contemporary preachers call their "holy imagination" to tell the story of Jesus's birth by fleshing out the details: the heaviness of pregnancy, the strangeness of the place, the lack of fire and light, the drunkenness, indifference and implied debauchery of the inn dwellers, carousing in that very inn from which Mary and Joseph had just been excluded. The sense of place is palpable, however imaginative the reconstruction of it!

But Luther allows his imagination such free rein not merely to entertain. Here is the next sentence of the sermon: "Therefore see to it that you derive from the Gospel not only enjoyment of the story as such, for that does not last long . . . But see to it that you make his birth your own." Here the reformer summarizes two of the most important reasons for employing story preaching; first, though he warns against enjoyment for its own sake, by implication what he has done is in fact very enjoyable indeed! The congregation that was there on that day will not soon forget (he may be too modest here) the dark and cold and terrifying circumstances of the birth of the Lord. But the second reason for using such a style is that "his birth must

20. Ibid., 228–31.

21. Pelikan and Lehman, *Luther's Works*, Sermons 2, 10–11.

become our own," that is, his birth is for us, and we must receive it in all of its wonder and mystery, in all of its earthiness and terror. No preacher since has combined these two aspects of the gospel, its mystery and its earthy reality, better than Martin Luther.[22]

Stories in Post-Reformation Preaching

It is interesting that in O. C. Edwards's history of preaching, the word "story" in the index is not mentioned from page 231 to page 712! That might imply that stories were not significant in preaching from the fourteenth century until the twentieth. As we have already noted, Luther used the narrator's art to great effect in the sixteenth century, and the subsequent four centuries saw their share of story in sermons as well. I am certain that Edwards knows this fact well, but just could not include all discussions even in a book of eight hundred pages!

When the Reformation made its way to England, it is interesting to observe that many of the greatest preachers were also among the greatest of poets. Thus, the relationships between preaching and literature were very close. The names are familiar: John Donne, Lancelot Andrewes, Jeremy Taylor, George Herbert. The latter wrote in "A Priest to the Temple": "A verse may find him, who a sermon flies," suggesting that poetry may possess a stronger evangelical power than a sermon. From these seventeenth-century divines, both poets and preachers, arose the narrative power of hymns in the eighteenth century, represented by the two greatest of hymn-writers, Isaac Watts and Charles Wesley, whose hymns often extended to great length in their attempts to tell a fuller story. (See, for example, Wesley's fourteen-verse version of "Come, O Thou Traveler Unknown" (1742), that expounds a Christological reading of Gen 32:24–32, based on Matthew

---

22. Each December at Perkins School of Theology two services of Lessons and Carols are presented as part of the celebration of Advent. In my early years on the faculty a central part of those services was the reading of a Christmas sermon by Martin Luther. I was privileged twice to perform this reading. I assume that this habit began due to the decided German tinge to our faculty in those days, several of whom were themselves German or had studied extensively in Germany. Each different Luther sermon brought home to me the extraordinary combination of the skill of biblical exegesis and wonderful imagination that the great reformer possessed. Luther sermons are no longer offered at these services, and I miss that feature greatly.

Henry's exposition.)[23] These long narrative hymns suggest the ongoing importance of story for the preaching and worship of the eighteenth century.

In that century, too, preachers were also writers of fiction. Jonathan Swift (*Gulliver's Travels, The Tale of a Tub,* "A Modest Proposal," among others), Samuel Butler (*The Way of All Flesh*), Laurence Sterne (*Tristram Shandy*), and others, turned their literary skills both to sermons and to literature. In addition, nearly every novel of the period had a prominent place for preachers and preaching. Henry Fielding, both in *Joseph Andrews* and *Tom Jones* (1749), finds preachers worthy of some withering scorn. This fictional, satiric attack on preachers and sermons continues unabated in literature of the next two centuries.[24] Such literature perhaps culminates in the twentieth century in Sinclair Lewis' *Elmer Gantry* and Peter De Vries's *The Mackerel Plaza*, two portraits of philandering, self-obsessed, money-grubbing clergymen that do not easily leave the mind.

In the United States, the first Great Awakening of the eighteenth century was fueled by preaching. George Whitefield was the epitome of the public, homiletical firebrand. Reports of his preaching beggar the imagination. Benjamin Franklin has left us a picture of Whitefield's preaching in his *Autobiography.* "His delivery was so improved by frequent repetitions that every accent, every emphasis, every modulation of voice, was so perfectly well turned . . . that, without being interested in the subject, one could not help being pleased with the discourse . . ."[25] Earlier Franklin claimed that Whitefield "might well be heard by thirty thousand," which one could chalk up to a "preacher estimate," save that Franklin was hardly a preacher. He was, in fact a rationalist Deist and not a regular churchgoer. His comments that even one not "interested in the subject" would still find the sermon "pleasing" perhaps referred to himself.

At the same time that Whitefield was wooing immense crowds with the fire of the gospel, and thereby gaining many converts, a quiet-spoken local church pastor named Jonathan Edwards was having his own important impact on eighteenth-century America. As pastor in Northhampton, Massachusetts, following the fifty-five year ministry of his grandfather, Solomon Stoddard, Edwards stirred his congregation and many others nearby on the Massachusetts frontier with strict Calvinist sermons, carefully constructed

---

23. This hymn may be found complete in *The United Methodist Hymnal,* number 387.

24. For details, see Bond and Jeffrey, *A Dictionary of Biblical Tradition in English Literature,* 631–35.

25. Franklin, *Autobiography,* 196–98.

and very quietly delivered. O. C. Edwards says that, "Whitefield was one of the most dramatic preachers of all time and Edwards one of the most staid."[26] Yet, both men had an enormous impact on eighteenth-century American religious life.

But neither of them used stories to any appreciable extent. Edwards focused his preaching on right doctrine, carefully conceived, while Whitefield used his vocal power and oratorical skill to draw and convert the people. It remained for another group of preachers to incorporate stories as the central mode of pulpit proclamation. Early African-American preachers, influenced by the emotional preaching of Whitefield, soon joined their African storytelling tradition with lively emotional preaching to create a uniquely American homiletics.[27]

In Henry Mitchells's discussion of black sermons he says,

> Generally speaking, Black preaching is probably as varied in structure as White preaching, except that more Black sermons are apt to consist of one single Bible narrative (with or without extended comments on the side).[28]

Whether or not this observation is statistically true, it is clear that Bible stories are often the backbone of African-American sermons. Mitchell earlier in his book points to two great tellers of tales, John Jasper (1812–1901), founding pastor of Sixth Mount Zion Baptist Church in Richmond, Virginia and Sandy F. Ray (1898–1979), long-time pastor of Cornerstone Baptist Church in Brooklyn, New York.[29] In the brief examples he provides from these two pastors' preaching, it is obvious that they combined a rich folklore tradition of storytelling with deep and profound acquaintance with the details of the Bible's stories. It is precisely this combination of storytelling technique and careful biblical reading that this book wants to suggest is the right road to powerful story preaching in the twenty-first century pulpit.

Though these African-American story preachers bring us well into the twentieth century, their roots are far older in the American soil. And, it must be noted, it was not only African-American preachers who were using stories extensively in their preaching. In fact, by the middle of the

26. Edwards, *A History of Preaching*, 478.

27. This story is well-told in Mitchell, *Black Preaching*, a revised and integrated version of two earlier books, *The Recovery of Preaching* and *Black Preaching*.

28. Mitchell, *Black Preaching*, 114.

29. Ibid., 69–72.

nineteenth century, preachers were, by one account "running mad for stories."[30] The author of that quip was no other than the famous Harriet Beecher Stowe, creator of a wildly popular story of her own, *Uncle Tom's Cabin*. In an introduction to a later book of hers, *My Wife and I* (1871), she comments on the style of preaching that has in her time become ubiquitous.

> Hath any one in our day, as in St. Paul's, a psalm, a doctrine, a tongue, a revelation, an interpretation—forthwith he wraps it up in a serial story, and presents it to the public . . . We have Romanism and Protestantism, High Church and Low Church and no Church, contending with each other in serial stories, where each side converts the other, according to the faith of the narrator. We see that this is to go on. Soon it will be necessary that every leading clergyman shall embody in his theology a serial story, to be delivered in the pulpit.[31]

In that same introduction, Stowe asserted that this love affair with fiction would soon displace Bunyan's *Pilgrim's Progress* and would lead to the following scene: "The way to the celestial city (see Bunyan) will be as plain in everybody's mind as the way up Broadway—and so much more interesting!"[32] It is not altogether clear whether Stowe deplores this movement toward pulpit fiction or celebrates its freshness and undoubted interest, but the result of its increasing use in preaching is a decline in doctrinal preaching. Perhaps Stowe saw herself in her most famous story of the fate of Little Eva as offering what was in effect a story sermon, though the point of that sermon remains even today the source of considerable dispute.

Reynolds's claim in his fascinating article is that the increased use of illustrations and stories in the upscale pulpits of the last quarter of the nineteenth century, led "both to the decline of theology and the rise in religious fiction."[33] He also suggests that "pietists, Great Awakening Revivalists, Methodists, and Unitarians shared the idea of a dissatisfaction with theological preaching and made a move toward secular illustration and example."[34] He cites the famous Horace Bushnell as an example. Bushnell tried to join together the "revivals' undisciplined emotionalism" and a

---

30. Quoted in Reynolds, "From Doctrine to Narrative: The Rise of Pulpit Storytelling in America," 479.

31. Stowe, *My Wife and I*, viii.

32. Ibid., x.

33. Reynolds, "From Doctrine to Narrative," 480.

34. Ibid.

"Boston liberalism's frigid literariness," and called instead for "a mediating combination of scholarship, stylistic talent, effective vocalizing, human feeling, and vigor."[35] That this combination was in fact an apt description of the preaching of Bushnell himself should come as no surprise.

Surely the capstone of this movement from doctrine to story in the pulpit is to be found in Charles Sheldon, who in the early days of the 1890s read to his Topeka, Kansas congregation the chapters of his novel that eventually appeared as *In His Steps*.[36] This novel of the Social Gospel movement had sold more than eight million copies by 1920, and remains in print over one hundred years after its initial publication. Thus, by the turn of the twentieth century, stories were deeply planted in the pulpit soil both of white and black preachers of whatever class in America.

However much the actual preaching of the early years of the twentieth century used stories, much of the commentary on preaching at the same time was not convinced of story's centrality. The most used introduction to the art and craft of preaching was John A. Broadus' 1870 work, *On the Preparation and Delivery of Sermons*, a work that has continued to be read in numerous institutions to the present day; a fourth edition of the work appeared as late as 1979.[37] Broadus had little good to say about stories. In his list of sixteen patterns of sermons, stories find no place.[38] In his discussion of the need for imagination in sermon preparation, at every turn, caveats are added to control an over-eager imagination. After calling a "historical imagination" "one of the most powerful allies of preaching," he quickly adds, "but here there is demanded a moderation and reserve, a care in distinguishing between the real and the supposed, which in some books and many sermons are sadly needed."[39] Stowe may have imagined that preachers were "mad for stories," but Broadus, whose book appeared only one year prior to Stowe's, thinks otherwise.

This is especially clear in a quotation I used in my earlier book on narrative preaching.

> A speaker must always subordinate narration to the object of his discourse, the conviction or persuasion which he wishes to effect. He must not elaborate or enlarge upon some narrative merely

35. Ibid., 498.

36. Ibid.

37. Broadus, *On the Preparation and Delivery of Sermons*.

38. Ibid., 68–74.

39. Ibid., 227.

because it is in itself interesting or follow the story step by step according to its own laws.[40]

Here are the implications of that statement. First, every story is always subordinate to the "object" of the discourse and must not be allowed to overwhelm that object. Second, the object of every sermon is "conviction or persuasion," and a story must not be told in such a way as to short-circuit that concern. Third, stories may be so interesting in and of themselves that they could overwhelm the basic object of conviction and persuasion. Fourth, and perhaps most important for the concerns of this book, the story must not be followed "step by step according to its own laws," because again the object of conviction and persuasion could be lost in the interest of the story, and the sermon reduced to a form of entertainment. In nearly every way he can say it, Broadus warns against excessive use of interesting stories, too wild an abuse of a storied imagination. Genuine conviction and persuasion can only occur through reasoned argument, carefully laid out, sequentially supplied, intellectually conceived and presented. Charles Sheldon may be selling a religious story by the boxful, but Broadus warns against an over-active, over-imaginative use of story in the pulpit. It could be said that the approaches represented by Broadus and Sheldon, so clearly in opposition, continued that opposition throughout the twentieth century.

That this opposition was too simplistic and finally not all that helpful for the practice of preaching, is made plain by a recent analysis of Paul Scott Wilson.[41] In an evaluation of Richard Eslinger's post-modern cultural-linguistic model of homiletics, Wilson accuses him of a sort of reductionism, pitting "symbols and imaginative constructs" over against "abstract reasoning" as "stark alternatives" rather than valuable approaches, each in their own right.[42] In short, one need not choose a story homiletics to the complete exclusion of a more abstract one, assuming thereby that one has chosen the better part. The reason for this book is not to present *the* homiletical approach that should always be used, an approach that will save a floundering pulpit ministry. Story preaching has great value for anyone who would proclaim the word of God in as many ways as may be conceived. To paraphrase the maxim of George Herbert, quoted above, "A story may speak to one from whom an abstract sermon flies." But hardly always.

40. Ibid., 132.

41. Wilson, *Preaching and Homiletical Theory*.

42. Ibid., 18.

Telling the Whole Story

The twentieth century's turn toward narrative and story has been well-catalogued in several places.[43] Wilson in his recent book is representative of this history. Modern movements toward narrative as a basis for homiletics began in the new hermeneutic (see Fuchs and Ebeling), which argued that when the word is an event, when language is an event, then words not only contain ideas but fashion events. Words do much more than convey ideas; they perform and create events.[44] Thus, since the Word of God encounters us as an event of God that *does* things, not merely *says* things, preaching should work hard to make that encounter possible. "As a result . . . , homiletics started to turn to narrative and plot to reflect the way people experience life and God, and away from abstract propositions or points."[45] The question of the structures of these sermons became very important as the movement grew, but Wilson argues that "the original strength of the narrative movement was its theological ability to generate experience through which God might be perceived."[46]

Add to this performative function of language the conviction, voiced most memorably by Stephen Crites, that human experience itself possessed a "narrative quality," and the interest in narrative and story grew ever stronger.[47] Books and articles appeared in profusion, trumpeting the fresh and exciting ways that narrative and story could invigorate the moribund pulpits of the late twentieth-century West.[48]

Disenchantment with Narrative/Story

So, had narrative/story triumphed? Hardly! Even while the tide of narrative preaching literature was reaching flood stage, huge dams were being built to staunch the flow. That the flow has turned into a trickle can be seen in

43. Wilson points to two such analyses: Rose, *Sharing the Word*, 40–41, 49–50, 60–61, 67–71; and Wilson, *The Practice of Preaching*, 20–35.

44. For the importance of this insight for a story homiletics, see Randolph, *The Renewal of Preaching* and Rice, *Imagination and Interpretation: the Preacher and Contemporary Literature*.

45. Wilson, *Preaching and Homiletical Theory*, 64–65.

46. Ibid., 65.

47. Crites, "The Narrative Quality of Experience."

48. Representative examples are: Jensen, *Telling the Story*; Brown, *Dramatic Narrative in Preaching*; Steimle, Niedenthal, Rice, *Preaching the Story*; Bausch, *Storytelling: Imagination and Faith*; Holbert, *Preaching Old Testament: Proclamation and Narrative in the Hebrew Bible*; Eslinger, *Narrative Imagination and The Web of Preaching*.

the 2005 Tom Long article, "What Happened to Narrative Preaching?"[49] In this article, Long offers some reflections on the reason for the decreasing interest in the kind of preaching that was talked about at length in the 1970s and 1980s. The critiques have come, he says, from the right, the left, and the center. From the right comes the charge that such preaching is "too soft, too doctrinally unclear, too ethically ambiguous, too shy about evangelism."[50] From the center comes the claim that story sermons too often tell the wrong stories, "anecdotes of human experience or alleged plot structures in the imagination, rather than the gospel narrative of Jesus."[51] From the left comes the charge that the very act of telling stories to a congregation has caused these story preachers to exercise "their privileged positions of power to grind down all human differences, have lifted their own views of experience to the level of the universal, and commanded the hearers to fit their lives into this frame, . . . all the while hiding behind a false front of seemingly neutral and objective but really power-laden language."[52] These are sharp critiques indeed and need to be addressed with seriousness if a story homiletics is to be practiced at all.

I believe that each of these arguments was preceded by the trenchant comments of Richard Lischer in his 1984 essay, "The Limits of Story."[53] I want now to give extended discussion to this piece, since I find it to be the most important and most carefully argued of the critiques of narrative/story preaching to have appeared. Lischer divided his critique of narrative preaching, as he conceived such preaching (there is, unfortunately, in the article no ready definition of what Lischer actually means by story or story preaching), into four categories: aesthetic, ontological, theological, and socio-political.

Aesthetic problems. "Art," says Lischer, "is intrinsically autotelic, not a means to an end." That is to say, a story has its own intrinsic meaning and always holds the danger of existing apart from the contexts of its production. Hence, in agreement with Erich Auerbach, Lischer says that the Bible is a

49. Long, "What Happened to Narrative Preaching?"

50. As an example of Long's point, see his assessment of Thompson's critique of narrative preaching in *Preaching Like Paul*, 9–14.

51. This is Long's reading of Campbell's critique of narrative preaching in *Preaching Jesus*, 192–93.

52. McClure, *Other-wise Preaching*, 81.

53. Lischer, "The Limits of Story," 27.

group of stories "fraught with background." This fact means that individual Bible stories ought never be told apart from their necessary background in the larger story of Israel and in the larger story of the mission of Jesus and the church. Isolated stories, however well told, however engaging and lively, inevitably lead to "moralism and universalism."[54] In the former, the preacher, rather than preaching the gospel of God's salvation, preaches instead a general moral code: "be kind," "be generous," be helpful." In the latter, the preacher assumes a universality of experience; we are all finally alike, s/he says, and the scandalous particularity of Jesus's sharp demands disappears into a fog of generalities worthy more of the Rotary Club than the church. Sermons are left with announcements of "transient expressions of grace,"[55] avoiding historical contexts and dogmatic underpinnings.

And this does not exhaust the dangers of aestheticism, according to Lischer. There are very practical dangers to address, too. Though these story sermons claim to be simplicity itself, they are in fact far from simple. First, there is a huge hermeneutical distance between *the* story and *my* story. The great story of God as found in the Bible is far different from mine, and to tell the Bible's story as if it were only an ancient version of the story I live is to reduce the Bible only to a mirror of things I already know, when it often is the sharpest of challenges to things I only think I know. Second, "the real irony is what began as a quest for authenticity in preaching (i.e., in telling a story) results in a thickening of the veil between the pulpit and the pew."[56] "Just telling a little ole' story" does not bring me closer to my hearers; it clouds their attempts to hear the gospel that would save them. Rather it offers them a snapshot of grace, a reduced and trivialized portrait of the saving work of Christ.

These are significant claims, calling into deep question any homiletics based on story. And I agree with Lischer that these critiques can and surely have surfaced in some of the story sermons I have heard (and preached). Nevertheless, as the saying goes, "the proof is in the pudding." I do not see how any of the four sermons I present in this book fall into these aesthetic traps, but I will, after I have presented them, return to Lischer's critiques to see if they have fallen short in the ways he has warned.

54. Ibid.
55. Ibid.
56. Ibid., 29.

Ontological Problems. Lischer here calls into question the claims of Crites (and Paul Ricouer) that "historicity is the form of life correlative to the language game of telling." Though we do tell stories to describe and to shape our lives, stories' very drive toward resolution is itself a large problem ontologically. ". . . the stories we tell may provide the sense of order so desperately needed or they may appear transparently palliative to those whose experience has resisted the broom that sweeps in one direction."[57] Resolved stories are not always the stories we know in our own lives. Much we experience is in fact non-linked events without chronological, logical, or organic order, more like the writing of Proust, Joyce, Kafka, and Beckett, than Dickens or Austen. The fact is, says Lischer, "many simply do not have stories."[58] They are the severely handicapped, the addicted, the poverty-stricken, the hungry, the imprisoned, "and many other marginated ones whose lives are structured not by the syntaxis of story but by immediate needs or bewilderment at the unrelatedness of things."[59] "This is not to say that they do not *need* story, only that it has ceased to be reputable currency." Lischer implies here that those who find themselves living lives generally unstructured have little patience with transient experiences of grace. Put another way, those who wait for Godot, imprisoned in trashcans, have a hard time hearing a nice well-rounded, resolved story. Lischer concludes his ontological critique by saying, "Before preaching says 'Once upon a time,' to the captive or the broken-hearted, it sits where these storyless, forgotten people sit and then proclaims the good news of the Lord's deliverance."[60]

Again, I wish to agree that neat and easily resolved stories do not at all exhaust the full range of human experience. Any preacher who would dare to utter a sweet story of personal victory into a congregation filled with persons whose own lives are a shambles of unconnected and devastating events is not worthy of the name preacher. I would like to think that Lischer is attacking the rare straw person here who only strides toward the pulpit occasionally. Alas, my own experience knows his critique is all too telling. I often wonder exactly whom the preacher is addressing when s/he tells the wondrous story of family unity into a room filled with broken homes and shattered lives.

57. Ibid., 29–30.
58. Ibid., 31.
59. Ibid.
60. Ibid., 32.

However, also again, stories need not be like this at all. Indeed, in the Bible few stories possess the neatness or roundedness that Lischer decries. They have an openness, a call to the deeps, that stand starkly over against the tales Lischer seems to be railing at. After I have offered my own story sermons in later chapters, I again wish to see if they have fallen into the ontological traps Lischer fears.

Theological Problems. Lischer agrees that "theology lives by story"; the great story (and stories) of the faith are the very stuff of theological reflection. However, theology must also have "precise modes of conceptualizing and interpreting" else theology will be "reduced to repetition or recital and lose its power and flexibility to address new situations."[61] In short, stories must always be conceptualized and interpreted, or they will be only stories, told again and again in the vain hope that they might one day serve as the means of transformation that is the essence of the gospel. Stories by themselves run the risk of meaningless repetition unless they are used as vehicles of meaning in ever-changing contexts. "How can they hear without a preacher," cries Paul in Rom 10:14, and surely he means by that someone who can expound just how the story of Christ can be for me, as it was for him, the center of my salvation.

By this critique, Lischer would seem to rule out some of the very sort of preaching I propose to do, namely, pure narrative, wherein the telling of the story itself is the sermon. But here, as I will try to demonstrate in my sermons, Lischer and I do not at all disagree. The very ways in which the stories are told imply clearly "precise modes of conceptualizing and interpreting." The art of these tellings is found in part in the subtle ways that the work of interpretation is hidden in the telling itself. But, as in the sermons themselves, it is far better to show how this works than to tell how it works. Hence, more on this subject later.

Socio-Political Problems. Perhaps here Lischer offers his most pungent arguments against stories in preaching. Several quotations attest to the disastrous dangers he fears. He observes that in the 1960s the very basic movement toward societal change, engendered by racism, the war in Vietnam, and other social earthquakes, moved toward a sense of "wonder" instead. "If we could not speak with assurance of God (note the 1960s 'Death of God' fad) and summon our hearers to faith and justice as the twofold

61. Ibid., 34.

telos of the Christian life, we could with growing theological warrant reflect with our congregations on the richness and interrelatedness of experience." This movement was "inevitably a turn from others toward the self."[62] In this general critique Lischer is surely correct. Gone from our pulpits with but few exceptions were the prophetic voices of Amos and Hosea and the prophetic Jesus whose deep concern with poverty and riches have all but been forgotten in the rush toward megachurches and mega budgets along with the concomitant reduction of moral concern to sexual behavior and reproductive rights. We now, much, much more than we should, "come to the garden alone," leaving our brothers and sisters to fend for themselves. Lischer's angry screed is not uttered without real provocation. He concludes, "It can be argued that story does not provide the resources for implementing ethical growth or socio-political change."[63]

A recent article by Brooks Berndt argues otherwise. In fact, he wants to claim that some of the recent movements for social change, both in the United States and elsewhere (he looks particularly at Haiti), are the direct result of the careful use of stories.[64] In fact, at one point in the article Berndt uses Lischer's own prize-winning work on the preaching of Martin Luther King, Jr., to demonstrate that King "did indeed use stories (i.e., the Exodus narrative presupposed and implicit) to galvanize action."[65] He further quotes Francesca Polletta, a scholar of social movements, who argues quite directly that "stories can elicit and guide emotions," rather more powerfully than any power of exhortation based on argument.[66] And finally Berndt examines more carefully a 1985 sermon of the Haitian leader, Jean-Bertrand Aristide, delivered on the Monday before Easter, wherein the ruthless tyranny of Baby Doc Duvalier was held up to ridicule and rejection. After examining the central place of stories in this sermon, Berndt concludes, "There are contexts in which narrative (stories) can play a vital role in social movements. In the tool chest of the preacher, one would be wise to not underestimate the value of narrative in the work of justice."[67]

In each of Lischer's careful critiques of the use of stories in preaching he has made significant points. Yet, each critique comes down to the

62. Ibid., 35.

63. Ibid.

64. Berndt, "The Politics of Narrative."

65. Berndt, 3.

66. Ibid.

67. Ibid., 11.

misuse of stories rather than a generalized claim that stories have no place in sermons at all. Each problem he names has appeared, and continues to appear, in pulpits in many churches. But I want to argue here that despite the important analyses that Lischer offers, story preaching can still find a significant role in our preaching. Yet, I find his work a touchstone to which I need always to return when I propose a story homiletics.

Now we turn in the next chapter to the sort of biblical reading we must learn to do if we are to preach significant, well-grounded story sermons. Also, in that chapter we will attend to the various skills one needs to do this sort of preaching along with the varying styles of that preaching.

TWO

Reading and Preaching
the Old Testament Stories

IN THE FIRST CHAPTER I argued that story preaching has a long history in the church, and that it remains a viable form of Christian proclamation, despite many serious challenges to that viability. Any preacher who would undertake such preaching will need always to have Richard Lischer's (among others') sharp questions sounding in their ears. I hope those sounds were in my ears when I composed the sermons that appear in the following chapters of this book. However, affirming the viability of story preaching does not by itself address how one might perform such preaching. In this chapter we turn to the basic tools needed to present powerful and memorable biblical story sermons.

Two very basic tools are needed, though each of those basic tools possesses several facets that must be employed if each tool is to work well. The first tool is the ability to read biblical narratives. The Bible writers were master stylists, but their style is not one especially familiar to twenty-first-century readers. In fact, it could be said that the largest single obstacle standing in the way of effective Bible reading today is this difference in their style and a modern style. The second tool is, of course, the ability to tell, to narrate, a story. The greatest gift that the Bible itself provides to the would-be storyteller is that of its wonderful stories that, when read well, offer central clues toward their effective telling. My assumption is that a story well-read leads then to a story well-told. So, first we must learn to read the stories of the Bible.[1]

---

1. I have gone over this same ground in my earlier book, *Preaching Old Testament*, in its third chapter. I refer the reader to that discussion for further explication of these basic narrative techniques.

READING THE NARRATIVES[2]

The Bible literature *is* literature at the same time that it *is* the Word of God for believers. This reality must be addressed before we examine the techniques these authors use to present their literature. Because the Bible is a sacred book, indeed *the* sacred book for countless readers, it was long considered immune to the usual ways of reading that were employed when other books were addressed and evaluated. If we are to read the Bible as we read, for example, Shakespeare, we should keep James Kugel's warning in mind:

> What is literary about the Bible at all? Certainly it does not identify itself as literature, and often such [God-oriented] self-definition as does occur seems clearly to . . . suppose a relationship between speaker and hearer which, we somehow feel, is being double-crossed by being looked at as literature, as artful composition, as anything more than a faithful and naïve recording.[3]

In other words, Kugel suggests that a faithful reading and a literary reading are potentially incompatible approaches to the Bible. (Of course, Kugel himself, in this book and in his many other books, goes right on to offer careful and nuanced literary readings of biblical texts.)

From another angle entirely, Kenneth R. R. Gros-Louis speaks to the issue of the relationship between the Bible's "literariness" and its "sacred uniqueness."

> We know, as students of literature, that the author's intention, his goals in writing for his contemporary audience, and his religious convictions, play a small role indeed in literary criticism and, more important, in the analysis of literary texts. *We* may be familiar with all this information, but we do not depend on it for interpretation, even with an avowedly religious poet such as Milton. For us, in fact, Milton's Satan, Adam, Jesus, God, and Samson are much more interesting than Milton himself. It is their views of themselves and their worlds, and not Milton's of his, on which we focus.[4]

2. There are numerous valuable books that can help preachers become better readers of the narratives of the Hebrew Bible. Alter, *The Art of Biblical Narrative*; Berlin, *Poetics and Interpretation of Biblical Narrative*; Sternberg, *The Poetics of Biblical Narrative*; Bar-Efrat, *Narrative Art in the Bible*; Brichto, *Toward a Grammar of Biblical Poetics*; Gunn and Fewell, *Narrative in the Hebrew Bible*; Fokkelman, *Reading Biblical Narrative*.

3. Kugel, *The Idea of Biblical Poetry*, 303.

4. Gros-Louis, *Literary Interpretations of Biblical Narrative*, 16.

What Gros-Louis implies here is that literary reading must be done precisely without any authorial intention (if such were ever readily available) or concern for religious implications in mind. The words of the story, how it portrays its characters, how they act and speak, will be all the guides we need to do interpretation.

Yet, as I said in my sentence above, the Bible is at the same time literature, and thereby subject to the laws of literary reading, *and* the Word of God. No preacher can or would desire to separate those two realities. In fact, my readings, over against Gros-Louis's claims, go further. The reality of reading any text, biblical or otherwise, suggests that reading can never be performed apart from careful attention to the contexts of the text and the contexts of the reader and the locations of the reading, physical, emotional, and social. Gros-Louis seems to imply that some sort of "pure" reading of the words of the text is possible, a reading unaware of those multiple contexts of text and reader just enumerated, a reading that brackets all those contexts. Such a reading simply cannot be done.[5] Such a reading, when its goal is a faithful preaching, *should* not be done. When the reader is at the same time a preacher, no "non-engaged, pure literary" reading ought be done nor can be done.

However, since the Bible is without doubt literature, it is in fact necessary to know the tools of reading literature if we are to plumb it as fully as we can for our preaching. The Bible's narrators chose to express themselves in the mode of narrative, so it is crucial that we learn to read them in recognition of that mode. If we do not, we run the risk of reducing the biblical text to a series of flat horizontal maxims and truths, refusing to accept the reality of its distinct literary genres, one of which is narrative.[6] Paul's famous metaphor of the truth of God's power contained surprisingly in "clay jars," (2 Cor 4:7) speaks directly to the necessity of our learning to read these narratives aright; the stories are narratives and must be read as such.

But they are also "old" narratives, written in a style unfamiliar to modern ears. Thus, we need to "get our ancient ears on" if we are to hear them. Fortunately, though they are "old," we can apply many of the familiar modern techniques to them with great profit, albeit adapted to recognize the significant differences presented by their unique styles of composition.

5. See, for example, The Bible and Culture Collective, *The Postmodern Bible*, for a detailed analysis of the complexities of reading any text.

6. See further on the necessity of taking the narrative genre seriously in Long, *Preaching and the Literary Forms of the Bible*, 66–86.

PLOT

Plot can be defined as the dynamic, sequential element in narrative literature. Insofar as character, or any other element in narrative, becomes dynamic, it is a part of the plot.[7]

Biblical stories all possess "dynamic, sequential elements," hence they have plots. Plots primarily work on the basis of expectations, either fulfilled or dashed. One could also speak of this as tension and resolution or lack of resolution. A familiar example makes the point:

> The King and Queen were married.
> The Queen died.
> The King died.

This is not strictly speaking a plot; it is sequential but hardly dynamic. There is no tension or resolution. It is probably true that when you read the sequence, you silently supplied various ideas to it to provide tension or resolution. Hence, you may have created something rather like this:

> The King and Queen were married.
> The Queen died.
> The King died of grief.

Now we have plot! There is still sequence, but the king's grief at the death of his wife adds the tension, and the expectation of the royal couple's long and happy reign has been crushed in their deaths. Though brief, this little story has all the necessary elements of plot. Obviously this bare outline could be, and has been, festooned with any number of elaborations, including the details of the royal wedding, the nature of the queen's death, the enormity of the king's grief, etc.

One more way to describe plot is offered by Wayne Booth. "Not only do we believe that certain causes do in life produce certain effects; in literature we believe that they should."[8] This is another way to say that the essence of plot is expectation. A Hebrew Bible example will be instructive.

The long story of Jacob and Esau (Genesis 25–50), comprising fully one-half of the book of Genesis, illustrates the importance of expectation for plot. At the very beginning of the story, the oracle of God reveals to Rebekah that her long-hoped-for, yet painful, pregnancy, is the result of a womb struggle between her twins. Rather than live in unity, as brothers

---

7. Scholes and Kellogg, *The Nature of Narrative*, 207.

8. Booth, *The Rhetoric of Fiction*, 126.

would be expected to do (Psalm 133), these twins will be "divided." And not only that; one will be stronger than the other and "the elder will be slave to the younger" (Gen 25:23). This pronouncement flies in the face of conventional expectations; in this ancient world the elder child always leads the way in the family. But not in this family. And though we are told one is stronger than the other, we are not told just which one is in fact the stronger, nor are we told whether strength means physical might or strength of mind. Expectations for this plot are decidedly ambiguous as the story unfolds.

Immediately, the descriptions of the twins give evidence of their vast differences. The elder is Esau (in Hebrew "hairy"), while the younger is Jacob (in Hebrew "taker," "grabber"). Esau is described physically while Jacob is given a description according to his actions. And in their first adult scene together, these descriptions are borne out (Gen 25:27–34). Esau is having a difficult hunting day while Jacob is making a bowl of stew. In desperation, the famished Esau bursts into Jacob's tent and demands, "Let me eat some of that red, red stuff!" The quintessential physical man identifies the object of his desire by its color, repeating the word for color to make the point. Jacob, the clever actor (is he in fact the "strong" one?) responds bluntly, "Sell now your birthright to me!" The birthright is, of course, nothing less than Esau's first-born status in the family. But Esau is ready to trade his elder status for a bowl of steaming "red stuff"; he apparently is not even too sure what the "stuff" is! "I am about to die; what good is a birthright to me!" Jacob then adds the equivalent of an ancient notary public: "Swear to me now!" And Esau does without a second thought. The scene ends in pathos and silence, save perhaps the loud slurping sounds coming from the gorging Esau. Jacob hands his brother the now more clearly identified "lentil stew," and Esau, "ate, drank, got up, left," offering no thanks or commentary of any sort. The narrator comments, "Esau despised his birthright."

Now our expectations are not quite as ambiguous after this scene. Esau, the elder, is a dolt, a man of appetites only who has thrown his future away for some unrecognizable bowl of stuff. Jacob, on the other hand, has played his brother like a drum, having gotten from him the elder son status and the spoken oath to make it stick. We expect little from Esau in the ensuing story save more foolish behavior, but from the wily Jacob we expect much. We will be both fulfilled in our expectations and surprised.

In short order, Jacob, with the help of his mother (who is operating, we remember, under the oracle of God) tricks his dying blind father out of the blessing of the patriarch, intended for the eldest son, and runs back toward the home country of Haran, leaving a howling and murderous Esau in his wake. Twenty years pass, during which Jacob is tricked by his clever uncle Laban (in Hebrew "white") into marrying both of his daughters, Rachel and Leah, though he is only said to love Rachel. However, Jacob eventually gets even by tricking Laban out of the very best of all of his flocks and herds. With this vast multitude, which includes eleven children, the now rich Jacob decides to head home to Israel.

In the famous scene at the ford of the Jabbok, Jacob, alone, wrestles with "a man" (the story names the mysterious stranger only that). Neither of the combatants wins the bout, but in the process the man renames Jacob as Israel, a name that according to the story means "wrestler with God," or perhaps "God wrestles." Limping away from the fight, Jacob exclaims, "I have seen God face to face, and my life is preserved!" (The Hebrew form of the verb could also mean "I have delivered my own life," which would perhaps provide a different nuance to the meaning.) It is, of course, only from Jacob that we hear that he has seen God; the storyteller calls him only "a man." Since Jacob has been witnessed again and again to be a consummate liar, we ought not immediately buy into his belief about seeing God.

In any case, the full surprise of the story does not occur until the next chapter, 33. Jacob now rejoins his family, after sending lavish gifts to his brother (donkeys, camels, slaves), whom he believes, even after twenty years, will bear his brother nothing but fury for his trickery. Jacob in abject terror looks up and sees Esau coming down the mountainside and four hundred men are with him. He is convinced that his doom is sure. He arranges his large family in such a way that Esau's coming onslaught will fall first on Bilhah and Zilpah and their families, then on Leah and her family, and last of all on Jacob's favorites, Rachel and Joseph. Jacob, in a last ditch effort for mercy, goes in front of all of them, "bowing seven times to the ground" as he approaches Esau. We readers, like Jacob himself, expect an enraged Esau to exact his revenge without a second thought; he is known to us as a physical man who gives little thought to his actions. But now we get a mighty surprise.

"Esau ran to meet him, embraced him, fell on his neck and kissed him; they wept" (Gen 33:4). It should be noticed that the brothers are weeping for very different reasons! Esau apparently weeps because he is thrilled to see his long-lost brother; Jacob apparently weeps because he is thrilled to be alive. But what has happened to Esau during these twenty years of separation? After meeting the whole of Jacob's large family, Esau asks him, "What did you mean by all that equipment I met (i.e., on my way here)? "To find favor with my lord," Jacob replies, admitting that the gifts were an attempt to buy Esau off. (Note, too, that Jacob never in this scene calls Esau "brother." He is Esau's "servant" [vs. 5] and Esau is his "lord" [vs. 8].) Esau quickly brushes aside all the gifts and says, "I have plenty, my brother (Esau regularly calls Jacob brother); keep what is yours." But Jacob, who has taken and grabbed for what he wants all his life, loudly demands that Esau accept his gift. "No, no! (I double the "no" because the Hebrew has an emphatic particle connected to its "no.") If I have really found favor in your eyes, then take my gift from my hand! Surely, to see your face is to see the face of God. You have accepted me with such favor" (Gen 33:10)! Jacob may have claimed that he saw God in that odd wrestler back at the Jabbok, but now he announces that he has really seen God in the face of his brother Esau, who has accepted him without question or recrimination.

And in that lies the plotted surprise of the story. No reader could have expected that the plot would turn in this way, that Esau, the famished dolt of chapter 25, would become the very image of God in his acceptance of his brother in chapter 33. The actions of Jacob go as expected; he is still buying the favor of all whom he meets or bargaining to maximize his own position and possessions. But Esau receives him generously and unexpectedly. Hence, the plot is both fulfilled and is not fulfilled. Perhaps it is often so in the very greatest of stories.

Of course, this long story is far from over; we have stopped our reading in midstream. Still, the great surprise of this part of the story should not be missed. At the level of plot, the story has offered to the preacher a memorable portrait of the surprise of grace, appearing here in the least likely of persons. If the reader reads to the end of this long tale (Gen 50 and the death of Jacob), s/he will likely find other plotted elements that are well worth reflecting on as the possible framework for a story sermon.[9]

---

9. There are several such places in the ongoing plot. Two example are: the complex story of Jacob's first-born, Judah, who visits a woman whom he believes to be a prostitute, but who is in fact his desperate and ill-used daughter-in-law, Tamar. Though he impregnates her, he attempts to cover the fact over in a craven and hypocritical way (Gen 38). Also, we note that as Jacob attempted to trick his father, Isaac, out of the divine blessing by means of a clothing deception (Gen 27), so his own sons attempt to trick him by means of a clothing deception (Gen 37).

CHARACTER AND CHARACTERIZATION

> What is character but the determination of incident? What is incident but the illustration of character? What is either a picture or a novel that is *not* of character? What else do we seek in it and find in it? It is an incident for a woman to stand up with her hand resting on a table and look out at you in a certain way; or if it be not an incident I think it will be hard to say what it is.[10]

Henry James, nineteenth-century novelist and critic, here points to one of the major ways that character is determined in any fiction: what they actually *do*. As an author allows her/his readers to watch characters act, that author is adding immeasurably to the portrait of that character and thus to the reader's expectations and evaluation of the character. The same is, of course, true in life; what people do tells us important things about just who they are.

The same is even more significant in biblical narrative. Because that narrative style is so spare, so lean in its presentation, quite unlike the very full characterizations found in modern fiction like that of Henry James, any reader must pay the most careful attention to the actions of the narrative's characters. Again, as in life, what people do is not fully determinative of who they are, but it is certainly revealing and builds expectations in those who are witnesses to the action. For example, we are first introduced to the character of Saul in 1 Samuel 9. He is son of Kish and is very tall and very handsome; that is all the physical description we get. (The Bible is notoriously reticent with its physical descriptions!) In his very first action, he is charged by his father to search for some stray donkeys. He takes a servant and goes, but after a fruitless search, and one for which he seems singularly unprepared (note his short rations and complete lack of money—1 Sam 9:7), he is ready to give up. But he finally seeks help from the local seer only after being urged to do so by the servant. This is a most inauspicious beginning for the future king of Israel! Saul is here ill-prepared, hesitant, and very cautious. If the reader has been paying attention to these actions, s/he will not be altogether surprised when on the great day of Saul's public coronation as king, he is discovered hiding in the baggage (1 Sam 10:22)! Just what sort of king will this be? Saul's actions speak volumes concerning his character, and readers must attune themselves to these actions if full characterization is to be gained.

10. James, "The Art of Fiction," quoted in Scholes and Kellogg, 160.

The second way that the Bible's storytellers present their characters is through their speeches; what Bible characters say adds important nuances to the sorts of characters they are. Let us listen to the pharaoh of Egypt as he responds to the magical ability of his Israelite slaves to multiply despite his best attempts to stop them from doing so. He first observes that "the folk, the people of Israel, are more numerous and more powerful than we. Come let us deal cleverly with them lest they increase (even more?), and if there is a war, they could join our enemies, fight against us, and leave the land" (Exod 1:9–10). This is a fairly lengthy speech by biblical standards, and thus deserves careful analysis. Pharaoh's first claim seems on the face of it patently absurd. Though it may be true that there are "more" Israelite slaves than Egyptian masters, however doubtful that may be, it is ridiculous to believe that they are "more powerful" than the hosts of Pharaoh, the most powerful people of the age. If that is so, then this speech from Pharaoh reveals advanced paranoia rather than an objective evaluation of one group of his many slaves. Yet, in the face of this paranoia, however ill founded in fact, he moves toward a "clever" response. The Hebrew word is more literally "wise," but has a broad nuance; surely here he thinks he is being clever in an attempt to deal with these numerous and mighty Israelites.

Because they are first of all "numerous," and perhaps capable of becoming in the future even more numerous, the monarch has a plan. That plan is enumerated in vs. 11. He proposes to work them to the point of exhaustion, most especially on some of his building projects. After such tiring labor, the last thing on their minds when they return home will be multiplication! Such a plan seems clever indeed, but unfortunately it is a complete failure, because "the more they were oppressed the more they increased and spread, so that they (Egyptians) were in dread in their presence." In vss. 13–14 the imposition of forced labor becomes "ruthless" in brick-making, all sorts of field work, every sort of labor, but even increased oppression has no effect on the rabbit-like Israelites. In the face of the defeat of his cleverness, Pharaoh devises a more fiendish plan. He invites two Hebrew midwives, Shiphrah and Puah, into the throne room and charges them, "Whenever you play midwife to the Hebrew women, seeing them on the stones of birthing, if it is a boy, kill him, but if a girl, let her live" (vs. 16).

A moment's thought should question the "cleverness" of this plan. The proposed genocide of the males may remove, over time, some of the potential recruits for a slave revolt or enemy army collaboration, but it may do very little to solve the presenting problem that Pharaoh himself diagnosed as a surfeit of Israelites. To stop excessive births, why not slaughter those who do that, namely, the women? In any event, this more brutal plan is also a failure. The midwives lie about their work with the Hebrew women, claiming that those women are so strong (literally "full of life" vs. 19) that they simply cannot get to the birthing place fast enough before the women are back to work, presumably carrying their newborns with them! In the midst of the lie they also quite directly demean the worth of Pharaoh's own Egyptian women. In response to this continued defeat of his plans, rather than punishing the midwives or investigating their ridiculous claims, Pharaoh blurts out a monstrously stupid command to "all his people." "Every boy that is born you must hurl into the Nile, but you must let every daughter live!" Though the Septuagint, the third–second century BCE Greek translation of the Hebrew text, adds "to the Hebrews" after the phrase "every boy that is born," that does not occur in the Hebrew. And the omission is significant for the characterization of Pharaoh. He began with his "clever" plan of exhausting the Israelites to prevent their increase, then suggested a more direct male genocide, and now concludes with the wild plan that "all boys born," whether Egyptian or Israelite, must be tossed to their deaths in the Nile. He is hell-bent on slowing the Israelite increase, and is now willing to sacrifice even his own Egyptian newborns to do so. He seals the complete absurdity of his final plan by again demanding that "every girl shall live." It could be said after listening to the great pharaoh that he is several bricks short of a load! The world's mightiest monarch is reduced by his own speeches to a spluttering, genocidal monster, who appears both terrifying and ridiculous at the same time. Such is the power of verbal speech in the narrative art of the Hebrew storytellers.

This portrait of an increasingly mad pharaoh demonstrates both the art of speech in characterization, but also the combination of action and speech as dual means to show character. Pharaoh's questionable words are well matched by his absurd actions to complete a picture of a man falling into a murderous madness. I am reminded here of the wonderful and terrifying Charlie Chaplin film, *The Great Dictator*, wherein Chaplin lampoons Hitler as both terrible and ludicrous at the same time. It could be said that Pharaoh's picture in Exodus 1 is nothing less than the archetype of all tyrants, simultaneously both dangerous and mad.

Other Means of Characterization

Physical Description

Though I noted above that the stories of the Hebrew Bible do not offer much in the way of physical description, nevertheless there are telling places where description is an important element of characterization. The classic example may be found in one of the Hebrew Bible's most famous stories, the battle between David and Goliath detailed in 1 Samuel 17. This story has become, of course, an archetypal depiction of the astonishing victory of little person over big person, often employed when there is a political or sporting upset, when the expected winner is defeated by the "dark horse." In this case, however, the physical description makes that simple meaning rather more complex.[11]

When David is first introduced to us in 1 Samuel 16 as the chosen king of God, he is described in three ways; he is ruddy (red-haired), has beautiful eyes, and is good-looking (easy on other's eyes). But as he goes out to fight the giant, Goliath in the next chapter, the huge Philistine champion scorns his adversary as one who is "ruddy with beautiful eyes." Goliath sees what we saw about David's physical description, but concludes that he is only a red-haired pretty boy, not a worthwhile combatant. But it is what Goliath does *not* see that will be his undoing. We are told that David enters the battlefield with his shepherd's staff in one hand and his sling in the other (17:40), but Goliath sees only the staff and even scornfully calls it a "stick" (17:43). He does not see the deadly sling.

And a further piece of physical description is crucial for the scene. Back in vss. 4–7, the narrator treats us to the longest single physical description of a human being in the Bible. Though we are not told anything about Goliath's beauty or lack of it, we are told numerous details about the image he presents on the battlefield. He is fantastically tall, nearly ten feet, if ancient cubit lengths be any guide. (This immensity was apparently too much for the translators of the Septuagint and certain Qumran manuscripts, since they reduced Goliath's height to the somewhat more reasonable 4 cubits from the Hebrew Bible's 6.) And on this vast frame is found a huge bronze helmet (no size given), an enormous coat of chain mail weighing five thousand shekels of bronze (perhaps between one hundred and

11. See Alter, *The Art of Biblical Narrative*, 81, for the impetus for my subsequent analysis of this scene.

one hundred fifty pounds)[12] and form-fitting metal greaves from knees to sandal-tops on both legs. Slung between his massive shoulders is a spear whose shaft has the mass of a weaver's beam, the main frame of a large loom, and a spearhead weighing six hundred shekels of iron (perhaps fifteen or sixteen pounds).[13] This formidable portrait has struck terror in the hearts of the readers of the story since first it was told. Indeed, one look at Goliath and the hearts of the Israelites turn to jelly (vss. 11, 24). But David has a different reaction.

It has long been understood that since David was a man chosen by God that he faced Goliath with a faith that Saul, his brothers, and the rest of the host of Israel did not have. However much that may be true, it is not the whole picture. The storyteller has made it clear that Goliath is characterized by size and weight, offering us actual measurements of both to make the point. Goliath is huge, all right, and in any close combat with any normal-sized human being would certainly prevail. David, on the other hand, is small, the youngest of eight sons of Jesse, but he is also adept at a skill that makes the battle far more even. He possesses a mobile missile-launcher, and knows as soon as he lays his beautiful eyes on Goliath that his weapon can win the day. In short, what David sees is not an impregnable fortress of a man, but rather a tank without an engine.

With that clarity of description in mind, listen to the scene of the battle as I translate 17:48 quite literally: "Thus, when the Philistine got up, and went out, and drew near to meet David, David rushed quickly toward the line of battle to meet the Philistine." Note the different descriptions given to the movements of the two figures. The massive Goliath takes three verbs to go into action (it likewise takes him three verbs to move in vs. 41, though most translations disguise the fact), while the agile David, dependent on speed and on staying away from Goliath's enormous size, "rushes quickly *toward* the line of battle," avoiding Goliath's spear range but within range of his sling. Alter summarizes well the significance of the physical descriptions in this famous scene.

> The thematic purpose of this exceptional attention to physical detail is obvious: Goliath moves into action as a man of iron and bronze, an almost grotesquely quantitative embodiment of a hero, and this hulking monument to an obtusely mechanical conception

12. Klein, *1 Samuel*, 175.
13. Ibid., 176.

of what constitutes power is marked to be felled by a clever shepherd boy with his slingshot.[14]

The Inner Lives of Characters

Though it is true that Hebrew narrative art shows little interest in its characters' inner lives, a very important feature of much modern literature, nevertheless there are important exceptions. Joseph, the pampered son and hated brother, becomes through a series of astonishing circumstances the right-hand man of the pharaoh of Egypt. A severe famine drives his brothers, who thought they had killed him long ago, to Egypt to find food. They are ushered into the palace of a mighty Egyptian who is in fact their brother. And there at the moment of confrontation, the narrator enters into Joseph's mind and invites us to follow. "Joseph saw his brothers and knew them . . . but they did not know him. And Joseph remembered the dreams that he had dreamed of them" (Gen 39:7–9). Here is a rich inner life indeed! Saying nothing, Joseph sees his brothers, recognizes them, immediately realizes that they do not know who he is, and remembers the dreams of power he had so many years before. After witnessing all that inner drama, Joseph's first words may come as something of a shock. He accuses his brothers of being spies! Why exactly he would say that, of all things, is the driving force behind the narrative for the next several chapters.

Even God on at least one momentous occasion is described as having an inner life. In Gen 8:21, God gracefully accepts Noah's pleasant-smelling sacrifice and then speaks in the divine heart, i.e., to God's own self, "I will never again curse the ground because of the human beings, because the imagination of their hearts is evil from their youth." The very reason the flood came in the first place was "the evil imaginations of the human beings from their youth" (Gen 6:5)! So the reader in this case hears from the inner monologue of God that God has changed God's grieved heart concerning God's human creatures. There will never again be a flood of destruction from God, because human shortcomings are an inevitable part of the human creation. Hence, inner life can be a significant element in biblical characterization.[15]

14. Alter, *The Art of Biblical Narrative*, 81.

15. Berlin, *Poetics and Interpretation of Biblical Narrative*, adds "contrasting characters" to her list of the means of characterization, noting the contrasting descriptions of Nabal and Abigail (1 Samuel 25), Jacob and Esau (as we noted in chapter 1), and Uriah and David (2 Samuel 11).

POINT OF VIEW

In addition to plot and characterization, it is important to examine briefly the complex subject of narrative point of view. To study point of view in story is to study just who is telling the tale, one of the characters (first-person) or the narrator (third-person). As Scholes and Kellogg have it: "In the relationship between the teller and the tale, and that other relationship between the teller and the audience, lies the essence of narrative art."[16] It matters a great deal just who is telling the story to me, whether or not I can trust that person in his/her telling, and thus how I, as reader/hearer, am to evaluate what I have been told. The great majority of stories in the Hebrew Bible are told from a third-person point of view; the narrator narrates the story to me. But within the bounds of the story, first-person narration can occur, and when it does, I need to listen carefully to determine whether or not what I am reading is to be trusted fully.

In the discussion of the Jacob/Esau story above, I noted that Jacob alone, in a direct speech, claimed that after his wrestling match with the man at the Jabbok River, he had "seen God face-to-face." No one else, including the teller of the story, makes that claim. And when in the next chapter he says that seeing Esau's face "is like seeing the face of God," it makes me even more suspicious that Jacob's claim to have seen God at the Jabbok may need to be taken with a grain of salt. Jacob's point of view as trustworthy truth-teller has over and over again been called into the most serious question in his story.

Or consider the famous story of Job. Twice in the first chapter the reader is told that Job is "blameless and upright," once by the narrator in 1:1 and once by God in 1:8. We thus have two witnesses to the peerless nature of Job. Thus when his "friends" begin in their speeches to impugn Job's morality and truthfulness, we, the readers, know that they are wrong. We know what they do not; Job is righteous, because we have been told that he is righteous while his friends have not.

One of the more significant examples of the importance of point of view for full understanding may be found in 1 Samuel 31 and 2 Samuel 1. In these two places the reader receives two very different stories of the death of Saul. In the former we read that Saul was killed by his own armor-bearer on Mount Gilboa after being mortally wounded by the Philistines, in order that he might be spared a humiliating death at the hands of the

---

16. Scholes and Kellogg, *The Nature of Narrative*, 240.

"uncircumcised," the unclean, pagan enemy. In the later chapter, a disheveled Amalekite warrior, showing all the appearances of deep mourning, claims to have wandered into the very middle of the battle between Saul's Israelites and the Philistines, to have seen Saul mortally wounded and in deep distress, and to have killed the king at his own request. He shows David Saul's crown and armband to prove his story, and, no doubt, to buy the favor of the one who will soon be king.

Are these merely two traditions of Saul's death? It was common for nineteenth-century historical critics to understand the disparate reports so. But narrative point of view provides another answer. First Samuel 31 offers a third-person report of the death of Saul, and since we have no significant reason to question such a report from such a narrator, we can be certain that this is a true account. Hence, when we are faced with another account in the next chapter, uttered in the first person by a foreigner bearing the emblems of kingship to the next king of Israel, we have every reason to be suspicious. This self-serving account by an Amalekite (David has been warring against Amalekites from his Philistine base in Ziklag for the previous several years) filled with dramatic speeches supposedly uttered by Saul and himself (2 Sam 1:6–10) has the express purpose of flattering the new king and gaining a reward from him. Unfortunately for this Amalekite, David has a consistent habit of destroying those who dare to "lay their hands on the Lord's anointed" (here again at 2 Sam 1:14). After all, David is himself the Lord's anointed and hardly wants the precedent of regicide established in Israel. So he has this Amalekite killed on the spot. Note that we never know whether or not David actually believes the report of the Amalekite; he could be telling the truth or not. In either case, it gets him killed. But in the face of the previous report of Saul's death, it is a good bet that the second report was a lie.

When thinking of point of view in stories, think of a camera. That camera's lens shows you only what it wants to show you. Other things are clearly going on outside of the lens—on the movie or TV set—but you are shown only what the lens, used by the director, allows. Think of a presidential news conference. The camera is focused on the president, while the reporters shout their questions from off-stage. The camera molds the viewer into thinking that the president is the central figure here, and the reporters are merely bit players in the drama. Occasionally, the camera will give us the heavyweight reporters in the front row, and even more occasionally, some less significant reporters in some middle rows, but the vast bulk of airtime is the president's. Point of view tells us what and who is important about this event.[17]

PREACHING THE NARRATIVES

The very best way to learn how to preach story sermons is actually to preach them after exploring some examples and their evaluations. I propose to do just that in the next four chapters. But in this brief section I wish to introduce some techniques for preaching in this style that might prove useful as you read the succeeding chapters with their examples.

Use the Narrative Carefully

You will soon see in the examples that follow that I have spent a great deal of time exegeting the story. As in all biblical preaching, extensive and careful exegesis is the key to serious preaching. This is doubly true if your sermonic goal is a story sermon. These biblical stories are in the main so well written that they offer quite specific guidelines to anyone who wishes to retell them in a sermon. The first rule of story preaching is: let the story itself be your guide.

I read Hebrew, and I imagine some of you do not. It is a great advantage if you are able to read and evaluate the language of the Hebrew Bible, but it is not any sort of an unmanageable hurdle if you cannot. Good modern commentaries can lead you into the vagaries of Hebrew a fair distance, and interesting modern translations can do the same.[18] There is no reason in the twenty-first century for you to remain at the complete mercy of any given translation of the Bible; the tools are too good and too numerous, so take advantage of them.

---

17. You might try applying these principles of point of view to the great narrative of Exodus 32. Watch where the narrator (camera) leads you, from the mob and Aaron at the base of the mountain, to Moses and YHWH at the peak, then back down the mountain with Moses and Aaron. And within these pairs of characters whose point of view is being portrayed? What effects do these shifting points of view have on the characterizations and thus on the meaning of the story?

18. Several modern translations attempt to capture in English some of the rich nuance of the Hebrew text. Three are: Fox, *The Five Books of Moses*; Alter, *The Five Books of Moses* and *The David Story*.

TYPES OF STORY SERMONS

In my 1991 book, I listed five possible types of narrative sermons. I will briefly summarize and add to what I said there.

Pure Story

A pure story sermon is just that: an unembellished story. In a sermon like this one, the preacher does not tell the story and then explain in more discursive language what the story may mean. The meaning of the story arises from the telling itself. The teller weaves into the fabric of the story the intended meaning for that particular telling. The adjective "pure" means only that no explanation of the story is provided outside the bounds of the narrative; the sermon's introduction is the introduction of the story, and the sermon's conclusion is the conclusion of the story.

This shape does not mean that the preacher merely reads the words of the story from the Bible, nor does it mean that s/he reads those words more dramatically than usual. The teller's imagination is fully engaged in the preparation of a pure story sermon as details revealed in the reading are elaborated, expanded, made more picturesque, modernized, illuminated in myriad ways in order to make the text live for the modern congregation.

My sermon in that earlier book, "The Best Laugh of All," based on Genesis 22, is an attempt at a pure story sermon.[19] As I have reflected on that sermon over the past 20 years, it is clear to me that it is in fact not absolutely "pure!" The final several lines of the sermon are a restatement of language from Hebrews 11 and not strictly language directly from the text. In effect, it is a multiple story sermon, I suppose (see below), but since the vast bulk of it is a direct retelling of the harrowing Genesis story, it is very close to a pure story sermon.

Frame Story

There are many occasions where the preacher wants to focus the story so as to help the listeners listen to the story with a particular goal for that story in mind. I can think of at least two reasons for using a frame for a story sermon. First, the biblical story is so rich in its multiple themes that if the

19. Holbert, *Preaching*, 79–92.

story is told without some framing help, the hearers may be drowned in the complexity and search frantically in an attempt to discover just what the point of this story for today's preaching actually is. Second, the familiarity of the story may make it necessary to help the hearer hear the story in a new way. In my reading of the very familiar story of the Two Sons in Luke 15 in the previous chapter, I noted that many have heard it as a story of repentance/forgiveness, based on a particular reading of the line, "when he came to himself." If I wanted to preach the story with another focus than that one, I could begin with a frame pointing to that different nuance, thus "clearing the decks" for a new hearing today. My story sermon on Genesis 2–3 in the next chapter is an example of a frame story sermon.

Frames can come from anywhere that typical sermon illustrations come from. The point of the frame is to focus the attention of the listener so as to help her/him gain clues concerning the reason the story is being told. The frame is not designed to explain the story but to lead the hearer toward the story's meaning for this telling. Such framing devices can help the teller avoid one of the dangers of this style of preaching, what might be called the "dazed story look." If the story is well told, it is possible that the hearer will get so caught up in the telling that the claim of the gospel will be swept away in the experience. I do not believe that the reason one preaches story sermons is to focus on the community experience of the telling itself, however delightful that may be. Shared experience is not automatically shared experience of the gospel. All sermons of whatever kind are preached to speak some portion of the gospel of Christ into a community always in need of it. Hence, the frame can help congregations avoid the danger of reducing the sermon event to one of generalized experience rather than a common experience of the gospel.

Multiple Story Sermons

This style of story preaching is precisely like the frame story described above, except that in this style the frame is always another biblical story. Two biblical stories are used to illuminate one another in some way, often to say the same thing in two different ways. This style is especially helpful to demonstrate the commonality of the gospel message in each of the two testaments. For example, my story sermon on Jonah in a later chapter could be paired with the story of the two sons in Luke 15, since in one reading the stories can be said to say something quite similar. Jonah at the end of the tale is outside the community of joy, represented by the sailors and the Ninevite humans and animals, just as the elder brother in Luke stands outside the party going on in the house where calf and joy are on the menu. Thus, Jonah and the elder brother refuse to join the respective parties of those who were lost, and each story asks the hearers, among other things, why that is so.

Such a style can go a long way toward demonstrating that the Hebrew Bible is rife with the gospel and stands not only as a foil to it. Preachers should avoid using the Hebrew Bible as what is "wrong" in order to provide New Testament "right answers" to solve that supposed wrong. By doing that the preacher adds to the dangerous stereotyping that has plagued the Hebrew Bible for centuries and has led to the horrors of anti-Semitism, surely among the most evil pages in the church's long history. Multiple story sermons can be helpful when done with sensitivity and care.

Fictional Stories

In this style the preacher writes a fictional story in response to a close reading of a biblical story. The decision is made to do this, because the preacher determines that the ancient story as it is presented does not speak as clearly or as forcefully as a more modern story might. Of course, such decisions have been made by numerous contemporary authors who have "updated" biblical stories in many creative ways. We can think of William Faulkner's retelling of part of the David story in his *Absalom, Absalom* or John Steinbeck's reworking of the Cain and Abel story in his *East of Eden*. Many examples can be provided.[20] Of course, to examine those great artists who have woven their authorial magic in response to biblical texts is surely daunting for those who would attempt to write any fictional story, however brief. My sermon on 1 Samuel 15 in this book is one such attempt. I am far from a great stylist, but I found the writing of that sermon quite exhilarating, and I would recommend the attempt to any who have any sort of writing tug lurking deep within.

20. See the massive *A Dictionary of Biblical Tradition in English Literature*, for hundreds of further examples.

A Threaded Story

In this style the preacher chooses to tell the story both by telling and commenting on the story at the same time. To do this effectively, that is to maintain the forward movement of the story, it is helpful to choose a storyteller who has full access to the story and to its meaning. In other words, the preacher needs an omniscient teller, one who is both engaged deeply in the telling of the story, but also is intent on telling the story so as to offer the meaning of it to the hearer.

My sermon on Judges 4 is an example of a threaded story. I chose an unnamed old person who knew the story very well, as well as I did, and who knew what I wanted to say about it. So he/she was able to tell and to comment simultaneously. In effect, this teller is my surrogate preacher, and I can manipulate him/her in any way I choose. I, of course, can just go ahead and tell the story myself, but using another person to tell may add an intimate sense of engagement to the telling and a sense of greater freedom for me as preacher. As I wrote that sermon, I felt quite free to tell the story with an eye on making it plain all along the way just why I was telling this story.

A threaded story is slightly different from a pure story in that the threaded story is more obvious in its commentary on the story being told. The pure story requires more art to avoid direct commentary, instead weaving the commentary directly into the fabric of the story. I suggest that the threaded story is easier to perform, but may lose something of the immediacy and freshness of the pure story sermon.

A Personal Story

Here the preacher relates a personal experience that is fully illuminative of the biblical witness. It may be this sort of story preaching that especially rankles those who emphasize the limitations of story preaching in general. A sharing of my experience runs the danger of reducing the power of the gospel to a passing and transient event that does not, indeed cannot, offer the specific power of the gospel as it is given to us in the scriptures (see especially Richard Lischer's important warnings about this in chapter 1).

Still, despite the dangers of trivializing that are endemic in the style, my own experience with listening to such sermons suggest to me that there is potentially great power here. I will never forget a personal story sermon I heard in my seminary chapel some thirty years ago that used the preacher's personal experience as a young pastor as illuminative of a particular biblical text. It was a Pauline text, and thus not a story text, but the theme of grace had never been made so memorable to me as that pastor's experience did that day. In his sermon, grace became an offered piece of pie, and even now as I think of God's grace that image will often float into my consciousness. I do not find this image trivial at all, but rather very helpful and very real as I attempt to understand the wonders of God's amazing grace.

I know all too well how personal experience can be misused for crass manipulation of emotions and to suggest that "my" experience is always just like "your" experience. Both are dangerous aberrations and can perform all manner of mischief among those hungry for the true word of the gospel. Yet, I know that when well and thoughtfully used, my reflective personal experience can be helpful to me and to my listeners. Surely, every preacher will want to have a sermon relaying to the congregation the call of the preacher, as that call is experienced in the light of calls from God as described in the Bible. Here our own experience is crucial if our congregations want to know us so they can better hear us.

How to Tell the Story

Once you know the Bible's story, you are ready to unleash your rich imagination to bring the story back to modern life. At this point, some of you will say, "Well, I am just not a good storyteller. I can't remember jokes, and when I do I often miss the punchline!" This may indeed be true for you, but nevertheless you can learn to tell a biblical story. I heartily recommend the brief but quite comprehensive "self-directed workshop" on biblical storytelling by my friend, Michael Williams, in any of the volumes of the Abingdon Press series, *A Storyteller's Companion to the Bible*. I happen to have in front of me the first volume of the series on Genesis that Michael and I published in 1991.[21] Let me reiterate the salient points of Michael's workshop for you, and update them a bit since twenty years have now passed. Please do the following, and in this order.

Read the story aloud at least twice. Stories always sound different in the ears than they do in the eyes. Pay attention to where the story takes place, when it takes place, who the characters are, what objects are important,

---

21. Williams, *A Storyteller's Companion to the Bible*, 23–24.

and what the general order of the plot is. I am assuming that your careful exegesis will already be done when you start the storytelling workshop, but it may be just as well to keep these particular questions in mind as you are doing the exegesis so as to keep the goal of the sermon in mind from the very beginning.

Close your eyes and imagine the story taking place. Here you are in control, and imagination is at a premium. Let yourself go! Don't be afraid to venture a bit, outside of what you have in the past found comfortable. In my experience, the danger of the sermons I hear is rarely too much imagination, but too little.

Look back at the Bible's story to be sure you have not left out important characters, places, things, or events.

Try telling the story aloud to your spouse, your friend, or even your dog. Of course, the dog will not help you in the responses you need, but spouse or friend can when you ask them for their questions. Where were they confused? What more information do they need? Is the story appropriate to those likely to hear it?

This step is my own addition to Michael's steps. No one tells a story, nor does anyone preach any sermon, without a clear goal in mind. I must have something in my mind that I wish to impart to my hearers. In other words, story sermons, just like all sermons, need to have clarity. There is little room in the church for stories for their own sake, stories that leave listeners confused or bewildered. And no story preacher should hide behind the notion "Well, I leave the meaning to them." Every hearer of every sermon is likely to create his/her own meaning out of the words you have spoken, but the goal of our preaching is to impart a meaning. In short, your story sermon has a point, and every part of the story needs to reinforce that point, so that by the end, few will be confused about what that point is. Part of the process of creating a story sermon is to clarify for yourself what the point of the story is for today. When in the future the same story is used, it may portray a different point, given the very different circumstances of its telling.[22]

---

22. A personal experience makes the point. I was preaching in Gulfport, Mississippi in Febuary of 2006, about six months after the massive hurricane Katrina had devastated that community along with numerous others along the shores of the Gulf of Mexico. My sermon was a retelling of the story of Job. As I told the part about the self-important and comfortable friends of Job, and their certainty that Job was on the ash heap because of his sins, many nods of recognition appeared in the congregation. The previous week, before my arrival, two nationally prominent politicians had surmised that the Gulf Coast had been so hard hit due to the influence of gambling there and due to the vice that

Read a modern Bible dictionary to find out more about places, characters, professions, etc. I suggest now the *Anchor Bible Dictionary*.

Practice, practice, practice! Revise as you go. You are not memorizing but getting the story into your heart and on your lips. Make the entire process as oral as you can, so that the story has an oral quality to it. I recommend that you never write a full manuscript of a story sermon, so as to avoid a written quality to your telling. However, you may feel more comfortable writing it out, if that is your practice. But if you do write, get away from the manuscript as soon as possible in your preparation.

Have fun! I have always found these kinds of sermons the most enjoyable to preach, since they allow me to become more of myself, and afford me the opportunity of engaging a part of myself that I do not always engage.

I hope that the next four chapters will prove helpful to you as you explore the possibilities of story preaching for yourself. I offer them as examples of how those sorts of sermons can work and examples of the readings on which they are based.

---

flowed forth from the casinos. After the service, a member of the church commented to me that if that idea were true then God's aim must be poor. Why not assault Las Vegas if gambling were the trigger for divine displeasure? And when I concluded the sermon with the certain notion that human behavior does not assure divine attack, the congregation was audibly relieved. Many of them thanked me for the story of Job that their terrible experiences had made them hear in a very new way. Stories can perform a healing function, too.

THREE

"To Give, To Take, To Eat"

A Reading of Genesis 2:4b—3:24

IT IS PRESUMPTUOUS TO imagine that anything genuinely new could be said about these two famous chapters. The written and oral reflection upon them has been both rich and strange. Also, the sheer number of books, articles, and sermons is little short of incredible.[1] Yet, the chief advantage of a fresh reading of the whole text, as I shall attempt to supply, is perhaps not that anything really new will emerge, but that a new combination of some of the familiar elements may spark the story preacher towards some new thinking. Our goal in this or any literary reading is to identify one major thrust of the narrative that may serve a preacher as her/his central focus for a particular telling of the story. By this focus on one major thrust, I do not in any way imply that another reading of the text might not yield a completely different focus. Surely, the history of the fantastic array of readings of these two chapters should be proof enough of that claim! But I hope that my reading has at least the advantage of taking the details of the text with great seriousness. Those who find fault with it must be willing to grapple with the actual words of the text as I have tried to do. I claim no exclusive "rightness" for the following analysis. I can only claim that I have wrestled with the text in its detailed wholeness; but as Jacob has taught us, those who would wrestle with mysterious strangers run the risk of coming up lame. If the following is lame, it will not be because of the lack of a game effort to seek at least one of the names of my awesome opponent.

---

1. Westermann, *Genesis 1–11*; Speiser, *Genesis*; Towner, *Genesis*; Brueggemann, *Genesis*; Vawter, *On Genesis* for a tiny sample.

READING GENESIS 2:4B-3:24

By nearly all scholarly accounts, the story that we will address in this reading begins in Gen 2:4b. I will not once again rehearse the numerous reasons that have led so many scholars to this conclusion: that information is easily available in any number of sources.[2] Nor will I engage in debate about the so-called two accounts of creation represented by the first three chapters of Genesis. Such questions are not primary to a literary reading in any case. Our first task is to *read* the text, and withhold as many judgments as possible that might tend to prejudice our reading in any way. I begin my reading in 2:4b because of the obvious introduction to the narrative that I find there, because the divine figure in the story is suddenly referred to in a different way than I have witnessed in chapter one, because the location of this narrative has moved to the desert from the vast ocean of the first chapter, and because the tone of the writing is now so clearly a story with plot, character, and dialogue as major features of its creation.

Genesis 2:4b–7

> *(4) On the day when YHWH God made the earth and sky, (5) there being no field shrub as yet on the earth, nor had any field grasses yet sprouted because YHWH God had not caused rain to fall on the earth, nor was there any soil creature to work the soil—(6) though a mist used to rise up from the earth to water the whole surface of the soil—(7) then YHWH God molded the soil creature out of dust from the soil, and breathed into its nostrils the breath of life so that the soil creature became a living being.*

Several comments need to be made about my translation. For those readers who do not use Hebrew, this text is replete with puns and word games. This playing with language is not at all incidental to a serious reading of the text, and so they must be indicated and discussed if we are to arrive at some satisfactory reading of the whole. I will attempt to capture as many of these word games in my translation as I can, but many of them are simply not transferable to English.[3]

2. See any of the above commentaries.

3. Two recent translations do their best to capture as many puns and word games as can be done from one language to another: Fox, *The Five Books of Moses*; Alter, *The Five Books of Moses*.

1. I have read *'adam* as "soil creature" for two reasons. First, the author puns on the relationship in Hebrew between the word for "earth, land, or soil" (*'adamah*) and the word used to designate this first creation of God, *'adam*. I like this reading better than Phyllis Trible's "earth creature" because the latter confuses the fact that the word for "earth" used in this section is *erets*, meaning "the whole earth."[4] The creature is not of the "earth"; it is of the soil, the dirt of the earth. Second, the author is not describing the creation of a male here; sexual differentiation does not occur in the text until the creation of the woman, as Trible has so clearly demonstrated.[5] This creature is hence not "Adam," the first male in the world. This is "soil creature," God's gardener, as the next section will point out.

2. When the narrator refers to God in the story, the two-pronged designation "YHWH God" is used. The fact that the characters of the story do *not* speak of God in this fashion is significant.

3. The word translated "molded" in vs. 7 is a verb often used in connection with the work of a potter (see, for example, Isa 29:16; 41:25; 45:9, 18; Jer 18:4, 6). God is often so described as one who molds or fashions the divine work in a very plastic way (see, among others, Isa 27:11; 43:1, 21; 44:21; 45:9, 11; Jer 1:5; Amos 7:1). Surely, the narrator presents the image that God is an artisan, carefully fashioning the divine creation with individual attention. (Compare the portrait of God given in chapter one of Genesis where God is described as one who creates by the sound of the voice alone.)

4. God animates the soil creature by breathing into its nostrils the "breath of life." Because of this divine breath, the soil creature becomes "a living being." In both of those phrases the operative word is "life, living," from the Hebrew *chayah*. Such life comes only from God. Later in the story (Gen 3:22–24), there will be real concern that the divine creation might steal the tree of "life" and live forever. By suggesting that life comes from God, rather than from an act of the creatures of God, the narrator frames the story by concern with the true origins of life; is life given or is it taken? This is a theme to which we will return.

---

4. Trible, *God and the Rhetoric of Sexuality*, 77.

5. Ibid., 96–97.

Genesis 2:8–9

> *(8) YHWH God planted a garden in Eden in the East and put there the soil creature just molded. (9) Then YHWH God caused to sprout from the soil all trees pleasant for seeing and good for eating, and the tree of life in the middle of the garden and the tree of the knowledge of good and bad.*

God now creates an environment for the soil creature, a fine Middle Eastern park of trees. Surely, the narrator has an oasis in mind, a spot of green in the heart of the vastness of the arid desert. And into this lovely oasis Yahweh puts the molded creation. What the little creature is to do is not revealed until vs. 15. Two trees are singled out for special mention among those of the garden. First mentioned is the tree of life. We are surprised by this tree, and wonder at its full significance. After all, we have just observed that life is God's gift to the creature in vs. 7; what possible meaning could a tree of life have now? And the second tree, the tree of the knowledge of good and bad, is introduced without any warning at all. But the fact that they are singled out raises tensions in the story. What relationship will the soil creature have to these trees? What is the knowledge of good and bad? How does the tree of life relate to the gift of life to the soil creature by God? These questions and others are deferred for a time while the narrator shows us the continued significance of water for the story world.

Genesis 2:10–14

> *(10) Now a river used to flow out of Eden to water the garden, and from there it was divided to become four branches. (11) The name of the first is Pishon; it flows around the whole land of Havilah where there is gold. (12) The gold of that land is good. There is bedellium and onyx stone as well. (13) The name of the second is Gihon; it flows around the whole land of Cush. (14) The name of the third river is Tigris; it runs east of Assyria. The name of the fourth is Euphrates.*

Many scholars insist on the secondary status of this passage.[6] Its interests in geography and the products of various countries seem wildly out of place in the story of the creation of the Garden of God, the soil creature, and

---

6. See Skinner, *Genesis*, 66; Von Rad, *Genesis*, 79; but see Westermann, *Genesis 1–11*, 214–22 for a more nuanced view.

the relationships between the two. However, at least three reasons for this section may be suggested.

1. The concern is with water, and that has been a concern from the very beginning of our story. There was at first "no rain"; the place from where water is to be expected, the sky, has yielded nothing. There is that mysterious "mist" that arises from under the earth and waters the whole surface of the ground. In lieu of water from above and the uncertainty and mystery of the water from below, the surface water of great rivers is needed to water the oasis of God. Two of the rivers are, of course, well known, the Tigris and the Euphrates, and provide to the reader the sense of verisimilitude needed to ensure the continuous supply of precious water for God's garden. Note how Eden and the garden are clearly separated in the story; the river rises *out of* Eden in order to water the garden. All of the world's water can be found to arise from the same source that waters the garden of God. This passage ensures to the reader that there will be water for the garden.[7]

2. Note also how the passage follows the pattern of the previous one. In verses 8 and 9, the trees are first mentioned as a general category, and then two particular trees are singled out for comment. So in this section, a generic river is mentioned, and then four specific rivers are noted. This movement from general to specific will be characteristic of the story's movement. Thus, the passage is well integrated into the overall scheme of the narrative.

3. I am struck by the use of the term "good" to describe the gold of the land of Havilah (vs. 12). It calls to mind the appearance of the tree of knowledge of good and bad. Has our narrator already eaten from the tree to be able to make the sort of judgments that would call things either good or bad? Are those the kinds of judgments one would be able to make if that tree were sampled? Is that all that is at stake in the tree? By announcing that simple judgment about the gold, our narrator again piques our curiosity about the tree, and points to the fact that we will need eventually to reckon with the tree of the knowledge of good and bad.

Thus, the "intrusive" passage about the rivers serves several important functions for the narration by solving for the reader the crucial need for water, by reinforcing the pattern established of the movement from general to specific, and by focusing the reader's interest ever more squarely on the

7. Westermann, *Genesis*, 216.

tree of knowledge. With these corroborative facts in mind, we may now return to the garden and the soil creature.

Genesis 2:15–17

> *(15) YHWH God took the soil creature and put it in the garden of Eden to serve it and protect it. (16) And YHWH God commanded the soil creature, "From any tree of the garden you may surely eat: (17) but from the tree of the knowledge of good and bad you may not eat from it, because when you eat from it you will surely die."*

The tensions of the story, hidden in the reading until now, finally burst to the surface, but without any final clarity. We are told that the soil creature is made by God for work; the creature of God is made for labor, however much pictures of an idyllic Eden where all loll about eating clusters of luscious grapes may be deeply embedded in our minds. The soil creature is to "serve it"; the noun form of this verb is the typical Hebrew word for "slave." And the creature is to "protect it," to guard it from whatever dangers may arise. But the first real danger arises, surprisingly, from within.

YHWH God speaks to the soil creature for the first time, and the speech is in the form of command. First, *every* tree is made available for eating; the verbal form at the end of the sentence of command is very strong—"you may surely eat," or more literally, "eating, you may eat." But, second, no sooner has this wonderfully general and generous word been uttered, when the commanding God points specifically to that tree of the knowledge of good and bad, and in much harsher terms strictly forbids its eating. Using the same verbal construction that magnanimously offered to the creature every tree of the garden, Yahweh God now warns it that "when you eat from it, dying, you will die." The syntax of the warning is ambiguous. In the first sentence of our story, a temporal clause reads, "When God made," or one might read "on the day of God's making." Now God warns, "When you eat," or again, "On the day of your eating." Does God here imply that the creature *will* eat, just as surely as God made the sky and the earth, or is it just a warning of what would happen *if* the creature eats? In either case the tension of the story screws tighter, and the mystery of the tree deepens. Why is the tree denied to the creature? Why is death the result of eating from the forbidden tree? Are we to see this tree as the tree of death and juxtapose it to the now unmentioned tree of life? The shadow of the prohibition is now cast over the remainder of the story, and our questions increase.

The theme of this particular reading is beginning to take shape. God has given life to the soil creature and has given it a task. The gifts of God were first unencumbered; "freely eat from every tree," says God. But God does not only give; God takes as well. First, God "takes" the creature, and puts it into the garden for work. Second, God takes away the freedom and inclusiveness of the gift by denying the tree to the creature. And third, eating will become the means of transgressing the command of the God who gives and who takes. To give, to take, and to eat will be the theme as this reading progresses.

Genesis 2:18–20

> (18) YHWH God said: "It is not good for the soil creature to be alone. I will make for it a companion like it." (19) So YHWH God molded out of soil every creature and every bird of the sky, and brought them to the soil creature to see what it would call them. Whatever the soil creature called them, those living beings, that was their name. (20) The soil creature called out names for every domesticated creature. But as for the soil creature, it did not find a companion who was like it.

The narrator earlier made a judgment about the goodness of the gold of Havilah; now Yahweh God makes a judgment about the soil creature. It is not good that it remain alone. Apparently, we may conclude that God has eaten from the tree that makes judgments of good and bad possible. Only the soil creature, and we, the readers, are not able to make such judgments. The tree becomes more and more intriguing!

God also returns in this passage to the molding activity that formed the soil creature in the first place. God is looking for a companion for the soil creature. A word about the text is important here. The word I have translated as "companion" is usually read "helper." This noun is often used of God in the Hebrew Bible, especially in the hymnic literature of Israel (see Deut 33:7; Pss 33:210; 115:9–11; 70:5; Exod 18:4). The verb, on which the noun is based, often has God as its subject (see Ps 10:14; 1 Sam 7:12; Isa 41:10, 13–14 and many others). The English word "helper" often carries with it the meaning "assistant," as in the phrase plumber's helper. This sense of assistant is not in the Hebrew word. *God* is most often the helper of Israel. Thus, when the narrator uses this word to describe the figure that God wishes to create for the soil creature, no thought of secondary or second best is in mind.

The second part of the phrase, translated by the KJV as "meet for him," a reading brought into the RSV as "fit for him," is plainly impossible in the Hebrew text.

One finds three small Hebrew words here. Those words are *c*, 'like," *neged*, "in relation to," or "over against," and *o*, "it" or "him." Thus, literally one could read, "like in relationship to it," or more simply, "like it." What God wants for the soil creature is a companion who is like it. So, in the attempt to find such a companion, God molds from the soil the world's animals and brings them to the soil creature which will give to them names.

But, in a delightful bit of humor and pathos, God's efforts to find a companion like the soil creature result in all the world's animals, yet none of those quite make the grade. None of them is a "companion who is like it." One could thus say that all of the animals are accidents, first attempts to find a companion like the soil creature! But God, not daunted by first failure, goes back to the drawing board.

Genesis 2:21–24

> *(21) So YHWH God caused a deep trance to fall upon the soil creature. It slept. God took one of its ribs, and covered the place over with flesh. (22)YHWH God built the rib that was taken from the soil creature into a woman, and God brought her to the soil creature. (23) And the soil creature said,*
>
> > *"This one is at last bone of my bone*
> > *and flesh of my flesh.*
> > *This one is called woman,*
> > *because from man this one was taken."*
>
> *(24) That is why a man abandons his father and his mother and cleaves to his woman, and they become one flesh.*

The soil creature no longer exists. It has become two, a man and a woman. The purpose of this memorable scene is not to indicate how the woman is dependent on a man for her existence, or how the woman was made after the man and is thus somehow secondary to him. The episode is an announcement of sexual differentiation.[8] With the unique creation of the woman (only of her is it said that God "built" her; she did not come from the soil), the purpose of God can be fulfilled; a lonely soil creature gives way to a man and a companion woman.

Their unity and equality are announced in vs. 24; a man abandons his own family to cleave to his woman, to symbolize in their "one flesh" the harmony and beauty of God's creation. Two equal creatures, a man and a woman, now are ready to live together in the garden of God.

Even though the joy of the creation of man and woman from the soil creature resounds through the text in vs. 24, the shadows of the divine prohibition have not disappeared. We know that this man and woman will need to reckon with the tree of the knowledge of good and bad, as well as the tree of life. The man's shout of recognition and satisfaction ("this at last," he says) is at one level a humorous chiding of God: "Ah, you got it right this time," he says. But we, the readers, are not certain that God can take a joke; there remains God's dread command, and the rest of the story revolves around it.

Genesis 2:25—3:6

> (25) The two of them were nude, the man and his woman, but they were not ashamed. (1) Now the snake was more shrewd than any of the field creatures that Yahweh God had made. It said to the woman, "So, God said that you [pl.] may not eat from any tree of the garden." (2) But the woman said to the snake, "From the fruit of the trees of the garden we may eat, (3) but concerning the fruit of the tree which is in the middle of the garden, God said, 'You [pl.] can not eat from it, neither can you [pl.] touch it, lest you [pl.] die." (4) But the snake said to the woman, "You [pl.] surely will not die, (5) because God knows that when you [pl.] eat from it, your[pl.] eyes will be opened, and you [pl.] will be like God, knowers of good and bad."

The unity and harmony of the man and the woman are immediately affirmed and attacked by the conversation between the snake and the woman. 2:25 announces the theme of harmony; both are nude and not ashamed. The announcement of nudity without shame serves two purposes. First, we, the readers, know that nudity without shame is impossible for us in nearly every case; even many husbands and wives are uncomfortable with

8. Trible, *God and the Rhetoric of Sexuality*, 100.

one another unclothed. If that is so in our supposedly liberated twenty-first century, in an ancient culture that stood in awe before the mysteries of sexuality, developing many laws to prevent the public display of nudity, open nakedness would surely lead to shame. Thus, by tying together nakedness and lack of shame, the narrator has symbolized a world far different from the one known by the readers.

Second, nakedness joined to lack of shame indicates a vulnerability without fear on the part of the man and the woman. They are open to one another, not separated by shame or fear. In short, nakedness without shame is a superb way of proclaiming the unity and harmony of this first couple.

But, just as the man and the woman are "nude," so is the snake "shrewd."[9] This English rhyme is an attempt to capture the pun in Hebrew; the couple is 'arummim, while the snake is 'arum. The fact that the narrator puns precisely here indicates to the reader that the snake's shrewdness is in some fashion going to confront the couple's nudity. But, we must be careful here not to over-read the text. The word chosen to describe the snake is an ambiguous one. It indeed can have a negative meaning. In 1 Sam 23:22, Saul is told to be wary of the "cunning" David, who is hiding from the murderous first king; the word is clearly used there in an unflattering way. So also in Ps 83:3, the enemies of the psalmist are said to lay "crafty plans against God's people."

Yet, the word may also mean "sensible" or "clever" in the best sense of that word. Especially in the book of Proverbs, the word is used as an antonym for the "fool" and the "stupid one." (See Prov 12:23; 14:15; 22:3; 27:12.) Thus, the snake's "shrewdness" need not immediately cause us to jump to the conclusion that it is thereby a figure of evil. I realize that avoiding such a conclusion is made doubly difficult by the centuries-long reputation of the snake as some sort of thinly disguised Satan. Yet, it is so far only called the shrewdest field creature created by God; that is all we know of the snake thus far. But now the dialogue begins, so we can expect to learn much more about all of the characters of the story.

The snake's first comment to the woman is a marvel of ambiguity. Commentators have long been divided on just how to translate what the snake says. Many read a question—"Has God really said . . . ?" or "Did God say . . . ?" But if the construction is translated as a question, it would be the only time in the entire Hebrew Bible that it would be so translated. I rather think that John Skinner was correct when he said, "It is a half-interrogative,

9. Fox, *The Five Books of Moses*, 21.

half-reflective exclamation."[10] "So, God said that you must not eat from any tree of the garden." If the line is read with the voice rising at the end, with an implied "huh?," the snake is clearly insinuating something that plainly is not true. In fact, the line cleverly borrows the grammar from God's prohibition of the *one* tree (2:17) and applies it falsely to *all* the trees, which, as we remember, were given freely for the eating of the soil creature (2:16). Thus, we could readily conclude that the snake is deliberately falsifying the command of God, however it discovered the content of that command.

On the other hand, the snake might simply be asking for information from the woman. It probes her knowledge of the command, having heard a whisper of it, but having no certain knowledge of its content. Yet, the detail of the text will not allow this second, more benign, reading. We are right to mistrust the snake. It does indeed know the command in detail, because, as I noted above, it borrows the precise words of the command, but distorts them for its own hidden purposes. God said concerning the garden, *"From any tree of the garden you may surely eat."* But concerning the one tree, God said, *"You may not eat from it."* Listen to the snake again. *"You may not eat from any tree of the garden."* The prohibition of the one has been verbatim applied to all. The snake has deliberately attempted to mislead the woman, or at least is interested in seeing how she will respond to the misstatement.

The snake's only alteration of the command's detail is that all the second person pronouns are in the plural; the snake sees the woman as the spokesperson for the couple, and as an equal in the partnership. She may certainly function precisely so, notwithstanding comments like those of Skinner: "The serpent shows his subtlety by addressing his first temptation to the more mobile temperament of the woman."[11] Skinner certainly did not derive his judgment of the woman from this text; she has said and done nothing to this point! This is a parade example of how hard it is to read a text without importing ideas and reflections into it, thus clouding what the text itself has to say. But the woman quickly responds to the insinuations of the snake.

Her response is fascinating. She first says: "From the fruit of the trees of the garden we may eat." She is the first to mention fruit; God in the command said nothing about fruit. The woman thus specifies what is implicit in the command. We noted earlier how this text often moves from general to specific. The woman also omits the word "any" from her brief recounting of

10. Skinner, *A Critical and Exegetical Commentary on Genesis*, 73.

11. Ibid.

what she and the man are able to do. This is an important omission, because in her summary she admits to the snake what is the clear implication of the entire command: *all* trees may *not* be eaten in fact. And she softens the generous inclusiveness of God's offer of all the trees when she says "we may eat," rather than God's "you may surely eat." Thus, the woman has been thinking about the words of the command, and her first summary of it reveals that she has well understood its fuller implications. First, the eating has to do with the fruit of the trees. Second, all trees are not available for eating; perhaps she has reflected on that one tree a good deal. Third, God's generosity is reduced to a rather mundane, "we may eat."

But her response goes on. "But concerning the fruit of the tree in the middle of the garden." She does not reveal the full identity of the tree; it is merely the one in the middle of the garden, not "the tree of the knowledge of good and bad." And about that fruit, "God said, 'You can not eat from it, nor can you touch it, lest you die.'" The woman has considerably toughened the command in two ways. First, her concern is with the fruit, not only with the more general "tree"; she makes the prohibition much more clear and specific. Second, she claims that God said that she and the man not only could not *eat* from the fruit, but could not even *touch* it. This second addition is an important one, and has led to much comment.

Skinner says that the woman "unconsciously intensifies the stringency of the prohibition," but gives us no clues about what that might mean.[12] Speiser claims, "In her eagerness to make her point, the woman enlarges on the actual injunction."[13] Thus, while Skinner calls the woman's addition "unconscious," Speiser calls it "eager." Von Rad says, "This additional word already shows a slight weakness in the woman's position. It is as though she wanted to set a law for herself by means of this exaggeration."[14] And Westermann, in agreement with Von Rad, adds, "This sentence makes it clear that a command that is questioned is no longer the original command, as the continuation of the narrative makes even clearer."[15] The latter two scholars present the clear implication that the woman makes her addition to God's command out of some sort of weakness, although neither explores that weakness at any length.

Compare Trible's reading:

12. Ibid., 74.
13. Speiser, *Genesis*, 23.
14. Von Rad, *Genesis*, 88.
15. Westermann, *Genesis 1–11*, 239.

> ... with these words the hermeneutical skills of the woman emerge. Not only can she relay the command of God; she can also interpret it faithfully. Her understanding guarantees obedience. If the tree is not touched, then its fruit cannot be eaten. Thus the woman builds "a fence around the Torah," a procedure that her rabbinical successors developed fully to protect the law of God and to insure obedience to it.[16]

For Trible, the woman is a rabbi, strengthening the command to protect it from those who would destroy it. With these disparate answers before us, we may simply summarize the problem: is the woman's addition to the command of God done with skill to protect the command or done from fear or weakness with the result that the command is put in serious jeopardy?

As in any textual reading, we can only adjudicate the problem by careful analysis of the context. The woman had altered the command of God in the three ways I have noted above, but unlike our analysis of the snake's obvious desire to mislead, the woman's reasons for the alterations are not so clear. Perhaps as the reading proceeds, we may be able to return to this question, as more light is shed upon it.

The snake responds to the lengthy statement of the woman in a flat denial of a small part of that statement. "You surely will not die," it says. The snake does not refer to whether or not she should eat the fruit, or touch the fruit, nor does it argue about what God has said about eating or touching. It turns to the question of dying, and it quotes the woman's rather unusual form of the verb about dying exactly. She had warned against eating or touching the fruit, quoting God as saying "lest you die" (*temuthun*, the "n" ending is unusual, usually described as "archaic.") The snake rejoins, strongly, "You surely will not die," quoting and denying God's stronger verbal construction of 2:17, while repeating the unusual verb form of the woman (*temuthun*). The snake is certainly a careful listener to all of the speeches of the story! Perhaps the snake now feels that if the woman can alter the exact words of the command of God, that she is at least open to a discussion about the precise meaning of the command. And, seeing that the woman is interested in engaging in a theological debate, it ceases its insinuations and offers a denial of a claim that the woman understands that God has given. But it goes on to suggest what the rewards of this different understanding of the mysterious tree might be.

16. Trible, *God and the Rhetoric of Sexuality*, 110.

"Because God knows," it says, "that when you eat from it, your eyes will be opened, and you will be like God, knowers of good and bad." This line is packed with innuendo and ambiguity.

1. Throughout the dialogue between the woman and the snake, they have referred to God by using the Hebrew term, *elohim*, a form that is a masculine plural noun. They have never called God what the narrator has consistently called God, YHWH Elohim. This difference in terminology reminds us of the question of point of view in Hebrew narrative. We said in chapter 2 that in the Bible's narrative first person narrators should be looked at with great care. Both snake and woman are suspect on this score. They appear to know the words of God, however much they both change them, but their constant reference to God as *elohim* tends to call their full knowledge of God into question. In short, all of their claims about God need to be carefully scrutinized.

2. The snake in vs. 5 does not quote God at all, but now claims to know what God knows. It does not even pretend to have heard God say anything that it claims in this verse. If the theological debate were a serious one, surely the woman would have demanded evidence of the staggering claims made by the snake, but her response is silence followed by disobedience. And what are those claims? First, fruit eating does not lead to death at all; it leads to one's eyes being opened. The implication is that the eyes of the man and woman are now closed in some way. Second, the result of this eye-opening experience is that the man and the woman will be *ca'elohim*. This may be translated in several different ways. It could be read "like God," perhaps the most natural meaning. If one reads in this way, the snake's promise is that the man and the woman will become in some way like God; more specifically, they will be "knowers of good and bad," which is apparently what God knows. One could also read the preposition to express identity: "You will *be* God." If this reading is used, the stakes of the eating are higher; the man and the woman can become God, and as God, they will be knowers of good and bad.

Another reading is possible. Because *elohim* is a masculine plural, the snake could mean that eating the fruit would make the couple "gods," some kind of divinity, but not God. Here the reward would be not quite as great but still considerable. Let me suggest one more reading of the words that will lend still a different tone to the snake's promise. In one place in the Hebrew Bible, 1 Sam 28:13, the word *elohim* must be translated "ghost" or "shade." The reference is to the dead Samuel, who is conjured by the woman at Endor, in order that a desperate Saul may consult his old enemy in a pathetic attempt to defer defeat at the hands of the Philistines. Could *elohim* possess that meaning here? What would it mean if it did? The snake's promise would be death, after all! Oh, you certainly will not die, it says, directly. But, if you eat the fruit, you will become ghosts, that is, in fact, dead! The woman must surely hear in the snake's promise one of the earlier possibilities; they will be like God or may be God. But the snake may in fact mean that God is right; to eat the fruit is to die. The irony between what the woman hears and what the snake intends would be a delicious one, if this latter reading is possible.

And now finally we must explore the meaning of the phrase, "knowers of good and bad." Again, the ambiguity of the grammar of the phrase is significant for its full understanding. My translation of the phrase implies that the snake's promise is that the man and the woman will become "knowers of good and bad" in that they will become "like God." To be like God *is* to be a knower of good and bad. However, the noun "knowers" could also be seen more directly as an explanation of what it means to be God. One would then translate: "like God, who knows good and bad," the plural noun being used because the form of God used is in the plural. In either case, the emphasis of the sentence should be placed precisely on the promise to be "like God" or to be "God." And when one achieves that state by eating the fruit of the forbidden tree, one will at the same time be defined most readily as one who "knows good and bad."

Note that I have not translated with the more familiar "good and evil." The latter word has assumed over the years of its use too close an affinity with questions of morality, of what is either right or wrong. And because the text refers several times to the nudity of the couple, commentators have talked as if the knowledge provided by the tree was in some sense a sexual knowledge; it is rather a divine knowledge, or perhaps one could say a divine power. What the phrase "good and bad" appears to mean is something akin to "everything." Skinner comments: "Hence the phrase comes to stand for the whole range of experience."[17] Knowledge in the Hebrew Bible is never limited to an intellectual exercise. Listen to Von Rad's more extended discussion.

> For ancients, the good was not just an idea: the good was what had a good effect; as a result, in this context, "good and evil" should

17. Skinner, *A Critical and Exegetical Commentary on Genesis*, 95.

be understood more as what is "beneficial" and "salutary" on the one hand and "detrimental," "damaging," on the other. So the serpent holds out less the prospect of an extension of the capacity for knowledge than the independence that enables a man (or woman) to decide for himself (herself) what will help him (her) or hinder him (her).[18]

In short, the knowledge of good and bad is in effect the knowledge of what is useful and harmful. Such knowledge does provide independence in decision-making, and it is this freedom that the promise of the snake holds for the woman and for her man. As Westermann says, "It is concerned with a divine and unbridled ability to master one's existence."[19]

Given this understanding of "good and bad," we need to return to the phrase to be "like God." How that phrase is understood will determine just how far the power offered by the tree is to be extended. The woman hears that the knowledge offered is divine, either *like* God's knowledge, or precisely God's knowledge. The snake either suggests that the knowledge is divine, at or somewhat below the level of God's full knowledge, or that the knowledge is in reality the dead knowledge of a ghost, who in effect has no power whatever in death. The text fairly bristles with possibilities; only the subsequent actions of the characters can determine just how they have heard the extravagant promises of the shrewd snake.

Genesis 3:6–7

> (6) *The woman saw that the tree was good for eating, and that it was a delight to the eyes. And the tree was desirable to make a person wise, so she took of its fruit and ate, and she gave also to her man with her, and he ate. (7) The eyes of the two of them were opened, and they knew that they were nude. They sewed fig leaves and made for themselves loincloths.*

The snake's glorious promise, as heard by the woman, is too much for her to refuse. After its bold announcement of vs. 5, its direct denial of God's warning about death and its promise of divine independence, the woman has nothing more to say. In a beautifully crafted verse, the narrator describes the inner thought of the woman as she moves inexorably to eat

18. Von Rad, *Genesis*, 89.

19. Westermann, *Genesis 1–11*, 248; he has very helpful extended discussion of the phrase on 242–45.

of the forbidden fruit. First, she reiterates to herself what she has already concluded: the tree is "good for eating." Is she showing her awakening independence of decision by making this judgment? Or is she beginning that process of rationalization for which humans have always been so justly famous? "It is good," she says, "it is useful. Why not, then?" Second, it is a "delight to the eyes." Not only is it useful, it is beautiful, an aesthetic marvel. Something so useful *and* so beautiful could hardly be detrimental. Both of these decisions have been made on her own. The third statement, however, is of a different order.

"The tree is desirable to make one wise." As we said in our discussion of good and bad, this phrase does not mean intellectual knowledge only. "To be wise" is "to be successful." To be wise is to overcome whatever limits have been set, either externally or internally. The snake has convinced the woman that the tree is not the tree of death but the tree of power and success. To eat of the tree is to gain independence, freedom to choose, power for decision-making. The command of God is forgotten; the snake has won the debate, though the woman has made her own choice.

Above, I asked the question about why the woman added the phrase, "nor touch it," so blatantly to the command of God. As her character has been filled out in the ensuing events, it seems reasonable to say that the woman was already most intrigued by the forbidden tree before the arrival of the snake. Her diminution of the command of God with regard to God's gift of the trees of the garden, in 3:2, but her strengthening of the command with regard to the prohibition of the one tree in 3:3, leads a reader to suspect that the one tree was her real interest all along. Far from in reality "putting a fence around the Torah," as Trible suggested, the woman revealed to the snake her deepest desire, namely, to eat from that tree. The snake merely played to that desire and gave her the information she needed to act out a desire she already felt. This is in no way to diminish the woman as a character; she is fully human. When faced with prohibition, desire heightens. Once the prohibition has been neutralized, the act is certain to follow. Nor does it follow that she is a weak character, because she ultimately submitted to the blandishments of the snake. She knew and respected the command, but in the face of a superior debater and of her own human desire, she gave in. Such compliments will not be afforded the man, as we shall see.

The woman, after eating the fruit, hands some to her man, "with her, and he ate." The implication of the text is that the man has been standing near throughout the preceding debate. If so, he has been silent, but he surely has had time to form a judgment of his own about the advisability

64

of eating from the forbidden fruit. Nevertheless, his entire reaction to the whole discussion is "he ate!" A father of the early church once said, "If the snake had come up to the man, this never would have happened!" How far from the text that insensitive remark is! After the spirited debate between the woman and the snake, we could have expected something more from the man. But he "ate." Period.

You will note that nothing happens until both of them eat. The narrator has prepared us for this unity in transgression by the constant use of plural verbs and pronouns throughout the debate, a plurality that now continues into vs. 7. The first occurrence after the forbidden eating is a real surprise. "The eyes of the two were opened." Immediately, the reader is reminded of the promise of the snake. "Your eyes will be opened," it said. The snake was right! Their eyes *are* opened! And now the tension of the story grows, because if the snake was right about their eyes, might it not be right about the rest? Will they perhaps become "like God"? Will they perhaps begin to exercise an independent divine power? The next words are crucial for our reading.

"They knew they were nude." It *is* a tree of knowledge, after all! The snake is once again right. But the first piece of knowledge that they are given is the fact of their nudity. At 2:25, the fact of their nudity was provided to us by the narrator, who joined that fact with their lack of shame. Now the fact of nudity, revealed to them by their newly opened eyes, brings a swift reaction from them, a reaction that indicates that lack of shame is no longer compatible with nudity. The snake is right, but the results of the tree of knowledge are far different from a glorious independence of power and decision.

"They sewed fig leaves, and made for themselves loincloths." The knowledge of nudity brings shame, which leads to the need to cover oneself; vulnerability is gone, and shame and fear take its place. The promise of independence and power, the promise of a divine ability to choose, is first tested by nudity. And the result is deliciously hilarious! The newly minted divine human beings solve their first problem, make their first choice, by making loincloths out of fig leaves. Readers from the South perhaps will get the joke sooner than those of you from the North. Have you ever felt a fig leaf? If you have not, they are rather like No. 2-grade sandpaper! I doubt whether you would have a fig leaf loincloth on too long, if you chose to don one fresh from the shower. How absurd these two are, standing in their itchy fig leaves, transgressors of the one simple command of God. Rather than Titans, storming the very gates of heaven, they are more like children, caught with their hands in the cookie jar by a bemused mother.

Human independence has been pilloried in the preceding scene. However, there is another side to all this; there is something positive in this story, so ridiculous on the surface. In those absurd fig leaf loincloths, our narrator wants us to see progress, however small, however silly. "And when this knowledge gives the man (and the woman) the ability to make something to cover himself (herself), the narrator intends this to indicate progress; they have also become clever (*haskil*, or 'wise')."[20] God does admit, at 3:22, that they have "become like one of us, knowing good and bad." This can only mean that the couple have become more than they were before; they do *know* more than they did before. And an interesting relationship demonstrates just how the humans have become at least in one sense like God. "Both God in 2:8f and the couple in 3:7f know that something is not good; both 'create' something to help the situation. But there is the widest gulf between what is actually done in each case."[21] Still, the remainder of the story will indicate in no uncertain terms that independent decision-making, apart from God, can lead only to division and disaster.

Genesis 3:8–13

> (8) *They heard the sound of YHWH Elohim, walking in the garden for the breeze of the day, and the man and his woman hid themselves from the presence of YHWH Elohim in the middle of the trees in the garden. (9) But YHWH Elohim called out to the man and said to him, "Where are you?" (10) He said, "Your sound I heard in the garden. I was afraid, because nude I was, so I hid myself." (11) God said, "Who told you that nude you were? Have you from the tree that I commanded you not to eat from it eaten?" (12) The man said, "The woman whom you gave to be with me, she gave to me from the tree, and I ate." (13) YHWH Elohim said to the woman, "What is this you have done?" And the woman said, "The snake tricked me, and I ate."*

The deed has been done; the newly wise couple, standing there in their fig leaf loincloths, seem frozen to the spot. Suddenly, from the dense growth in the garden, they hear a familiar sound. It is YHWH Elohim, the maker of the garden and of them, taking a walk, hoping to catch some of the gentle

20. Ibid., 251.
21. Ibid., 252.

and cooling breeze that wafts through the leaves in the late afternoon. The implication is that this divine stroll is a regular occurrence, but its effects on this day are not regular at all. "The man and his woman hid themselves from the presence of YHWH Elohim in the middle of the trees in the garden." It is significant that the couple go to hide from God precisely "in the middle of the trees of the garden." It is the location of the two forbidden trees (2:9), and it is the way in which the woman identifies the one forbidden tree to the snake (3:3). It is in the story the "exact scene of the crime." It is appropriate that the trial scene to come is conducted in the very shadow of the fateful trees.

For eight verses now the references in the story have all been in the plural. The woman debates with the snake as representative of both the man and the woman, and the snake includes both of them in all of his insinuations. Also, the eye opening does not occur until both of them eat the fruit; they both sew the foolish leaves to make the clothes; they both hide from the sound of God. At verse 9, all the references become singular. The man is called first. "Where are you (*sing*)?" The adverb translated "where" here anticipates the answer "nowhere" in the majority of its uses in the Hebrew Bible; it is usually used rhetorically (see, for example, Job 14:10; 20:7; Jud 18:6). Thus, it offers to the reader here another set of possibilities for its understanding.

1. The question could be understood quite literally. So the proper response would be something like, "I am over here!" or "50 yards to your left!"

2. The question might be heard as a rather more general salutation, something like "What's going on?" in the modern idiom. To that sort of question the answers could range anywhere from "fine" to a twenty-minute recitation of one's physical and emotional aches and pains.

3. As often in Hebrew narrative, both 1 and 2 could be intended, depending on the point of view of the questioner and questioned. We cannot know yet what God has in mind by asking the question, but we can learn what the man heard, or wanted to hear, as we listen to his reply.

"Your sound I heard in the garden"; that is true enough, and it could be the beginning of a fully appropriate reply to a question of location. The man might go on to say, "So I rushed to meet you." Instead, he says, "I was afraid because I was nude." The question was not heard by the man as one asking him to reveal his current physical location. He quickly announces an emotion to God, his fear, and just as quickly informs God of what brought the emotion on, his nudity. "And I hid myself," he concludes. This remarkable response reveals two things about the man that are important for the story. First, he has in effect divorced himself from the woman. Four separate ideas make up his reply to God; three of them have appeared before in the story, but in each of their earlier appearances both the man *and* the woman were involved. "*I* heard," he says; in 3:8 "*they* heard." "*I* was nude," he says; in 2:25 and in 3:7, *they* were nude. "*I* hid myself," he says; in 3:8, "*they* hid *themselves*." The unity and harmony are no more. Whatever else has been the result of the eating of the fruit, "one flesh" has been effectively sundered.

The second thing that is suggested about the man by his reply is his inability to hide very well, either himself or what he has done. A curt and simple reply like "over here" would have been the proper way to respond if the man's intention were to deny everything or to debate his way out of trouble. As a debater, he is hardly the match of the woman! To the open-ended question of God, the man offers a rambling response, words tumbling out on top of one another, and each word revealing far more than a clever liar would ever want to reveal. "I am afraid, and I am nude, and I am hiding," he shouts, hardly the speech of a wise deceiver.

As usual in the story, something general, God's first question, is followed by something more specific. God's second question is, "Who told you nude you were?" God echoes precisely the syntax of the man's reply; the snake is not the only careful listener in this story! And then in a truly torturous bit of syntax, God pops the most direct question of all. "Have you from the tree that I commanded you not to eat from it eaten?" The narrator wants to get the key verb at the end of the sentence, flying in the face of common Hebrew syntax, namely, the verb "to eat." So, now the question is not in the slightest open-ended: "Who told you?" and "Have you eaten or not?" The man's response is both justly famous and revealing.

"The woman (he places her first in the sentence, a rather unusual Hebrew word order), whom you gave to be with me, *she* (an unnecessary use of the pronoun; it is already contained in the verb to follow) gave to me from the tree and I ate." The man has in his first reply to God divorced himself from the woman by his use of singular forms; now he objectifies her, emphasizes her primary role in the drama, and implies that he was an innocent bystander who took the fruit from the clever woman, who of course had it long before he did. And just to top off his denial of any responsibility for what has happened, he reminds God that the woman was *given* to him by God; he did not ask for her! It is directly her fault, but at base all of this is God's problem.

And this marvelous "passing of the buck" is reinforced by the words used by the man. Just as the woman "gave" him the fruit (3:6), so God "gave" him the woman (3:12); because he asked for neither he is in effect responsible for neither and washes his "clean" hands of the entire affair. This treatment of the woman is a far cry from the delighted man, who when first seeing the woman, broke into excited song, praising God's wonderful and unique handiwork (2:23). His first reply to God may have hinted that he wanted to confess; perhaps God hoped that he would and pressed him to do so with those second very specific questions. But now we see the man for what he is; he is a craven coward, hurling blame in every available direction, completely forgetting his relationship with the woman and with his God. The man who would be God is fully worthy of his fig-leaf clothes!

The spotlight of the story moves back to the woman. Though she was out-talked by the shrewd snake and finally duped by it, we might expect a more rousing response from her than we received from the man. God asks, "What is this that you have done?" It is again a rather general question. If the little particle, *zoth*, "this," is translated as enclitic, that is as an emphasizer of the sentence, the question might be closer to a cry of anguish: "What in the world have you done?" But the narrator has more in mind by the use of *zoth*. It was this demonstrative pronoun that the man used three times to express his overwhelming delight with the gift of the woman, that same woman whom he has just blamed for the whole deed. God asks her, "What is this one who has done it?" Perhaps God expects once again some sign of confession or remorse; the woman's reply is curt and no less an evasion than that offered by the man. "The snake (she, too, puts the one to blame first in the sentence) tricked me, and I ate." It was of course not my fault; it was the snake. She does not blame God, but she exonerates herself from all blame. She announces last in her sentence what has been last in the previous three speeches; it is the bottom line. "Have you eaten?" asked God. "I ate," said the man; "I ate," said the woman. The deed has been done and admitted by both, however much they attempt to deny responsibility for it. God has given, the man and the woman have taken, and they have eaten. The result of this interplay of verbs is deception, disharmony, and disaster on the intimate plane of the garden. Now the disaster will assume a more dangerous significance.

Genesis 3:14–19

(14) YHWH Elohim said to the snake, "Because you have done this, be cursed more than every domesticated creature. On your belly you shall walk,
And dust you shall eat all the days of your life.

(15) And struggle I shall put between you and the woman, between your seed and her seed; she will bruise you on the head, while you will bruise her in the heel.

(16) To the woman God said,
"I will greatly increase your childbirth pain;
in pain you shall bear children.
For your husband will be your desire,
And he will rule over you."

(17) And to the man God said, "Because you listened to the voice of your woman,
and ate from the tree about which I commanded you
"Do not eat from it,"
I curse the ground because of you;
In pain you will eat of it all the days of your life.

(18) Thorns and thistles will sprout for you;
you shall eat the field shrubs.

(19) In the sweat of your nostrils you shall eat food,
until you return to the soil,
because from it you were taken.
You are surely dust, and to dust you shall return.

These curses or punishments have been much discussed. It seems certain that our narrator has one particular purpose in mind for these verses. The narrator notes a disturbing reality in the actual world in which the story is written, the world of the author. First, there is the continuous and dangerous battle between snakes and human beings. This, says our author, can be traced back to primordial time. Second, a woman's fulfillment in the ancient world came in the birth of children; to be a mother was to find hope and joy. Why, then, asks the author, is this great event always accompanied by pain and struggle, and why is sexual desire joined to male dominance; where did the equality and harmony of God's creation go? This mysterious and sad state of affairs, too, can be traced to the primordial garden, where equality was thrown away by desire for independence and power.

Third, why is the act of agriculture, so necessary for the survival of the community, accompanied by such heavy toil and sweat, and often by such poor harvests? The release from this backbreaking labor comes only when one returns to the very soil which one must work and from which one was taken. This, too, is grounded in the story set in primordial time. It is important, as we examine these punishments, to note something; these disturbing "why" questions are never answered. If the intent of our narrator had been to give an answer, the snake would have received some extended interrogation from God. God asks it not a single question. The "why" of the origins of sin, death, toil, sorrow, pain is given no clear explanation in this story. However, it is ultimately the human beings in the story who stand in the spotlight of responsibility; our reading has led to that conclusion, and the remainder of the chapter will emphasize that finding.

The snake's unique and mysterious form of locomotion is a result of "this," says God. What is included in "this" (3:14) is not made clear, another sure sign that the narrator is not interested in the snake as the ultimate cause of the transgression in the garden. Nevertheless, the snake remains a dangerous enemy of the woman, and all of its offspring remain dangerous to all of hers.

The woman's most distinctive feature, her magical ability to give birth, is accompanied by great pain, and is the result of the dominance of the man. It is most important to see here that this state is neither the one intended by God nor is it seen as the normal one. In 2:18, when God announced that the soil creature should not be alone, God immediately sought for a "companion who was like it," as we saw. This companion, the woman, was in every sense the equal of the newly differentiated man. Verse 25 described in metaphor the will of God for the human creation; nude together but not ashamed. The domination of men over women is thus an aberration in a world intended for equality and harmony. We ought to weep in the face of such suffering, not rejoice that it is so.

The man, who in the garden was called to serve and protect, must now toil in "pain" (the same word describes his work as describes the woman's work of giving birth). The blessings of labor are now joined to sweat, toil, and limited success.

In so many ways, the punishments of vss. 14–19 recapitulate and round off the ideas presented earlier in the story. The key terms are "eat," "dust," "all the days of your life," and "return." The word "eat" is a veritable leitmotif in the story. It is used no fewer than 21 times in the 46 verses. It first appears in the prohibition against eating in 2:16, and appears last in the statement of fear that the people might eat from the tree of life (3:22; I shall say more of this verse below). In the punishments, it occurs six times. It is a wonderful irony that the snake, which incited the woman and her man to eat of the forbidden tree, now must "eat dust all the days of its life." "Eat this fruit," says the snake, and as a result it is forced to eat dust.

The man, who accepted the fruit without comment from the woman, and who attempted to deny all responsibility for his actions, is told that he will eat all right, but "in pain all the days of his life." In this way, the man is united both to the snake and the woman, not in the intended harmony of God, but in "pain" (see vss. 16 and 17) and in the endlessness of the punishment. Like the woman, the man will be in pain, and like the snake the man will eat and work in pain all the days of his life.

Some further irony may be seen in the use of the word "dust." The snake, which for reasons unexplained incited the woman to eat from the tree, now is cursed to struggle with her and her seed. The man will only end his struggle by a return to the soil, more specifically to the dust, from which he came. It is this same dust that the snake will eat all the days of its life. Thus, the snake will struggle with the woman and consume the man. One could see here a terrible cycle of human and animal creation. The man dominates the woman, who in turn gives birth to men and women in pain, who in turn struggle with the snake and a recalcitrant soil and dust, only to be consumed by that snake and that dust in their death.

And, of course the most obvious circle is drawn by the creation of the soil creature, the forebear of the man and the woman, out of dust (2:7), and the return of the man to that same dust at his death (3:19). The cycle of birth and death is thereby established, but the portrait of that cycle has a terrible harshness etched into it. The creation of the soil creature, done with such care and artistic skill by God, the differentiation of that creature into the man and the woman, done by God to prevent the loneliness of the soil creature, and praised so loudly and lovingly by the man as he first spied the woman, has resulted in frustration, sorrow, struggle, pain, and death. Can this be the end of the story? For our narrator, the answer is a resounding "No!"

Genesis 3:20–21

> *(20) The man called the name of his woman Eve, because she was the mother of all life. (21) So YHWH Elohim for the man and for his woman made skin tunics and clothed them.*

In the face of the dark picture of human existence provided by the punishments of the preceding verses, these two verses come as a breath of fresh air. The reader would ask, "How shall the couple react to this grim existence as it is described in vss. 14–19? Will they refuse to go on? Will they persist in their isolation one from the other, only engaging in dominating sexual encounters which lead to painful births?" I cannot agree with Trible that vs. 20 assigns the woman to a "position of inferiority and subordination."[22] Surely, the title given to her, "the mother of all life," is one of great honor. Earlier, we saw how God was the giver of life by animating the soil creature with the breath of life. Then God was the controller of life by creating a tree of life that was unavailable to the soil creature and to the man and the woman. To call her mother of life is to raise her in fact to the near level of divinity. From her body the spark of life, given first by God, will be offered to the world. Also, note that though the man names her Eve (*chawah* in Hebrew, close in sound to the word *chayah*, life), a fact that signals to Trible her subordination to him like the animals of 2:19, he provides a name only in response to a fact known already to the narrator; he named her Eve *because* she is the mother of life. His naming her does not *make* her the mother of life; the name announced to the world her enormous significance in the continuation of the human species. In the same way, Abraham names the child born to him and Sarah, *Isaac* ("laughter" in Hebrew, see Gen 21:3) to announce publicly what the narrator has already told the readers in chapters 17 and 18: both Abraham and Sarah have laughed in the face of the promise of God. What else could he name the child of their extreme old age but "laughter"?

By this announcement to the world that Eve is the mother of life, the man and the woman proclaim that they will go on, even in the face of the grim realities described in the punishments. There will be a future for humanity! And one can almost catch a small smile on the face of God, who now clothes the two of them in the tunics of animal skins. This action of beneficence on the part of God rounds off an earlier absurd action of the human beings right after their disobedience. "Take off those silly fig

22. Trible, *God and the Rhetoric of Sexuality*, 133.

leaves," says God. "Let me give you something more suitable, more durable, and much more comfortable!" The tunic offered by God is the principal garment worn next to the skin and is far more substantial than a fig leaf loincloth, not to mention far less irritating! (See Gen 37 and 2 Sam 13:18 for examples of the garment described.) Given the shape of the story, one could say that God is pleased by the human decision to go on in the face of life's vicissitudes, and as a sign of that pleasure offers the couple together these new God-made garments. Perhaps their forfeited unity can be found again in the rich light of the gifts of God.

It should be noted that only here in the entire Hebrew Bible does an author have God "making" something (*'asah*) in the manner of manual labor, creating something out of material at hand. Yet, again this unique expression may be understood in the context of the use of the verb in our story. Three times in the first part of the story, God is said to "make" something: "skies and earth" in 2:5, the announcement that God will "make" a companion for the soil creature, although the actual creation of the world's other creatures falls under the verb "to mold" (2:18), and the *post facto* statement that the snake was the shrewdest of the creatures "made" by God. As the story climaxes, the man and the woman "make" their fig leaf loincloths (3:7). And as God questions the woman about what has happened, the question is "What is this you have done?" ("Made"; the verb is the same.) In 3:14, the snake is told of its punishment because of what it has "done" (again the same verb). And now, in the final use of the verb in the story, God "makes" for the disobedient but resolute couple skin tunics and clothes them (3:21). The verb is applied to each of the characters in the story, but the humans have made only fig leaf loincloths and the snake has only made disaster possible. God it is who made skies and earth, the snake, the companion for the soil creature which results in the man and the woman, and the final gift of the skin tunics. The making of God quite literally surrounds and supplants the makings of snake and people.

But still the story is not ended. The disobedient couple cannot remain in the garden of God for the reasons provided in the last passage of the tale.

Genesis 3:22–24

(22) YHWH God said, "The human beings have become like one of us, knowing good and bad; what if they should reach out their hands and take also from the tree of life, eat, and live forever!"

(23) So YHWH Elohim sent them from the Garden of Eden to serve the soil from which they were taken. (24) God drove them out, and placed east of the garden the cherubim and a whirling, flaming sword to guard the way to the tree of life.

This section has always proved troublesome to readers of the story of the garden. Once again, if we can remember the movement of the story itself, this section will be seen to have its role to play. First, God recognizes what the narrator implied by the account of the events at the forbidden tree; the human beings in a certain sense have indeed become like God in that they do have a knowledge of good and bad. They do understand, in however limited a way, some things that are helpful to them and some things that are harmful. If this statement of God is taken from its context, it will sound as if God is fearful of the human beings. It is certainly true that the ancient east is replete with stories like this one where the gods express their fear of the increasingly powerful humans. But is it possible to assume from our reading of the story at hand that God is *afraid of* these human beings in the sense that God fears that they will resolve to dislodge, and be capable of dislodging, God from the divine throne? The hilarious scene of the bewildered people, standing uncomfortably in their fig leaf clothes, makes God's fear less than likely. God might indeed be afraid, but certainly not afraid that the man and the woman will storm the gates of heaven. God's fear might rather be that immortal life for these creatures might not be a very good idea. They have eaten from the one tree, and look at the result. Were they to eat from the tree of life, and live forever *as they are now*, what would be the result? An eternity of struggle, painful childbearing, and difficult agriculture, characterized by pain and suffering, is hardly a prospect that would tantalize the hardiest of human souls. Thus God, in mercy, protects the rather unpredictable human beings from the tragedy of an eternity of a grim life. In this context, the gift of death is welcome indeed, ending a life of desperation.

If such a reading of vs. 22 is a possible one, one further idea may find its expression here. Death becomes, in this reading, the great orderer of life. The narrator announces to the reader that without death life can have no final meaning. Immortality in this existence would remove any need to act in any way whatever. If I know that I am to live forever, why would I be motivated to act in any way as opposed to any other way? An infinite amount of time would lead to an infinite number of rationalizations. A finite amount of time removes that one major reason for not being about one's business;

one will not be around forever. God's denial of immortality to the human beings in the denial of the tree of life merely reiterates the announcement of mortality in 3:19: "dust you are and to dust you will return." We called that statement punishment above; now we see it is also a gift.

So God sends the humans out of the garden, but the divine charge to them remains the same as that given in 2:15. They are to "serve the soil," and the certainty of their mortality is reiterated in the phrase "from which you were taken." Thus, God's crowning creation is driven from the Garden of Eden, and the way of return is denied them by a huge and ancient creature, a cherubim, and by a magically revolving and fiery sword, both stationed to guard the way back to the tree of life. At the beginning of the story, the soil creature was asked to protect the garden of God. Its failure to do so has brought a more fearsome guard who ironically is asked to guard against any return of the would-be guard.

Our reading of this rich tale has merely introduced the complexities of its construction. Another reading of it would yield different emphases and a host of other concerns. I have entitled this reading, "To Give, To Take, To Eat." I did so because I find that verse 6 of chapter 3, along with vss. 12 and 22 of that same chapter, encapsulate the theme of this reading. The story is begun by the gifts of God: the skies and the earth, the soil creature, the breath of life, the other animals, the man and the woman. In 3:6, the woman herself "gives," but her gift is of the forbidden fruit to her man. After God gives in the story, God also takes. In 2:15, God takes the soil creature and puts it in the garden. In 2:21, God takes a rib from the soil creature and makes from it a woman, in the process creating the man. And in the fateful 3:6, the woman takes the fruit of the tree in disobedience to the God who took only to benefit the divine creation.

And finally, to eat. Eating, for our narrator, becomes the very symbol of obedience and disobedience. That is set up by the announcement of the command of God in 2:16–17, where eating is forbidden three times. In the dialogue with the snake, it and the woman discuss eating and its consequences four times. And then in our central verse 6, three times the word appears: the tree is good for eating, she eats, and the man eats. In the trial scene God asks if they have eaten; both say that they have. In the punishment scene, the snake is forced to eat dust, while the man is forced to eat in pain. And finally, in 3:22, God once again forbids eating, not in a verbal command, but in the awesome presence of an ancient monster and a terrifying sword. The plot of the story began with a command not to eat. The plot ends with the denial of eating.

God gives and takes for the creation, while the man and the woman give and take for themselves in disobedience. In 3:12, the man accuses God of being like the woman; God gave the woman to the man just like the woman gave the fruit to the man, and the man wants no part of either one. And in 3:22, God must deny the tree of life to these humans, and performs that denial by saying, "What if they take?" After all, when humans give or take in this story, they do so only to satisfy their own desires. Such creatures must not be allowed to take the great gift of immortality. The story thus begins in gift, God's gift of life and breath, and ends in gift, God's gift of skin tunics and God's gift of death. The story finds its wholeness in the God of gift.

A Narrative Sermon on Genesis 2:4b — 3:24

A narrative sermon on a rich and complex text such as the one we have just examined will necessarily need to be narrated carefully for clarity. The nearly two chapters of the story we have just analyzed spread its story over forty-six verses and includes many diverse elements in its structure. There is, of course, the movement from the garden to expulsion from the garden, the complex changes of giving and taking, and the many uses of the actions of eating. I have chosen in my story sermon to focus on the relationships of the two human coverings: the fig leaves of the humans and the skins of God. In these two articles of clothing, the story of Gen 2–3 finds an immediate theological power, both ancient and contemporary.

Fig Leaves or Skins?

I was raised in a very politically conservative home in Arizona. Barry Goldwater was a liberal in my house. For those of you old enough to remember, that should tell you something. I fancied myself a conservative, too. If I had been able to vote in the 1964 presidential election, I certainly would have voted for Mr. Goldwater. But, alas, I was only eighteeen at the time. Still, I did my bit by denouncing the slain John Kennedy, the allegedly living Lyndon Johnson and all of their minions every chance that I got. Living in Arizona made such denunciations not only acceptable but suggested that you were a sane, freedom-loving, and red-blooded American.

> I frame my sermon with an exaggerated portrait of my conser-
> vative up bringing, somewhat tongue-in-cheek. I do this to an-
> nounce one of the most pronounced and well-known divisions
> between Americans, that between so-called liberals and so-called
> conservatives. I know that this division is a caricature of reality,
> but I plan to use that division later in my sermon, and it is one that
> is very familiar to any American listener. Also, the lighter tone of
> the introduction will prepare the hearers for the light tone of the
> story of the text, and, I hope, will thereby aid their listening.

Though our home was politically conservative, we were allowed to read anything we could get our hands on. Indeed, my father subscribed to *Playboy* magazine in a time when that was the filthiest rag you could receive through the U.S. Mail. It seems closer now to *Reader's Digest*, given what else is available. Oh, we also subscribed to *Reader's Digest*. But, in the manner of reading, my father was not so conservative after all.

But there was an exception. *Pogo*. Do you remember *Pogo*? I like to think of it now as Walt Kelly's pre-*Doonesbury* blast at the world he knew. We were not to read *Pogo*. It was communist-inspired at best and satanic at worst, although in our home there was not much difference between those two inspirations. Now, I was a dutiful son. However, when it came to *Pogo*, I dutifully rose each morning, before my father, and most undutifully read *Pogo* first thing!

One of *Pogo*'s own inspirations has become world-famous. One of the creatures, while tramping through the beloved swamps, is carrying a wooden toy gun on his shoulder. He meets one of his fellow creatures, who asks him, "Have you met the enemy?" "Oh, yes," he replies, "We have met the enemy, and the enemy is us." "We have met the enemy, and the enemy is us." That reminds me of another story, older than *Pogo*, set not in a swamp but in a garden.

> I now extend my story of my childhood toward the *Pogo* quota-
> tion, which is crucial for the way in which I plan to tell the story
> of the garden. Remember that the purpose of a frame for the nar-
> rative to follow is to pre-establish the thrust of the story to be told,
> especially when that story is well known; in this case, the story has
> become part of the natural lore of the culture, however confused
> its understanding in that culture may be. And because it is so well
> known, and so variously interpreted, it is important to point the
> emphasis in any sermon on it, but not in such a way as to give the
> possible surprises away.

Once upon a time, in a magic garden, far away, there lived a creature who was made out of the soil, from the very dust of the ground. This creature had no name, but for this story, let's call it Dusty. Dusty wasn't a man or a woman; Dusty was, well, Dusty. There had never been another creature like Dusty. After all, it had just been made by God. God was lonely, and decided to do something about it. So, God knelt in the dirt of the freshly made earth, scooped up a lump of clay, and swiftly molded something on the divine potter's wheel.

God was pleased, indeed, but a lump of clay is just a lump of clay, no matter how pleasing its shape. So, God breathed into the shapely lump the breath of life, and there at last was Dusty! Dusty took a deep breath of this gift of God and came fully alive.

But Dusty's new eyes fell on a vast and treeless plain. So God went back to work. God made trees, so many trees that an oasis appeared in the vast plain. And right in the middle of all those trees, God made two special trees: the tree of life and the tree of knowledge of good and bad. But Dusty knew nothing of that yet; it was too busy looking at the great rivers that flowed in the oasis and out into the world. Soon Dusty was looking at a garden, and, quick as a wink, God had taken Dusty and put it right into that garden.

One day while Dusty was hoeing a row of corn near the middle of the garden, God announced something. Dusty listened carefully; it was the first time God had said anything to it! "From any tree of the garden you may surely eat." Lovely, thought Dusty. Just like God to give so freely. But then God went on. "But from the tree of knowledge of good and bad you may not eat, because when you eat from it you will die." Something I should not do, thought Dusty; my first prohibition! I wonder . . .

> I begin the story in the beginning, namely, the creation of the soil creature in the desert, the shaping of the garden of trees, the placement of the creature in the garden, and the prohibition of the tree of knowledge. I call the creature "Dusty" for obvious reasons; hearers will hear a name easier than something like "soil creature," and Dusty has the twin advantages of direct relation to its origin from the dust and no special connection either to male or female naming. I have tried to include in this introduction only those items of information and background that will play a role later in the sermon. Please remember that as you shape a narrative sermon, one of the chief dangers is to get carried away with your own descriptions and your own re-creation of the clever scenes

and rich dialogue. The possibility for excess is very real, and if allowed to run unchecked can drown the sermon in a flood of "cuteness." Note, however, how readily and excitedly the children of a congregation will hear this story. Preaching that can be heard by the children as well as by the youths and adults has distinct advantages over preaching that has led some churches to resort to that infamous hybrid worship known as "children's church." To my mind, children's church is nothing less than the result of the preacher's failure to communicate in his/her word and worship.

Time passed. And God, remembering the divine loneliness, decided that Dusty needed a companion, too. So God dragged out the potter's wheel once again, and this time made many interesting creatures very different from Dusty. God's imagination ran wild, as curious shapes poured from the flying wheel. When God had finally finished, these newest creatures were led to Dusty so that they could have some names. Dusty called out, "Horse, dog, platypus, mosquito, aardvark, cockatoo, snake," pointing to each creature in turn. These are all very nice, thought Dusty, but hardly suitable companions for a creature such as I. And God couldn't help but agree.

So, Dusty suddenly got very sleepy, and during its sleep, God took just one rib from its side and built that rib very carefully into something really new and different—a woman! God did not use the divine potter's wheel this time; even God saw that this creature was different indeed. And there was another surprise in store. When God brought the woman for Dusty to see, Dusty was no longer there! Instead, Dusty had become another new creature—a man! And when the man saw the woman, he broke into song! "At last, God, you got it right! This one is bone of my bone and flesh of my flesh! She is woman, because she came from man!" Well, the man *was* excited. What had actually happened is that the man and the woman had both come from Dusty. But no matter. They were both so thrilled with one another that they danced far into the night. They didn't even notice that they were both completely nude. Who cared, anyway! And as they danced, God could hardly repress a smile of pleasure. God's gifts were certainly good. That old tree was just about forgotten . . . but not quite.

I try in this section to highlight the sheer fun and enjoyment of the text, which we saw in our reading. And at the end, I try to introduce the growing sense of tension as the harmony and joy of the story are blunted by the dialogue with the snake and the subsequent eating of the fruit. I chose to emphasize the creation of the animals and their naming for three reasons. First, it is one of the most delightful examples of the playfulness of the narrator. Second, one of those creatures is about to take center stage in the story. Third, later the man will announce the name of the woman in the face of the sorrow of life after the eating of the fruit; that act of naming will be reminiscent of this act. I have the naked couple dance and show God smiling to suggest what the narrator wants us to feel, namely, something of the harmony, unity, and joy of this man and this woman.

Time passed. One day, as the woman was hoeing a row of corn near the middle of the garden, a snake, one of God's fanciest creations, stopped by and wanted to chat. Now the man and the woman were nude, but the snake was shrewd. "So, God said *you all* may not eat from any tree of the garden." The snake was from the south side of the garden; and besides it wanted to include both the man and the woman in what it was saying. Actually, the snake didn't know what it was talking about, or at least it didn't get right what God had said. God had said that they could eat from *any* tree of the garden, and only from the *one* tree of the knowledge of good and bad were they not allowed to eat.

The woman knew all that. "From the fruit of the trees of the garden we may eat, but concerning the fruit of the tree in the middle of the garden, God said, 'You cannot eat from it, neither can you touch it, lest you die.'" Now, wait a minute. She didn't name that tree correctly; it is not just that "tree in the middle of the garden." It's the tree of the knowledge of good and bad. And besides; where did she make up that stuff about touching the tree? God didn't say anything about that. She is afraid even to touch that tree; she has made God's prohibition even worse. What is she trying to protect herself from? The tree?

The snake knows; he knows she wants that tree and could care less about any of the rest of them. He pushes her a step closer to it. "You all surely won't die! God knows that when you all eat from it, you all's eyes will be opened, and you all will be like God; you all will know good and bad!" Well, that did it. All other trees disappear from her sight. That tree was luscious; it was beautiful besides. And now the snake has taught her that it was desirable because one bite will lead to wisdom, to success in life, to freedom, to the independence of God! She ran to the tree and grabbed the nearest piece of fruit and thrust it into her mouth. The man was nearby, so she handed him some, too, and he bit right in without a single comment. At least she said something and thought something! The man just eats!

And immediately their eyes are opened. It was just like the snake said! It *was* a tree of knowledge, and the first thing they knew was that they were nude. Well, eight verses ago, the fact was not a problem. But this knowledge does make a difference, and now their nudity *is* a problem. And so, these newly minted would-be divine human beings now proceed to solve their first problem, armed as they are with the knowledge of good and bad. And what do they do? They sew fig leaves together and make for themselves underwear. Have you ever *felt* a fig leaf? For those of you who haven't, they feel like No. 2 sandpaper. If you decided—I don't know what kind of fool would—but if you decided to try on a fresh pair of fig leaf underwear after a refreshing shower, chances are you would not have them on too long. But that is precisely what this man and this woman decide to do.

Well, it is just like human beings, isn't it? When trying to solve problems on their own, armed with great knowledge and what seems to be complete independence, they tend to make fools of themselves. Oh, they have to learn, else they do not grow and progress. But growth and progress bring with them foolishness and disaster when knowledge is unaccompanied by God. So, here stand the man and the woman, filled with knowledge and power, scratching away in their figleaf underwear. My, they need something now. And here some*one* comes.

> The reader will perhaps note that in this section, I, as narrator of the story, am commenting a bit on the story. I find this is necessary for this narration because of the potential multiple understandings that a more direct telling might engender. Such multiplicity is a result of the extraordinary richness of this story and the fact that it has entered the common folklore traditions of much of the western world.
>
> I dwell on the humor of the fig leaves because it is precisely there that this particular reading finds its basic metaphor. The human brings thought that the fruit led to wisdom. In a hilarious irony, it has led instead to an absurd and most uncomfortable response to a very simple problem. The humans in their scratchy leaves are the perfect representation of radical human independence, an independence exercised apart from God. The importance of this picture necessitated that I stand back from the story long enough to comment upon it in the paragraph that begins, "Well, it is just like human beings."
>
> Yet, I do not want to neglect the positive side of the story, the necessity of seeking for knowledge, notwithstanding the dangers inherent in the search. Thus, I make a comment about that in the same paragraph mentioned above.

In the rest of my telling, I try to pick up on the ideas that the detailed reading has provided; for example, I emphasize some of the subtleties of the dialogue between woman and snake, I note some of the puns in the text (e.g. nude, shrewd), I make certain that each member of the congregation can feel the fig leaves for themselves and the silliness of their making. Each of these emphases is designed to enliven the telling, to thus engage the hearers, and to share with them the real power and wonderful humor of this magical tale. What the original narrator has done I try to do for my hearers, even though I know that I can never fully recapture for twenty-first century ears the quite remarkable flavor of this superb story.

I end this section of the story with the humans standing frozen to the spot, scratching their ridiculous creations, waiting for something to happen. What happens is God.

Meanwhile, God is strolling through the lovely garden, trying to catch the cool breezes of the late afternoon. It is God's custom to stroll in the garden and to engage the humans in a bit of pleasant conversation. As God approaches, the humans hear the familiar divine step and scurry like rats toward the trees of the garden. God stands near the trees in the middle of the garden, but the humans are not there. God is somewhat surprised, not a common emotion if you are God. "Where are you?" God calls out to the man only. A male voice answers from somewhere among the trees. "I heard your sound in the garden; I was afraid, because nude I was. So, I hid myself." It is a *very* long answer to an apparently quite simple question.

The answer does not satisfy God, whose curiosity is now fully aroused. "Who told you that nude you were? Have you from the tree which I commanded you not to eat from it eaten?" It is a simpler question than the first one. "Have you eaten or not?" The man says, "The *woman,* whom you gave to be with me, she gave to me from the tree, and I ate." This is the same woman, you will remember, who just 14 verses ago was the subject of a love poem from this same man. "This at last is bone of my bone and flesh of my flesh," he sang. Now the tune has changed. "That hunk of trash you made over there—she did it!" And besides, God, it is ultimately your fault; you made all of this stuff, didn't you? It is the most classic passing of the buck in the history of the world.

But it is not only the man's problem. God confronts the woman with the question, "What in the world have you done?" She immediately blames the only one left to blame, the snake. And what has happened? In precisely thirteen verses, the world has gone down the tubes. The harmony and joy of the human couple, working together in the wonderful garden of God, has been replaced by a terrible alienation between God and the humans, between the man and the woman, and between the snake and the humans. Harmony has given way to separation; it now sounds more like the world we know. And as God metes out the punishments, like a parent reprimanding the children, the harshness of our world appears. Snakes are not often our friends, and we are at war with them. Women will have children, but always in pain, and always as a result of the dominance of the men, and the men will work the rocky and unyielding soil, gaining a meager harvest. All will return to the soil from which they came, for that is what they really are—soil creatures after all. Death would be a welcome relief from such a grim existence.

How would you act, if you thought that your future held so much pain and sorrow and so little joy? The man in our story announces that the woman is called Eve, because she is the mother of all life. The two of them together will face the rigors of the world and will persist. The harmony lost is here given the promise of return. And God likes that sort of spunk, and makes for them garments of skin and clothes them. First, of course, they have to take off those fig leaves, their own ridiculous creations, to make way for the good gift of God. As they leave the garden, they are wearing the grace of God. Though they cannot live in the garden forever, they can live in the world literally surrounded by the presence of God, who loves them still.

> I move rapidly through the text now, wanting to make the focus of my reading clear. The fig leaves for me are the key, and the human response to their creation of them. I have tried to expose the absurdity of the act itself, and I have attempted to portray the very funny responses given by the man and the woman to God's questions. I would suggest that when the man and the woman speak gestures of an exaggerated kind can help to picture the humor. When the man blames the woman, one should point to the woman, and when the woman blames the snake, she should point to it. This whole scene is the stuff of low comedy and should be seen as such.

That is an *old* story, but it reminds me of another one, one that may be rather more familiar to you. One day, Jesus and his disciples were walking together toward the tiny village of Caesarea Philippi. The day was hot, so they paused for a rest. But Jesus had a question. "Who do people say that I am?" The disciples had heard the conversations about their leader, and they were quick to supply answers. "Some say John the Baptist," one said. That surely was a peculiar thought, due to the obvious fact that John had been beheaded not too long before. "Others say Elijah," another shouted. That was a more reasonable response, given the Jewish belief that Elijah must return before the Messiah could come; perhaps Jesus was the Messiah's forerunner. "Still others say one of the prophets," called out a third. Here was the safest answer of all. Obviously, Jesus was some sort of prophet, one who claimed to speak for God.

But now the first part of the quiz is over, and Jesus asks the question that is uppermost on his mind, and perhaps on ours. "Who do you say that I am?" Without a moment's hesitation, Peter cries out, "You are the Messiah!" Immediately, Jesus rebukes Peter against telling anyone what he has just said. Jesus goes on to tell the disciples what Messiah must do: it is a grim litany. Messiah must suffer many things, be rejected by elders, chief priests, and scribes, and be killed. But after three days, Messiah will rise. Jesus said all of this plainly.

And Peter, the one who thought he knew about Messiahs, grabbed Jesus and loudly rebuked him for such evil talk. And Jesus, gazing at his disciples, even more loudly rebukes Peter, and calls him Satan. "You are on the side of human beings," says Jesus, "and not on God's side at all."

Jesus immediately turns away and shouts for the multitude to join the disciples; he has something to say that he wants everybody to hear. "If anyone wants to come after me, let them deny themselves, take up their cross, and follow me. Whoever would save life will lose it; whoever loses life for my sake and the gospel's will save it."

Deny yourselves. Take up your cross. Follow. Note the order of Jesus's commands. Self-denial comes first. You must step out of the center of creation long enough to see that the world does not revolve around you and your needs, but around God and God's will. In other words, to eat the fruit of divine power is to assume the role of God. The result is fig leaf underwear. The result is confusion about just who does have ultimate power and freedom in the universe. To embrace independent power is to embrace fig leaves. To deny oneself is to embrace the cross.

Without self-denial there are no crosses to pick up. If I am the final authority in the world, I need take no responsibility for anyone else. I need not worry about the crosses of hunger, racism, sexism, or any of the other crosses of hatred that divide the human family. Conservative parents need not be reconciled to not-so-conservative sons. By shouldering one of these crosses, I then, says Jesus, will be following him to the hill of crosses, and will be joining him in the shattering of every barrier, the removal of every fig leaf that would divide us and make us foolish.

We are Peter. We are the man and the woman in the garden. We want to speak of discipleship, of being the children of God, without speaking of the cross. And like Peter, we are Satan. Like the man and the woman, we divide ourselves from one another by blame, by refusal to admit our weaknesses, by denying God's power in our lives.

But God stays with us. Jesus comes to Peter, even after his craven denial, his desire for fame and power, and says, after the resurrection, "Go tell the disciples, and especially Peter." Especially Peter. Especially us, our own worst enemies, as Pogo would have it. Tell Peter to take off his fig leaves and accept the skins of God. And God's offer comes to us, as well. We can keep on scratching or we can follow God to the cross, dressed in our divine skins. That's the choice: fig leaves or skins. Choose.

> I close this frame narrative sermon by using another biblical story and by commenting on that story, using the threads of the earlier parts of the sermon: my parents and I, Pogo, and the story of the garden. This ending part of the frame sounds a good deal like a more traditional sermon. And it well could be that an exceptionally rich story could often lead to a more direct attempt to point that story in a particular and very clear direction. Still, this is, in my judgment a narrative sermon, because the telling of a story was the heart and soul of its content. That is, the two stories have served as the major vehicles of the sermon, carrying the thrust with memorable metaphor and sharp dialogue. I want the hearers to remember the scratchy fig leaves and the skins of God, the basic metaphors of this sermon on the human tendency to desire absolute independence and the tragic-comic results of that tendency. And I want those metaphors to be memorable, because that is precisely what my careful literary reading led me to want. I hope that the reader can begin to see how enormously valuable this kind of textual reading can be for narrative preaching.

Is This an Effective Story Sermon?

I have said that I wish to explore in my four story sermons whether or not they have fallen into the traps that Richard Lischer warned are laid for narrative preaching. Because I have tried to take my content from the most careful reading of the Bible, this sermon does not run the risk of a vague universalism or a "transient experience of grace." There can be no confusion here between my personal story and the great story of God. God's gift of grace in the face of our denials of that gift is clear in the Bible and in the sermon. The sermon is about God, first and foremost. Is the story too neat and too simply closed? Not at all. The choice to accept the grace of God and to sew fig leaves is a choice we all need to make, whatever our individual stories may be. At the close of the sermon I offered straightforward conceptualizations that could please any hearer fearful of a story without a stated point; I do not here merely repeat the Bible's story, as if such a thing were in reality possible. And I make the connection between the choice the sermon demands and the socio-political implications that follow from the choice. In short, this sermon has avoided the traps Lischer warned against.

FOUR

"Vulture, Son of Wretchedness"

A Reading of Jonah

JONAH HAS LONG BEEN seen as a story, some kind of narrative fiction, and though there remain a few persons who still spend time attempting to prove the historicity of the book, from reports of actual big-fish swallowings, to accounts of obscure fast-growing and fast-withering vines, to tenuous geographic surveys of the dimensions of ancient Nineveh, the fact remains that Jonah is a story. Its author wrote the tale precisely as a story and would no doubt be horrified (or perhaps vastly amused) to hear any attempt to find real history in the narrative. The author's horror would not be the result only of the futile attempts of would-be historians to validate the "facts" of the story; what would be especially painful is their complete misapprehension of the author's concern precisely to *write* a story. In their quest for fish and vines, they run the serious risk of missing the point entirely.

In that sense, a narrative reading of the book of Jonah is not only possible, it is in fact necessary if we are to hear the tale in the way in which it was intended to be heard. That the book is some sort of narrative fiction is in my mind beyond discussion.

And just what sort of narrative fiction is it? In an earlier article, I argued that "Jonah is a short story characterized by the use of satire."[1] Many scholars would agree that Jonah is a short story or a novella,[2] but it is equally

---

1. Holbert, "Deliverance Belongs to YHWH!," 60.

2. See the concise summary of this question in Burrows, "The Literary Category of the Book of Jonah."

significant to note that the chief means of the literary construction is satire. Satire is indicated by the presence of at least five discernable characteristics.

1. Satire is humor based on the fantastic, the grotesque, the absurd.

2. Satire has a definite target that must be familiar enough to make the assault meaningful and memorable.

3. Satire is characterized by indirection of attack. The charge comes from the flanks rather than head on.

4. Satire pillories inferior excesses; hypocrisy is one classic and familiar example.

5. Satire is usually external in viewpoint. The actions of the character or the overt effects of the satirized idea are emphasized rather than the interior realm of the individual or idea.[3]

The following narrative reading of the Book of Jonah will have these characteristics of satire firmly in mind. It is important in this case to get these assumptions named before the reading begins, in order that the reading has a definite shape and point from the very start. You will soon see how the author very quickly moves us into a fantastic and grotesque world and thus announces that satire is afoot.

The reader should know that the following reading is only one that can be made of this delightful story. Its validity as a reading may only be judged by how effectively it accounts for the literary material presented by the author, how effectively the reading communicates a clear and forceful meaning for the story. In a very real sense, you, the readers, also become judges of the reading as you evaluate the effectiveness of the reading. But, as always, when one reads a biblical narrative, one soon finds that one has ceased playing the role of judge, and has become, in fact, one who is being judged by the very story one is reading.

Jonah 1:1–3

> *(1) Once, the word of YHWH came to Jonah, the son of Amittai, (2) "Arise! Go to Nineveh, the great city, and cry against it, because their evil has come up in my presence!"(3) But Jonah arose to flee to Tarshish from the presence of YHWH. He went down to Joppah and found a ship bound for Tarshish. He paid the fare and went*

3. Holbert, *Preaching Old Testament*, 62.

> *down into it to go with them to Tarshish away from the presence of YHWH.*

In these three verses, the author sets the tone for the entire tale. The central subject of the book is established in the pointed first verse. It is clearly a prophetic call from YHWH, nearly identical in form to the opening verse of the prophet Joel. There is here no historical detail as is often provided in the introductions to the prophets of Israel, no lists of kings (e.g., Hos 1:1 or Mic 1:1), no other chronological determinants (e.g., Amos's earthquake, 1:1). Indeed, the author provides for us stark simplicity in this prophetic call, the better to focus our attention on the author's primary concern, namely the subject of that call, Jonah, son of Amittai. While it is certainly true that Jonah is nowhere in this book called "prophet," he is most assuredly called to be one in the opening verse of the story.

And just who is this Jonah ben Amittai? A prophet with the name is mentioned in 2 Kings 14:23–29. He is there described as a prophet who was involved in the great expansion of the Northern Kingdom under the long reign of Jeroboam II. H. W. Wolff claims that this eighth-century Jonah was a "typical prophet of salvation," and, as such, was used by the author of our book in part to criticize similar prophets of an easy salvation in the author's own day.[4] On the other hand, Fretheim notes that the prophet Jonah of 2 Kings is in no sense the central concern of that text. Rather, God's willingness to save Israel, in spite of the continual wickedness of the evil Jeroboam, is central to the story. Thus, Fretheim thinks that the prophet called to mind for our author the major theme of the proposed work, namely, despite great wickedness, God resolves to save. Hence, Jonah was chosen as "hero" of a work that wanted to proclaim in narrative guise this same theological point.[5]

I readily grant that the Jonah, son of Amittai, of 2 Kings calls to mind the twin concerns of God's resolution to save in the face of wickedness and the demand for a prophetic announcement. But *that* Jonah proclaims glad tidings in the face of wickedness, while our prophet is called to announce evil tidings in the face of wickedness. The concerns are on the surface similar, but the respective contexts are quite different. In short, I think it is premature to decide just how these two Jonahs relate to one another.

4. Wolff, *Obadiah and Jonah*, 98.
5. Fretheim, *The Message of the Book of Jonah*, 41–42.

I think rather that "Jonah, son of Amittai," is chosen as the main character of the book precisely because of the meaning of his name. He is "Dove, the son of faithfulness or fidelity."[6] It is really quite an astonishing name, and builds certain expectations into the minds of the readers. Of fifteen non-sacrificial uses of the word "dove" in the Hebrew Bible, all save one are quite positive in tone, best represented by that most famous image, the dove of Noah (Gen 8:8–12), whose olive branch has become one of the most recognized images for peace in the western world. With a name like "dove," we might have a right to expect wonderful and dutiful activity from this prophet.

But, as Wolff points out, the other, more negative image of "dove" as silly and flighty (Hos 7:11) should perhaps warn us that this "dove" may not be quite what he is cracked up to be.[7] And yet, he is said to be the "son of faithfulness," another certain indication that YHWH has indeed chosen well in the quest for a prophet to the Ninevites. And YHWH's call could hardly be clearer. "Arise! Go to Nineveh, the great city, and cry against it, because their evil has come up in my presence." The command, the place, the means, and the reason all are provided by a YHWH who obviously expects instantaneous obedience.

But, astoundingly, that is exactly what YHWH, and we, do *not* get. The one called to "cry out" without a single murmur "arises" all right in apparent intention to fulfill the command, but instead of "crying out," "flees" to Tarshish! In response to the call to "go East," the would-be prophet heads West![8] And the narrator tells us that Jonah is fleeing more precisely "from the presence of YHWH," the very place to which the evil of Nineveh arose to instigate the whole process in the first place. Note, too, the obvious locational disparity represented in the verse. YHWH's call is to "arise." In response, Jonah "goes down" to Joppah, and upon finding the west bound ship, "goes down" into the ship's hold. He is thus about as far away from

---

6. Several commentators note this fact: Good, *Irony in the Old Testament*, 42; Fretheim, *The Message of Jonah*, 43. Burrows has the surprising statement, "Dove, the son of Fidelity is hardly an appropriate appellation for the prophet Jonah" ("The Literary Category of the Book of Jonah," 90). Perhaps Burrows himself is being ironic here; if satire is the key to the book's proper understanding, no better name could be chosen.

7. Wolff, *Obadiah and Jonah*, 99.

8. The exact location of Tarshish is unimportant for the story. That it is far west of Israel is the key. See a summary of the speculations for the location of Tarshish in Ibid., 100–102.

YHWH's presence as he can get, that presence which knows of the evil of Nineveh, that presence with which Jonah apparently wants nothing to do.

The structure of these three verses is designed to demonstrate the total disobedience of our prophet, Dove, the son of faithfulness. It opens with YHWH's word coming to Jonah and closes with that Jonah fleeing headlong "from the presence of YHWH." Verse 3 beautifully exemplifies the flight of the prophet, as two infinitives ("to flee" and "to go") frame four rather dry finite verbs ("he went down," "he found," "he paid," "he went down.") Both infinitives are tied to the phrase "from the presence of YHWH," this repeated phrase highlighting the central concern of the narrator. At both the level of scene and at the level of language, Jonah is portrayed as disobedient.

It is, of course, hardly unprecedented that a Hebrew prophet has proven reluctant to follow the call of God without hesitation. Moses, when called out of the flame of a burning bush, offers five increasingly lame excuses why he should not go to Egypt and fulfill the call of YHWH. Isaiah claimed that he was a man "unclean," surrounded by people equally unclean, and thus was unworthy of the mission of his God (Isaiah 6). Jeremiah said he was too young (Jer 1). Yet, Jonah's wordless flight is quite unique (Elijah does flee, at first silently, but it is *toward* the mount of God and not the opposite direction, 1 Kgs 19). God's prophetic call has been more thoroughly rejected here than at any other place in the Hebrew Bible.

And, of course, the question is: "Why?" And thus the gap in the text yawns wide. The call is clear, and the call is rejected. In this reading, this gap is the chief one. We must read on to attempt to close this basic gap; we must know what has driven the prophet so far away from all he is called to be and do. In this reading, that gap will not be closed until the end of the tale.

Before proceeding with the analysis, we would do well to return to the discussion of satire. The flight of the prophet is described as completely at variance with the call of YHWH. It can thus be named for what it is, a grotesque reversal of expectation. And, the prophet himself is in the spotlight and becomes thereby the object of the attack of the narrator. It certainly cannot be said at this point in the story that Jonah is representative of prophets in general, prophecy in general, or anything other than himself as disobedient prophet. Jonah alone is the target, and his story has begun with a grotesque and wholly unexpected action on his part, which should at least put us on our guard against this fast-moving refugee, running away from his God.

Jonah 1:4–10

> *(4) But YHWH hurled a great wind at the sea; thus there was a great tempest on the sea, so that the ship thought to be broken up. (5) And the mariners were afraid, and each cried out to his gods. They hurled the things of the ship at the sea to lighten it for them. Meanwhile, Jonah had gone down into the hold of the ship; he had lain down and was sound asleep. (6) The captain of the vessel came near to him and said, "What are you doing asleep? Arise! Call to your God! Perhaps that God will give a thought to us so that we do not perish." (7) Then they said to one another, "Come now! Let us cast lots in order that we might know on whose account this evil has come to us." So they cast lots, and the lot fell on Jonah. (8) So they said to him, "Tell us right now on whose account this evil has come to us; what is your occupation, where do you come from, what is your homeland? Who are your people?" (9) He said, "A Hebrew I am, and YHWH, God of heaven, I fear, who made the sea and dry land." (10) Then the men feared a great fear, and said to him, "What is this you have done?" For the men knew that he was fleeing from the presence of YHWH because he had told them.*

If Jonah thinks that he can actually escape the presence of YHWH by taking an extended sea voyage, he is quickly disaffected of the notion. YHWH, pictured as one standing on the mound of heaven, "hurls" a great wind at the sea with the result that a great tempest engulfs the tiny vessel, so great that "the ship thought to be broken up." The text is worded in such a way as to ascribe thought to the ship itself. In such a tale of fantasy, a detail like that is surely not out of place.

As the sea begins to boil, we are introduced to some new characters, the ship's sailors. Quickly, we are told two things about these mariners. First, they are "afraid" because of this "great storm," with the clear implication that it is far from an ordinary squall at sea. We, the readers, know that their fear is not misplaced; this is nothing less than a divine storm, brought on by the flight of the reluctant prophet, Jonah. Second, we are told that these sailors are polytheists, because they "each cry out to their own gods." Thus, we are presented with a picture of pagan sailors, caught in the unseen grip of a struggle between YHWH and the would-not-be prophet, terrified by a storm of supernatural proportions. Yet, even as pagans, they immediately turn to their gods whom they assume to be the cause of the tempest. They are certainly religious, as the narrator tells us, even if their religion is suspect on theological grounds.

Not only are they religious, they are good sailors who do their utmost to save the vessel that is entrusted to their care by "hurling" (they perform their actions with the same verb used to describe the actions of YHWH) items off the ship in a valiant effort to save the threatened craft. This furious activity of "crying out" to their gods while acting to attempt to save the ship is marvelously contrasted with the "actions" of Jonah. Where is the prophet through all of this? "Gone down" into the very deepest part of the ship, lying prone on the floor of that very deepest place, sound asleep! The contrast between Jonah and the sailors could hardly be greater. While it was he who was called by YHWH to "arise" and "cry out" to the Ninevites, he has "gone down," first to Joppah, then into the bowels of the ship, was lying down there, fast asleep; all of this activity was accomplished without the aid of a single word. Meanwhile, it is the pagans, uncalled by any god, who are "crying out" (the verbs are different but are synonyms in Hebrew) for relief from the storm from any god there may be who caused it, and who are trying their utmost to salvage the ship.

The reader should note that the verb used to describe Jonah's sleep has interesting connotations as it appears in the Hebrew Bible. Jonah's "sleep" here is rather more like a trance, induced by the divine. It is this sleep that descends on 'adam prior to YHWH's act of divine surgery (Gen 2:21). It is this sleep that falls upon Abram just prior to God's gift of the mysterious covenant sealed by the flight of a smoking fire pot and a flaming torch between the halves of sacrificial animals (Gen 15:12). It is this sleep that comes to General Sisera, as he lies exhausted on the floor of Jael's tent, just prior to her brutal murder of him (Jud 4:21). It is this sleep that Eliphaz, the so-called friend of Job, claims to have fallen on him before he is visited by a nocturnal divine spirit from whom he learns "great" truths about life. By using this verb, the rather pathetic Eliphaz attempts to class his own experience of divine trance with these other experiences from the sacred past of Israel's worthies (Job 4:13). When this word for sleep is used, the reader can just about bet that God is involved somehow in the situation. And so it is here; God is involved, but in ways hardly imagined by this sleeping prophet.

Indeed, Jonah, asleep and hidden on an unnamed ship, bound for the wilds of the far-western ocean, must at this point in the story feel that he has actually escaped the call of his God. But the incongruities we have witnessed, from fleeing prophets to praying pagans, warn the reader, who knows far more than Jonah about his relationship to the commanding God, that Jonah's sense of safety, evidenced by his quiet sleep, is actually seriously threatened. And, as often in the story, the bearer of the news of the inescapable presence of God is an unlikely one.

The captain of the ship comes upon the sleeping Jonah, and rather rudely arouses him with the phrase, "Why are you sleeping?" (He uses the same "trance" word discussed above.) Why, indeed? The storm is growing, the ship is sinking, all other persons aboard are praying and working. Only the comfortable "Dove" rests unaware and uncaring. The captain then commands the sleeper, "Arise! Call to your god!" He uses both verbs that YHWH used in verse two to call the prophet to action. Thus, the captain says more than he knows when he wakes his mysterious passenger. He, in effect, reiterates the call of God to him, and the reader does not miss the repetition. And he concludes his wake-up message by asking, "Who knows? Perhaps that God will give a thought to us so that we may not perish!" Crying out for help to a possible source of help may lead in fact to help; that is good religion. One might imagine that the prophet would have thought of that, but not this prophet.

It is significant that another pagan in this book, the king of Nineveh, utters a nearly identical suggestion in the face of divine annihilation at 3:9: "Who knows? That god might change, be gracious, and turn from divine fierce anger in order that we do not perish!" Are the pagans teaching prophets proper religion? The startling incongruities of these scenes suggest that this prophet has much to learn, and they further suggest that satire may be loose in the story and that the object of the satiric attack is none other than Jonah.

After the captain's commands are completed to the drowsy Jonah, the sailors decide to attempt to discern the will of whatever divinity is the source of the "evil." They see the storm as "evil," using the same word by which YHWH described the "evil" of Nineveh in verse 2. It was this evil that brought about the call to Jonah in the first place, and his refusal to address the source of that evil, this evil drawing in innocent sailors and putting them at risk of their lives.

> Jonah, by his flight and inaction, has tacitly announced doom on the pagans—but they are the wrong pagans. Jonah has not only not done his duty for YHWH; Nineveh's evil has fallen on him, and upon his unwilling and undeserving companions, due to his pronounced willfulness. Could the satire be more pointed? Jonah, by refusing to announce judgment that might lead to repentance, has instead brought judgment upon the innocent.[9]

9. Holbert, *Preaching Old Testament*, 66.

The sailors cast their lots, and the lot "falls" on Jonah, just as the reader knows that it must. Note that the descending motif, in opposition to YHWH's initial call to "arise," continues as lot casting involves both throwing and falling. The throwing down of the lots here surely prefigures the sailor's later action of "hurling" Jonah into the sea. Once the lot has accused Jonah, why then do the sailors begin their flurry of questions to him with the demand to "tell us now on whose account has this evil come upon us?" They have just determined the answer to that question by the throwing of the lots. But perhaps we need to ask: why do persons ask a direct question of someone when the questioner already knows the answer? The question at this point does not seek information; it seeks confession. Like the question YHWH asks 'adam in the garden of Eden, after the consumption of the fruit, "Where are you?" does not necessarily expect an informational reply, so here the sailors want Jonah to tell them that it is indeed his fault that they all find themselves on the point of death.

But they do not ask only that one question. They fire a volley of questions at the guilty one, asking about his occupation, his general place of origin, his specific homeland, and finally his people. As Edwin Good noted, the scene is "wildly incongruous," as the sailors, in the teeth of a howling, life-threatening storm, ask Jonah for a "thumbnail autobiography."[10] Jonah answers in part, and at the same time his answer is only to the *last* of the questions in the series. But, also, it offers a response to a question that was not even asked. In this his first speech in the book, he announces that he is a "Hebrew," and the reader hears this as an answer to the question of his "people." But he continues by saying that he "fears YHWH, the God of heaven, who made the sea and the dry land." No one had asked about his theological inclinations, but he spills them out to the sailors unbidden.

His announcement has the sound of a creed, long known and oft quoted. The reader might ask: in what exactly does this 'fear' consist? How does it relate to the great fear of the sailors because of the storm? Wolff claims that the word in the mouth of Jonah here means little more than an "impersonal pointer" to a very general "religious affiliation." He goes on to conclude that "there is no trace here of that elemental dread of destruction" suggested by the sailors' fear in verse 5.[11] Further, is it not peculiar that Jonah has just uttered a claim to believe in a God who made the sea at the

10. Good, *Irony in the Old Testament*, 44.
11. Wolff, *Obadiah and Jonah*, 116.

same time that he is running away from that very God on the very sea that God supposedly made?

To return to the Genesis reference alluded to above, just as 'adam blunders out a very long response to the simple question, "where are you," so Jonah announces more to the sailors than he perhaps intended. In the garden story, God goes on to ask two further questions of 'adam, which engender the hilarious and tragic "passing of the buck" responses both of 'adam and his companion (see my comments in the previous chapter). Jonah's creedal response to the many questions of the sailors reveals and hides. Unfortunately for Jonah, it reveals more than it hides, as the response of the sailors makes all too clear.

Their first reaction to this creed, so easily tossed off by Jonah, is "they feared a great fear"; that is, the fear they feel as they hear the creed is greater even than the fear they felt in response to the storm. What makes them so afraid now? After all, it was only a simple creed. In apparent horror, they say to Jonah, "What is this you have done?" With this question, we are once again reminded of the Garden of Eden. At Gen 3:13, God asks Eve verbally the *identical* question. God, astonished by the disobedience of Eve in her eating of the forbidden fruit now mirrored by the sailors, is equally astonished at this disobedient prophet, running away from the God who made the sea. Just as God's "hurling" of the storm is matched by the sailors' "hurling" of the things of the ship at the sea (later they will "hurl" Jonah at the sea as well), so their question to the prophet is God-like in its formulation. Remember, too, that the captain of the ship uttered to Jonah the same two commanding verbs that God spoke to Jonah to begin the tale. The narrator seems intent on connecting these pagan sailors with God. Thus, incongruities mount.

The anguished question of the sailors arises, "because they knew that he was fleeing from the presence of YHWH, because he had told them." Some scholars claim that all of Jonah's speech is not reported; in the missing lines he must *really* have told them that he was fleeing his God.[12] But that is only an argument from silence and does not attempt to address the text as it stands.

Jonah has proclaimed belief in a God who made the sea. The sailors already know that the reason for the sea's raging is to be found with Jonah. Thus, the sailors conclude that Jonah's God, who made the sea, is upsetting the sea precisely to chasten, or even to destroy, a wayward subject. In effect,

12. Fretheim, *The Message of Jonah*, 85.

Jonah *has* told them he was running from God; the sailors have simply deduced the truth from the prophet's creed. But, and this is the important fact, they were able to so conclude that Jonah was running away from his God only because they *believe* immediately what the prophet has said about God. Jonah, with his creed, has made instantaneous YHWH worshippers of them all! It will not be the last time in this book that a very brief phrase brings surprising conversion experiences to a group of unlikely pagans.

And so at the end of vs. 10, grotesque incongruities abound. We see pagans who sound religious, while a prophet says nothing as he denies his religious vocation. Indeed, this prophet only speaks when he is forced to do so, but his off-hand creedal statement results in great fear and conversion among the pagan sailors. And all of this unexpected missionary work is accomplished in the midst of a howling supernatural storm, and it is accomplished by a prophet who is running away from the very God who is the source of his mission. In fact, it was the refusal of the missionary to go on his mission that has made this other wholly unintended missionary work possible! And yet the major gap remains open: why did Jonah flee in the first place?

Jonah 1:11–16

> *(11) So they said to him, "What shall we do to you that the sea might calm down around us?" For the sea was growing even more stormy. (12) He said, "Pick me up and hurl me at the sea so that the sea might calm down around you. For I know that it is because of me that this great storm has come upon you." (13) But the men rowed hard to return to the dry land, but they could not because the sea was growing even more stormy against them. (14) So they cried out to YHWH and said, "Ah, YHWH! Please do not let us perish because of this man's life; do not lay on us innocent blood!" (15) Then they picked Jonah up and hurled him at the sea. And the sea stopped its raging. (16) Then the men feared YHWH with a great fear. They sacrificed a sacrifice to YHWH and they vowed vows.*

The sailors now know beyond the shadow of a doubt that the cause of the evil and awesome storm is this Jonah, this prophet who has stupidly attempted to escape the very God who made the sea. Surely, their course should be clear: to rid themselves of Jonah is to rid themselves of the storm and the furious God who has brought it down on their heads. But instead of hurling Jonah at the sea forthwith, they ask *him* what they should do with him! One wonders whether or not they demonstrate a certain reluctance to murder the wretch, even though they know that his death will mean the saving of their lives. In response to their gracious question, allowing Jonah to determine his own fate, though he apparently would have let them die without a word had he not been discovered, he insists that they "hurl him at the sea," and assures them that the entire debacle is his problem alone. When he hits the water, their trial will be over.

Some have found an enormous magnanimity on the part of Jonah here.[13] He appears to be offering his life on behalf of the sailors in an act of selfless devotion to the threatened strangers. However, readers should be cautious before reaching such conclusions too quickly. What is the evidence so far? Jonah has received a call from God to go to Nineveh and cry out against them. In silence, he goes in the opposite direction. In a crisis, he remains silent and inactive until aroused to speech by some pagan sailors who act and speak in the sorts of ways we might have imagined the prophet of God would have acted and spoken. We have been offered no suggestion at all that Jonah would be willing to sacrifice himself on behalf of anyone. Surely, Good is correct when he says, "perhaps we must see Jonah's offer not as a sudden burst of generosity but as his perception that death might yet be a way out of his frightful mission. Jonah will express the same thought again."[14]

But we note that once again, a speech from Jonah is not met with the fulfillment of his expectations. His simple creed above resulted in the conversion of the sailors to a working belief in YHWH (vs. 9). Now, instead of death, and supposed escape from the dogged YHWH and the divine calling, the sailors "row hard" in a valiant attempt to save their ship and the cause of their plight, Jonah. Such amazing characters are these sailors! They can easily save themselves by the simple dispatch of the wretch who put their lives in jeopardy. Indeed, saving was hardly in the mind of Jonah when he silently boarded their vessel and attempted to sleep through the storm that brought the innocent sailors close to death. They have every right to be furious in the face of the callous disregard for them demonstrated by this Hebrew. Nevertheless, they row hard to save him.

---

13. Brynmor et al., *A Translator's Handbook on the Book of Jonah*, 24; Fretheim, *The Message of Jonah*, 46.

14. Good, *Irony in the Old Testament*, 45; for still another explanation of the verse, see Magonet, *Form and Meaning in the Book of Jonah*, 86.

But they cannot, for the storm's fury intensifies. Thus, in intense piety, the once-pagan sailors now turn to YHWH by "crying to" that God who made the sea and the dry land. What Jonah resolutely refused to do in response to the direct command of YHWH, the sailors now do in response to the great crisis of the storm; unbidden by the command of YHWH, they "cry out." They humbly ask two things. First, "Do not let us perish because of the life of this man." The prophet of God, called to preach YHWH's word to Nineveh, has in fact become a man of death from whom the sailors now pray to be saved. Second, they cry, "Do not lay on us innocent blood." They do not see Jonah as innocent; they merely ask that his blood, about to be shed by them in innocence, not stain them. Wolff points to a possible parody in connection with the sailors' requests of YHWH.

> The ironic undertone becomes perceptible when we remember Jonah's antitype, Jeremiah, and the words of Je. 26:15: "If you put me to death, you will bring innocent blood on yourselves." There a true prophet warns a wicked people (Jerusalem!) against shedding his innocent blood. Here good non-Israelites, who are face to face with a prophet who is not good at all, pray that they should not acquire guilt through his death. Only a satirist switches roles like this, in order to convey a humiliating lesson to his readers.[15]

Exactly what sort of humiliating lesson this is remains to be seen, but this "satiric switching of roles," as Wolff would have it, furthers the narrator's portrayal of the "good guys" and the "bad guys." But the incongruity is that the Hebrew prophet is the latter, while the pagan sailors are the former.

And the good guy sailors conclude their heart-felt plea to YHWH with a phrase designed to demonstrate their complete and total submission to that God, a phrase not unlike the line of Jesus in his garden prayer: "Not my will, but yours be done" (Luke 22:42; Mark 14:36; Matt 26:39). "Surely, you, YHWH, have done just as you pleased." And with that line, the satire has come full circle. "The total obedience of the sailors is now vividly etched against the total disobedience of the prophet Jonah."[16]

At the conclusion of that prayer, the sailors pick Jonah up and hurl him at the sea. The sea immediately calms; the literal phrase is "the sea stood still from its raging" (note the exaggeration in the satire). And, as a result, "the men feared YHWH with a great fear." Note, too, the growing

---

15. Wolff, *Obadiah and Jonah*, 120.
16. Holbert, *Preaching Old Testament*, 69.

use of the word "fear" in the chapter.[17] The sailors' fear is first of the storm (*s' ahrah*) (vs. 5), a natural fear at the power of some unknown god. Jonah's "fear" of YHWH is little more than a religious cliché, as we noted above, but the two words are here introduced to us together, namely, "fear" and "YHWH." At 1:10, the men "feared a great fear" upon hearing Jonah's creed, a creed that included his supposed fear of YHWH. And finally, at 1:17, these same men (they are not again called sailors after vs. 10, because they are now identified clearly as YHWH's men) "feared YHWH with a great fear," as they witness the instantaneous calming of the raging waters just as Jonah slips below the waves. "Fear" has in effect become "worship," two possible meanings of this Hebrew word, in the transformations of these pagan sailors into YHWH's men. To seal the fact that they really are people of YHWH, the men "sacrifice sacrifices" (the word used refers to that most ancient of feasts where the God receives the blood and the fat of the sacrifice while the people enjoy the flesh), and they "vow vows" (an ancient way to promise fealty and acceptance of the covenant commitment).

While the smoke of their sacrifices and the words of their vows rise into the now-placid sky, Jonah is dropping like a stone into the depths of the sea, surely at last escaping from the God who called him to go to Nineveh. A watery death is apparently preferable to that call, and to such a death Jonah goes. But, once again, he will learn that escape from this God is not quite as simple as he imagined.

Jonah 2:1–11

(1) But YHWH appointed a great fish to swallow Jonah, and Jonah was in the belly of the fish for three days and three nights.
(2) And Jonah prayed to YHWH, his God, from the belly of the fish.
(3) He said, "I cried out of my distress
*   to YHWH who answered me;*
*   from the depths of Sheol I cried for help;*
*   you heard my voice.*

(4) You threw me into the deep,
*   into the heart of the seas*
*   where the stream surrounds me;*
*   all your breakers and waves passed over me.*

17. For a discussion of the technique of "the growing phrase" in Jonah, see Magonet, *Form and Meaning in the Book of Jonah*, 31–33.

> *(5) Then I said, 'I am cast out*
> *from before your eyes;*
> *nevertheless, I will again discern your holy temple.'*
> *(6) Waters encircled me up to the neck,*
> *the great deep surrounded me,*
> *weeds wrapped around my head*
> *(7) at the roots of the mountains.*
> *I went down to the land*
> *whose bars closed on me forever.*
> *But you brought up my life from the Pit,*
> *YHWH, my God.*
> *(8) When my spirit fainted away,*
> *YHWH I remembered.*
> *My prayer came to you,*
> *to your holy temple.*
> *(9) Those who keep worthless idols*
> *abandon their covenant loyalty.*
> *(10) But I, with a voice of thanksgiving,*
> *I will sacrifice to you.*
> *What I have vowed, I will complete.*
> *Deliverance is YHWH's!"*
> *(11) Then YHWH spoke to the fish, and it vomited*
> *Jonah onto dry land.*

A significant number of commentators on the book of Jonah have concluded that the psalm of chapter 2 is a later, and quite inappropriate addition to the text of Jonah. In the main, three arguments have been used to sustain this claim.

1. The psalm simply does not fit the situation described in chapter one. This psalm is quite obviously a song of Thanksgiving. If Jonah were so intent on dying, why would he, after his saving by the fish, offer such a prayer to YHWH? We would have expected some angry words, perhaps in the form of a complaint/lament.

2. The Jonah described to us in chapter 2 seems quite different from the one we see in chapters 1, 3, and 4. The seemingly "pious" Jonah we find in the psalm appears to be very remote from the disobedient Jonah we saw in chapter 1, and the angry Jonah we find in chapters 3 and 4.

3. It is odd to find Jonah in prayer at all. Why is he now so willing to pray when he had to be coerced into speech by the pagan sailors in the first chapter?

I will attempt to offer answers to the questions in the course of the analysis of this chapter.[18]

It is immediately clear that the mood of the grotesque, established so obviously in chapter 1, is continued at the beginning of chapter 2. YHWH "appoints" a "big fish" precisely to swallow Jonah. The employment of the adjective "big" or "great" *(gadol)* is reminiscent of its use in the first chapter in connection with the city of Nineveh (vs. 2), the storm against the ship (vs. 4, twice), and the sailors' "fear" in its two meanings of vss. 10 and 17. The word will come up again in the final two chapters. The fish is, of course, miraculous, a unique divine appointment, no less than the several divine appointments that Jonah encounters in chap. 4. It must be "big," divinely so, so that it can comfortably swallow down a fleeing prophet, who would rather be dead than prophesy, and maintain him alive in its alimentary system for three days and nights. It is not a threatening creature, but a salvific one, designed for the one task of rescuing Jonah from drowning in the sea. From its fishy entrails, the prophet prays and thanks YHWH for the rescue.

Because I have already decided that Jonah's primary interest was escape from YHWH, a desire so overwhelming that death was preferable to the divine call to cry out to Nineveh, it is disconcerting to hear Jonah thanking YHWH for saving him. I might have expected Jonah to tell YHWH in no uncertain terms to ply the divine trade of rescue somewhere else! But before we jump to conclusions that might lead us to embrace this supposedly new more pious Jonah, we must examine the words of the prayer along with their functions within the story.

The very first word of the prayer is a familiar one to readers of chap. 1. YHWH called Jonah to "cry out against Nineveh"; his response was to flee in silence. At last, at 2:3, Jonah "cries out" but not to Nineveh, rather to YHWH. The prophet is at last "crying out" all right, on the surface fulfilling the command of YHWH, but his cry is only for *himself.* Note the numerous first person singular uses in this verse: "*I* cried," "*my* distress," "answered *me*," "*I* cried," "*my* voice." YHWH's command to "cry out to Nineveh, "the great *city*" is answered by a prophet concerned only with the first person. Jonah cries out because of personal "distress" brought on by his desire to die, realizing that escape from this God is impossible.

Thus, Jonah "cries out" but only for individual reasons, his own distress. But in vs. 4, he suggests a more peculiar reason for that distress. "*You*

---

18. The following is a summary of my own earlier work, Holbert, *Preaching Old Testament*, 70–75.

threw me into the deep, into the heart of the seas." The five first-person references of vs. 3 are abruptly countered by a second-person flurry in vs. 4. Jonah accuses YHWH of throwing him into the water, but the reader knows quite well that that is not true. Jonah asked to be thrown into the water and he was so thrown by those wonderful sailors, only after a thrilling attempt to save their nemesis. The second person finger-pointing continues as Jonah says, "All *your* breakers and *your* waves passed over me." In effect, YHWH is the guilty party according to Jonah's recounting of the events of chap. 1.

And to emphasize Jonah's own innocence, in verse 5 he employs the passive verb (*nigrasti*) and claims, "I have been *cast out* from before your eyes . . ." But again the reader must raise a quizzical eyebrow. Jonah was not by any means "cast out" by some unnamed third party (YHWH by implication?); he was in fact running from YHWH as fast as his disobedient feet could carry him. We remember how the narrator went out of the way in the first three verses of the story to emphasize the certain fact that Jonah was "fleeing from the presence of YHWH." To claim that he was "cast out" is nothing else than a lie.

Could it be that this pious-sounding prayer, like the ready creed of 1:9, reveals more of Jonah to the reader than he had in mind? Magonet calls this technique on the part of the narrator a "partial confession."[19] Surely there is hypocrisy here.

> Jonah has fled from YHWH; he has fled so far as to demand to be drowned in the sea. But, instead, that same God has saved him, and in return, Jonah, the pious, prays an unctuous thanksgiving prayer. In 5a, however, the real Jonah, our satiric target, has appeared. Indeed, in the first three verses of the prayer, Jonah accuses God of his plight, while thanking (God) for rescuing him from it. "O mea culpa" has become in Jonah's mouth "O sua culpa!"[20]

The entire surface intent of this "thanksgiving" is called into question by these several anomalies.

Jonah continues in vs. 5b: "Nevertheless I will again see your holy temple." What possible meaning could this mention of the temple have? The temple in this context must mean the very presence of YHWH, as

---

19. Magonet, *Form and Meaning in the Book of Jonah*, 24, 52, 56, 119 for a description of this literary device.

20. Holbert, *Preaching Old Testament*, 72.

the parallelism of "your holy temple" and "from before your eyes" in vs. 5 makes certain. What, then, has Jonah said? He claims that even though God has cast him out of the divine presence, Jonah still longs for that very presence. But the one who is praying is the one who is in flight headlong *from* that presence. Though his words claim that he longs for God's presence, his actions say just the opposite.

The reader should note that the descending motif of chapter 1, wherein Jonah rejected the call of God to "arise" and instead beat a steady path downward, is continued and completed in chapter 2. Jonah literally sinks from the "stream" of vs. 4b to "breakers and waves" in vs. 4c to the "great deep" of vs. 6b to the "roots of the mountains" of vs. 7a and finally to the "earth's bars," in vss. 7b and 7c, apparently the very bottom of the seas. Jonah's descent from YHWH finally ends at 2:7c, and precisely there we find the catchword "go down" (*yarad*) which was used twice in chapter 1 at vss. 3 (twice) and 5. This fact makes it even more certain that chapter 2 is an integral part of the book.

Jonah admits that his ascent begins as an act of God at 2:7d; the great marine creature, Jonah's private submarine, has saved him from a watery death. It is from this very creature's belly that Jonah is recounting his adventure in prayer to God and demonstrating to the reader his understanding of that adventure, which we have seen to be thoroughly one-sided and quite often false. In vs. 8, he offers his reading of just what sort of ascent he is undergoing:

> When my spirit fainted away,
> > YHWH I remembered.
> My prayer came to you,
> > To your holy temple.

At best, we have "fox-hole" religion here, or perhaps better, "fish-belly" religion. Jonah remembers YHWH only when his spirit, his *nephesh*, has fainted from him. Still, we cannot chide him for the words alone; they are common in the Psalter (e.g., Ps 18:7). The danger here is to make too much of the words.[21] Jonah is telling us only the facts as he sees them; these words are in no sense a confession. Just because Jonah prays at this point is no reason to be swept away by the certainty that praying itself as a clear sign of piety. As we shall see, he will pray at 4:2 also; the prayer found there is no

---

21. Holbert, *Preaching Old Testament*, 73; Magonet, *Form and Meaning in the Book of Jonah*, 43, claims that Jonah here submits to God's will; Landes, "The Kerygma of the Book of Jonah," 26, finds here "a sincere cry to God."

sign of piety at all. But now we must ask: what is the conclusion of Jonah's prayer, and what are the results he claims to gain from it?

> (9) *Those who keep worthless idols*
>   *abandon their covenant loyalty.*
> (10) *But I, with a voice of thanksgiving,*
>   *I will sacrifice to you.*
>   *What I have vowed, I will complete.*
>   *Deliverance is YHWH's!*

Note carefully the theological claims of vs. 9. Who are those in this story who have "kept worthless idols"? It is clear that this tale is filled with pagans. We have already witnessed the sailors, but they are thoroughly laudable people and are, at this very moment, in the process of sacrificing and making vows to YHWH. They have certainly not abandoned their "covenant loyalty," their powerful relationship with YHWH. In the next chapter, we will meet the Ninevites, all of whom are pagans. But the minute they hear the word of YHWH, they convert, and become followers of the only true God; why, even their beasts will become YHWH followers! But it is Jonah, the one we have seen who has publicly abandoned loyalty to YHWH, who will quote a very famous description of YHWH that includes that famous word *chesed*, translated here "covenant loyalty," at 4:2 precisely to *disparage* that loyalty, to decry the fact that YHWH has, because of *chesed*, spared Nineveh. Who is it then, who in reality "keeps worthless idols"? Is it not in fact Jonah himself?

Jonah proceeds to announce that he will both sacrifice and complete vows he has made to YHWH. He never sacrifices in this book, neither are we told that he either makes or completes a vow. Is it not ironic that while Jonah is claiming these mighty intentions, which he will never fulfill, the real men of YHWH are on the prow of their ship sacrificing and vowing to YHWH in heartfelt gratitude for YHWH's salvation?

Jonah's psalm ends, "Deliverance is YHWH's!" In my judgment, this is one of the key statements of the book. No one in the tale would at this point dispute that claim. YHWH can indeed deliver in the most unlikely of ways and through the most unlikely of persons. Who should know that better than Jonah? After all, he has been rescued from the very bottom of the world by a magic fish even against his will. Who should know that better than the sailors? They began a west-bound voyage to Tarshish as contented pagans, but ended up sacrificing and vowing to a God they learned of from a prophet of that God who was, however, running away from that very

God! In other words, they were evangelized for YHWH by a missionary whose very last desire was to evangelize anyone and had gone out of his way to avoid any such possibility. And, finally, who should know that better than we, the readers? We have witnessed the flight of the prophet away from the command of his God only to see him convert all those sailors with a half-formed creed and a desire to drown! And we have seen the reluctant prophet saved, while wanting to die, and then heard him utter an appalling hypocritical prayer, accusing God of his problems while claiming he will do the right religious things but never doing them at all. After a prayer like that, it is no wonder that the big fish throws up![22]

And we have also learned that Jonah will not escape this persistent God; God has called and God will have the missionary perform the divine command. Thus, we can expect Jonah to go to Nineveh. But, the central gap of the story, the one that is driving us to read on, is still wide open. Why is Jonah reluctant to go to Nineveh? We could make some guesses at this point in the story, but the narrator is saving *his* answer for the end of the tale. And so we must read on, urged by the art of this narration to discover the true identity and rationale of this Dove, the son of Faithfulness.

Jonah 3:1–4

> *(1) The word of YHWH came to Jonah a second time. (2) "Arise! Go to Nineveh, the great city, and cry to it the crying that I speak to you." (3) So Jonah arose and went to Nineveh according to the word of God. Now Nineveh was a great city; even God walking (through) it is a three-day journey. (4) Jonah began to enter the city, walking one day. He cried out and said, "In forty days, Nineveh will be overthrown!"*

Jonah, having been rather ignominiously vomited out of the big fish, immediately hears the "word of YHWH" a second time. The call begins in exactly the same way: "Arise! Go to Nineveh, the great city." But now the similarity stops. It is obvious that the actions of Jonah in the preceding two chapters have taught YHWH just what sort of prophet this chosen one

---

22. This wonderful joke is not my own. I heard it first orally in a sermon given by Professor W. J. A. Power in the chapel of Perkins School of Theology, sometime in the late 1960s. I have since read it in Magonet, *Form and Meaning in the Book of Jonah*, 53 and Williams, *Understanding the Old Testament*, 246. Williams was a student of Power's, as was I.

really is. Note the specificity of this second command. "Cry to it the crying [the roots of the two words are identical] that I speak to you." Far from the open-ended call of the first chapter—"Cry against it, for their wickedness has come into my presence"—YHWH now gives Jonah explicit instructions to cry to the Ninevites only the exact words that YHWH will provide for him. The reason for this change of command seems obvious; Jonah is hardly to be trusted to answer a call that provides any latitude for response. And so Jonah at last "arises and goes to Nineveh." After all, he has learned by now that escape from the call of this God is impossible, whether on land, on sea, or undersea.

We might note, however, that though YHWH warns Jonah to tell the Ninevites only what YHWH determines that they must hear, the narrator does not give us those words. When Jonah does cry out, we could assume that the words he uses are the words of YHWH. However, our experience with this prophet should warn us to listen very carefully to what he says; he is hardly to be trusted.

The second part of vs. 3 provides several options for translation. The usual way is something like the reading of the Revised Standard Version: "Now Nineveh was an exceedingly great city, three days' journey in breadth." The word rendered "exceedingly" in that translation is literally "to God." It is true that this may be a way for the narrator to indicate a superlative condition; the city of Nineveh was "the biggest city of all." Wolff reads, "Nineveh was then (even) for God a great city."[23] Even through divine eyes, the city of Nineveh was immense. Though the nuance is slightly different, the effect is the same.

My reading provides a different emphasis. I suggest that the narrator describes the city as so immense it would take *God* three days to traverse its boundaries. Such a fanciful notion fits well with the fairy-tale quality of the story, and establishes an important relationship to Jonah's movement into the city that is about to begin. The city of Nineveh is so vast that the Almighty would walk for three long days to get through it.

Contrast the vastness with Jonah's entry into the city. "He began to enter," the text reads, indicating a tentative process, and he walked "one day." Thus, in comparison to the divine immensity of Nineveh, Jonah's one-day human walk into the city hardly brings him to the center of the metropolis, as Wolff says;[24] he has barely penetrated the giant place. Thus, his five-word

23. Wolff, *Obadiah and Jonah*, 143.
24. Ibid., 149.

sermon is uttered not at all in a place where it would be likely to "spread like wildfire in every direction."[25] On the contrary, Jonah speaks on the fringes of the city with very little likelihood that he will be heard at all. Such a reading makes the results of the sermon to follow all the more astonishing and incongruous, and matches the picture of the reluctant prophet we have seen portrayed to this point in the tale. Jonah will preach the word of God, all right, but he will do so in such a way that any hearing of that word will be most difficult.

And the sermon itself is couched in ambiguity. If this be the word of YHWH, it is not at all clear exactly what that word is intended to say as it pours forth from the mouth of Jonah. "In forty days, Nineveh will be overthrown." What does this mean? We were told by God at the beginning of the story that the "evil" of Nineveh had reached the divine presence, and that this evil had moved YHWH to call Jonah to "cry out against" the city. We should note that when Jonah finally does come to cry out, it is neither "against" the city, as YHWH's first command indicated (1:2), nor is the cry "to" the city, as YHWH's second command insisted (3:2). The word is used in a very general way; Jonah is said to "cry out," not to or against anyone in particular.

Are we to assume that this message is to be one of warning with the possible expectation that the sinners might change their evil ways? Or are we to think that the message is one of irrevocable doom? Here is another gap in the text. Up to this point in the story, we have no way of adjudicating this gap, because we have no clear notion yet of the prophet Jonah. Would he care at all what happens to Nineveh? Is he not only intent on fulfilling this onerous task to "cry out," but to do so in the least painless way possible for him, enough at least to get this hounding YHWH off his back? Yet, he has announced to us and to YHWH that he claims to believe that "deliverance is YHWH's." What might that mean for Nineveh? Does he hope that his sermon will effect deliverance for them, or does he want them destroyed? At this point in the story, I cannot be certain. The narrator thus bids me to read on.

But I have said that the sermon is ambiguous. By announcing the number "forty," Jonah of course harks back to the many occasions of divine activity accomplished in that exact period of time. We remember the flood of Noah and its forty-day rain and the wandering of Israel in the wilderness that lasted for forty years. God is plainly at work again, and the number

25. Ibid.

forty makes that certain. But the verb that Jonah uses leaves us wondering at his intent. The verb I have translated "overthrow" can mean "transform" (e.g., "I will *turn* their mourning into joy" Jer 31:13) or "destroy" (e.g., "God overthrew those cities," that is, Sodom and Gemorrah, Gen 19:25). Which is it here? Good points to the ambiguity of the word, noting various places where it is used in the ways I have suggested, and concludes, "the latter (the 'transforming' sense) is certainly not in the prophet's mind, but, given the response of the populace, may we not say that it is in the author's mind?"[26] In my judgment, we cannot at this point say what is in the mind of Jonah at all. From what happens to Nineveh, we can say what they *heard* the prophet say, and we may finally be able to conclude that the narrator was in sympathy with their reaction. But about Jonah's *intentions* for his sermon, I do not think we can conclude anything, at least not yet. And this is significant. Our narrator is purposely withholding information about the "hero" from us, forcing us to read and ponder his actions. If I jump to conclusions too soon, I will have short-circuited part of the narrator's way with me; I will have denied myself the pleasure of the surprise that I have in store about this Jonah. But that the Ninevites heard what he said, and drew certain implications from the sermon, is made abundantly clear from the incredible scene that follows.

Jonah 3:5–10

> *(5) The men of Nineveh believed in this God. They called for a fast, and they dressed in sackcloth from the greatest of them to the least. (6) The thing reached the king of Nineveh. He arose from his throne, put off his royal robe, put on sackcloth, and sat in ashes. (7) He proclaimed in Nineveh an edict of the king and his great ones, "Human beings and animals, cattle and flocks must not taste anything: they shall not feed or drink water. (8) But they shall cover themselves with sackcloth, human beings and animals. They shall cry out to God mightily. And each one shall turn from their wicked way, and from the violence which is in their hands. (9) Who knows? This God may yet be sorry and turn from fierce anger so that we do not perish." (10) When this God saw their actions, that they turned from their wicked way, this God was sorry for the evil which "he" intended to do to them, and did not act.*

26. Good, *Irony in the Old Testament*, 49.

As pathetic and reluctant as Jonah's five-word sermon appears to be, the effect is positively breathtaking, not to mention appropriately absurd. The entire city is possessed with a fever for contrition and repentance. Immediately, the entire human population of the city "believed in God." The verb translated "believed" (*'aman*) is closely related to the word that was first used to describe Jonah in chapter one. We remember that he was Dove, son of faithfulness (*'amittai*). The reluctant, hence unfaithful, "faithful one" has struck again: in five words, the worst city in the world has been converted to belief in a God heretofore unknown and unacknowledged. We note that Jonah is a master of the passive, as we saw in his prayer of 2:5, when he indirectly accused God of "casting him out" of the divine presence, although he did not mention God until the final word of his prayer.

No matter. When the word of YHWH is made public, no matter how poorly, no matter how indirectly, human beings (not to mention cows!) are changed. Just as in chapter 1, where a simple creed, uttered in partial answer to a flurry of questions, led directly to the conversion of pagan sailors, so now a vague, ridiculously short, undirected announcement at one place on the outskirts of an incredibly large metropolis, filled with people saturated with evil, has led to another great conversion. This time the conversion is only to "this God," because Jonah has not bothered to speak the name of the God who called him, commissioned him, and who dragged him, kicking and screaming, to his prophetic task. But Jonah and the reader know who "this God" is, and that God's true name will reappear in the next chapter.

The wildfire of repentance soon reaches the king of Nineveh, who, without a word, joins in the sacred acts of contrition by leaping off his royal throne, tearing off his robe of office, putting on a garment of sackcloth and proclaiming a fast that goes beyond even that one already proclaimed by the people. Not only are the "men" (*'enos*) of Nineveh to fast and refuse to drink water. The king insists that "all the people" (*'adam*) and all the beasts, both herds of cattle and flocks of sheep and goats, are to wear sackcloth and are to avoid eating and drinking as well. In words that echo those of the ship's captain in chapter 1, the contrite king says, "Who knows? This God may yet be sorry, and turn from fierce anger so that we do not perish." Once again, good religious motives for confession come out of the mouth of an unexpected one. We might have thought that the prophet would have thought of such a thing, but not this prophet.

And so all of the people of Nineveh are crying out to "this God," and all of the beasts of Nineveh are mooing and baaing to "this God." And when this God saw all of that, this God was indeed sorry for the "evil" planned for Nineveh; the divine mind was changed. The "destruction" of the city has indeed become its "transformation." Nineveh, that great and evil city, has fallen under the protection of the "God of deliverance."

If the tale concluded there, a reader might decide that several themes had been explored.

1. One theme is the overarching power of the God YHWH, who indeed is creator of sea and dry land. Escape from the call of this God is foolhardy and plainly impossible, and the story of Jonah is a particularly clever and humorous attempt to illustrate that theme.

2. Another theme is the power of the word of YHWH. No matter how absurdly that word is made public, through rote creeds or half-baked homilies, the word simply does not return empty. In spite of the most recalcitrant of messengers, YHWH's will is done through the speaking of the divine word.

3. Another theme is related to number two. The word of YHWH is to go into all the world. Even the Ninevites, the epitome of evil and all things hated in Israel and the ancient Near East, are to hear the word of YHWH, and the people of Israel are to take it to them. Far from gloating over the death of Ninevites, as the prophet Nahum does so appallingly in his small book, Israel is to move toward these quintessential enemies with the word of God.

Any one or all three of these may be themes of the book of Jonah. But the close reader remains decidedly uncomfortable with any of them, because the basic gap of the story has yet to be closed. We *still* do not know what led Jonah to flee the presence of God at the very beginning of the story; that most basic of questions remains unanswered as we move to the end. The world of Jonah is now peopled with YHWH-worshipping sailors and God-protected Ninevites. It may be that he will have to respond to this world of his that is changing so rapidly around him. And respond he does!

Jonah 4:1–5

> *(1) But it was evil to Jonah, a great evil, and he was angry. (2) And he prayed to YHWH. He said, "O YHWH! Was this not just what I said while I was in my home country? That is why I fled to Tarshish in the first place, because I knew you were a gracious and a merciful God, slow to anger and full of covenant loyalty, who is sorry for evil.*

*(3) So now, YHWH, please take my life from me. It is better for me to
die than live." (4) And YHWH said, "Is it good for you to be angry?"
(5) And Jonah left the city, and lived east of the city. He built for
himself there a shelter and sat under it in the shade until he could see
what would happen in the city.*

The key to understanding vs. 1 is the reference of the implied "it" in the
translation. The most obvious answer to the question is found at 3:10.[27]
YHWH's change of mind about Nineveh, YHWH's sorrow over the evil
planned for Nineveh, and the subsequent refusal to perform that evil, have
infuriated the prophet. The narrator, as always, describes Jonah's fury in
hyperbolic language. "It was evil, a *great* evil," says the teller, using a word
used often before to describe the events and objects of the story from great
wind, to great fear, to great city, to great fish. Here again the satire cuts deep.
As Wolff notes,

> Nineveh's violence and God's threat of disaster aimed to do harm.
> Now—since Nineveh and God have both turned away from their
> intention—this will to do harm overcomes Jonah. He is especially
> obsessed by the thought of Nineveh's wickedness, now that God
> has withdrawn his threat of disaster. Thus the repeated catchword
> ("evil") does not merely accentuate Jonah's opposition to God's
> judgment; it also stresses that Jonah and Nineveh have actually
> exchanged roles. That it should be God's very mercy that brings
> "great wickedness on Jonah" is both dramatic and satiric.[28]

Wolff, in his claim that Jonah and Nineveh have "actually exchanged roles,"
the former replacing the latter as that which is evil in the world, points to
another possible meaning of the "it" of vs. 1. If Jonah is obsessed with the
wickedness of Nineveh, might not the "it" refer to that unexpunged evil
that still pervades the city? They may all be crying and mooing to God, but
evil still clings to them in the mind of Jonah.

And, of course, the "it" could also mean the entire ludicrous scene
of all of these Ninevites and their livestock now incredibly entering the
realm of YHWH, and precisely because of Jonah's own paltry sermon in
the "sticks" of Nineveh. It appears that the reader need not choose one of
these alternatives; all three may indeed be intended by the narrator, as the
remarkable statement of vs. 2 indicates. Once again, Jonah prays, and the
reader immediately remembers the hypocritical prayer of chapter 2 and

27. Wolff, *Obadiah and Jonah*, 160.
28. Ibid., 165.

wonders just what the prophet is about this time. At last, the gap of the story is closed.

Jonah now tells us and YHWH the precise reason for his flight to Tarshish, and his admission helps us to understand the earlier actions of this prophet. Jonah announces that it is exactly the character of God that forced him to flee in chap. 1. He quotes again an ancient formulation (see 1:9) describing the kind of God YHWH is as found in numerous places in the Hebrew Bible (e.g., Pss 86:15; 103:8; 145:8; Ex 34:6; Neh 9:17; Joel 2:13). This ancient creed about the nature of YHWH fairly drips with sarcasm in the mouth of Jonah, as his own character is revealed to us in all of its grim colors. "I left," he says, "because I knew that you were a God gracious and merciful, slow to anger, filled with steadfast love (covenant loyalty), and sorry because of evil." Jonah left silently and swiftly for Tarshish and the oblivion of escape, and finally the escape of death in the sea, because to speak for this God is to speak words of grace, mercy, love, and the desire to seek repentance. Jonah wants no part of any of that. It is the final part of this snarling "confession" that galls him the most. The "evil" of Nineveh is real, all right, but Jonah now admits that speaking any word from this God to them would result not in the proper treatment of such evil, namely swift destruction, but sniveling love and whining repentance. Even a five-word sermon, uttered in a tiny corner of the place would affect such a disastrous result. And it has done just that!

And so, Jonah reiterates his desire for death. He would rather be dead than live in a world where such a God is ruler, a world where pagan sailors and evil Ninevites can find their way into the love and favor of such a disgustingly merciful God. And that God is understandably astonished by the behavior of the chosen one. "Do you do well (or "is it right for you") to be angry?" God has finally gotten a prophet who is successful, and the character is furious! The great prophets of Israel were only minimally successful in terms of any kind of acceptance of their messages. With a simple creed and a five-word homily, Jonah has converted every person who has heard the sound of his voice. But instead of joy, God hears only complaint and a desire for death. The movements of the satirist are becoming clearer and clearer.

Jonah, his appalling beliefs now presented for all to see, rushes out of the city, builds himself a small shelter, and sits down to wait. He waits in a scornful silence "to see what would become of the city." Perhaps, he reasons, if the divine mind has changed once, it may change again; Nineveh may yet get what it has coming to it. This absurd expectation again indicates how little Jonah understands of the words and phrases that he utters so easily from his tradition. He just made it completely clear that YHWH's will is for deliverance for all, because mercy and slow anger are the divine way. Yet, he still thinks that God is finally not what God so certainly is by his own continual admission. But God is not through with Jonah yet.

Before concluding the reading, let us look back at the problematic actions of Jonah with our new knowledge of him as a character. He told us that he left for Tarshish because God was merciful. This explains his silence, as I have already said. He fears that any speech will present the word of YHWH, the merciful one, and the results will be that many undesirables might find their way into the realm of God. His first speech, the creed of 1:9, wrenched out of him by the terrified sailors, is now seen for what it was, namely a grudging partial confession, designed to say as little as possible about himself and the reasons for the storm. However, as Jonah later admits, any talk even related to the actions of YHWH tends to have profound effects. So it is here. The creed not only reveals to the sailors precisely what Jonah did not want to admit—his guilt for the storm—but also leads them on the road to worship YHWH, a result far from the mind of this appalling prophet.

His request to be thrown into the sea (1:12) now must be viewed as a request for death, and hardly a magnanimous attempt to save the sailors. The long prayer of chapter 2 was indeed a hypocritical attempt to blame YHWH for his miseries and to claim a deep religious conviction that he obviously did not feel. His cry that "deliverance is YHWH's" was nothing else than religious demagoguery. Jonah is perfectly willing to claim the deliverance of YHWH for himself, but others whom he contacts need not apply.

So, of course he is angry when the Ninevites are spared; indeed, he has been secretly angry from the beginning. This YHWH is impossible to escape and equally impossible to live with. As long as Ninevites and their beasts and pagan sailors can find their way into the realm of God, Jonah would be more than happy to leave the wretched world to them and their disgusting God.

But we must note again how the narrator has disguised certainty from us almost to the last. He has been able to do that because of that wide gap that moved the story from the very beginning. Only now, when the gap has been closed, can we see the actions of Jonah for what they are. But the narrator is not yet through with Jonah, perhaps because he is not yet through with the readers of the tale.

Jonah 4:6–11

> *(6) But YHWH God appointed a large plant, and it grew up for Jonah, becoming a shade over his head to save him from his evil (or "discomfort"). And Jonah rejoiced over the large plant with great rejoicing. (7) Then this God appointed a worm at the break of dawn on the following day, and it struck the plant so that it dried up. (8) And when the sun rose, God appointed a scorching east wind. The sun struck Jonah's head and he grew faint. And he asked his spirit to die. He said, "It is better for me to die than to live!" (9) God said to Jonah, "Is it good for you to be angry because of the plant?" He said, "It is good that I am angry enough to die!" (10) YHWH said, "You pity the plant that gave you no trouble and that you did not make grow, that appeared one night and perished the next. (11) Should I not pity Nineveh, the great city, in which there are more than 120,000 people who do not know right from left, and many beasts?"*

God now assumes the role of teacher as the Divine One attempts to lead Jonah away from his twisted conclusions about the world and about God. Just as God "appointed" the big fish to save Jonah from his desire to die, so now God goes into a frenzy of appointing in the attempt to instruct Jonah about the real implications of belief in the God who has called him to be prophet. In very short order God appoints a large plant (*qiqayon*; the exact horticultural reference is impossible to determine, because our author is no more an agronomist than he is an ichthyologist when he has God appoint a "big fish") to provide shade for Jonah's head. Yet, the more significant purpose for the plant is "to deliver him from evil." The phrase could also be translated "to save him from discomfort" (so RSV), but to render it thus is to miss the irony of the clause. Yes, in the simplest sense, God provides the plant to give Jonah a bit of leafy shade. But when we remember that Jonah has already made a shelter for himself precisely designed to provide "shade" (4:5) for him, it is certain that the plant of God is not offered to Jonah to provide shade, although he takes it in that most literal of ways. The plant is designed by God to "deliver him from his evil."

We noted above that Jonah and the city of Nineveh had just exchanged places, the former becoming the evil character in the story, replacing the latter. Thus, the narrator tells us, there remains only one evil character in the tale, and he is now being dealt with in the series of illustrations provided by God, the professor. In effect, the object lessons for Jonah in 4:6–11 are the rhetorical equivalent of Jonah's own five-word sermon of 3:4. The work that that sermon performed for Ninevites, God's lessons should now perform for Jonah.

Jonah's response to the plant is given in the narrator's typical hyperbolic language; he "rejoices" with a "great rejoicing." The reader is, of course, immediately suspicious of such unbounded joy over a one-day plant that provides him shade that he does not need. Jonah assumed a supposed posture of joy during his long prayer of chapter 2, but we saw the hypocrisy that laced that prayer. Also, we have just heard Jonah announce to us his complete rejection of the world as ruled by a merciful God and his desire to depart from it. Such a petty joy from the joyless prophet stinks again of hypocrisy.

God's series of appointments continues, and in the process Jonah's joy is revealed for what it is. First, a worm attacks the plant, and it dries up. Second, the sun rises with an extraordinary heat, and God appoints a scorching east wind that, in combination with the sun, attacks Jonah's head so fiercely that he thought he would faint. Apparently, his own shelter was not sufficient to withstand the assaults of the teaching God. Jonah's response to this climatological disaster is his usual one, though he phrases it this time in a slightly different way. "He asked his spirit to die." We need to compare this phrase with Jonah's earlier request to die in this same chapter. At 4:3, Jonah asked YHWH *directly*, "Take my spirit from me!" Now at 4:8, Jonah no longer speaks directly to God; he addresses his own spirit (*nephesh*). Thus does the narrator separate his main character ever further from all other human characters and from God.

This act of separation began in the first chapter when Jonah set off alone and silent to escape God and the city of Nineveh. His descent to Joppah, to the bottom of the ship, and finally to the bottom of the sea, mirrors his inexorable descent into himself, a descent that eventually cuts him off from all those in the tale. In 4:8, that isolation and separation are now complete. Jonah is alone. And by cutting Jonah off from the other characters of the story, the narrator has effectively thrown the spotlight directly on to him. He may think that he has escaped from all humans and God, but his continual attempts to hide have had precisely the opposite effect. Rather than being hidden, Jonah is caught in the harsh light of his own petty desires for escape and death. There can be no doubt that the author is intent on keeping the light squarely on Jonah, and this fact will be very important when we attempt to determine the central concerns of this reading of the book.

God brings the divine lesson to a close by asking the prophet, once again consumed by fury, due to his loss of his "beloved" plant, "Is it good that you are angry over the plant?" "Angry enough to die," the prophet retorts. "You pity the plant," says God, though you had nothing to do with its growth. Besides, the thing was only a one-day wonder. Your anger over this insubstantial thing, and your pity for it, are really touching, says God, who is not above a little sarcasm, as one can see. But if you get so overwrought about a little weed, should not I, God, find pity for the great city Nineveh that contains more than 120,000 people who often do not know right from left, not to mention all of those beasts?

And, of course, the answer is "yes"; of course God shows pity to Nineveh, which after all is filled with God's creatures, too. The trap is sprung. Jonah's pathetic pity for a weed is contrasted with God's immense pity for Nineveh, and the petty prophet is skewered on the spit of his own self-centeredness. Some have claimed that because God gets the last word, the book is ultimately about God's character as universally merciful. I agree that this is *an important* theme of the book, and the narrator with his interesting uses of divine names in the last section emphasizes this theme. In 4:6–11, the deity is named by the narrator five times. An important pattern is followed. First, at 4:6, God is called "YHWH Elohim," the only time this title is found in the book. Indeed, this designation is quite rare in the Hebrew Bible, being confined almost exclusively to Genesis 2 and 3 and the Chronicler. Yet, we find it here, in my judgment, because the author is summarizing his picture of God. Both titles, "God," ('elohim) and (YHWH), have been used in the story up to now. Note especially that in this last chapter "this God" (ha'elohim) was used since Jonah did not mention God's "true" name to the Ninevites in his little sermon; all they knew was that they must change their ways to please "this God."

At 4:7, "this God" (ha'elohim) is again mentioned. By using "YHWH Elohim" first in this series, the author wants the readers to know that "this God" is in fact identical to "YHWH Elohim." The next two references are to "God," ('elohim) (4:8, 9). This designation has also been used in the book and occurs here again to remind the readers that a God by any of these names is the same God. And finally, and not accidentally, the last designation of God in the book is "YHWH" (4:10). The book began with YHWH calling the prophet (1:1), and the book ends with YHWH lecturing the recalcitrant Jonah on the ways of YHWH in the world. Whatever name the peoples of the book give to God, this God is finally YHWH, God of the skies, who made sea and dry land.

But God is not the final subject of this book; we are not reading "The Book of God," but "The Book of Jonah." God may have the last word in the book, but the fact that that word is precisely a rhetorical question, asked directly to Jonah, throws the glaring spotlight right back on the prophet. Though rhetorical questions do not call for any verbal answers, the answer already being implied in the question, still the audience of the tale shifts its gaze to Jonah and wonders how he will respond. The fact is, he says nothing at all. We are given no indication that he hears the lesson of God, that he takes it to heart, or that he acts in any way. The last picture we have of the prophet is sulking in his poor shelter, sweating uncomfortably in the sun and wind, hoping for death and escape. In effect, the end of the book reinforces the character of this Dove, son of faithfulness, a character that has not changed at all throughout the entire tale. At the beginning, he ran away in silent rejection of the call of YHWH, and at the end he sits in silence in the face of the divine teaching. There can be little doubt that Jonah is the central figure and ultimate interest of the narrator.

But just who is Jonah? I have claimed at the beginning of my reading that the book was primarily interested in satire, and that for a satire to be effective it must have a pointed object of attack. If that object is Jonah, then I must know who he is if I am to see the satirist clearly at work. Let us see what our reading has uncovered about him. First, he is certainly a prophet. He was called to proclaim the word of God, which he finally did, albeit in a most pathetic way. Second, he tries very hard to prevent, or at least to limit, the prophetic word of God. He does so, he tells us, because he loathes the character of that God. Third, when he finally does proclaim the word of God, and when deliverance is effected through his paltry words, he calls the entire experience nothing less than a "great evil" and says he would rather die than live in a world where such events can occur. With those actions, he directs our attention to those who would limit both the scope and intention of God's word.

Fourth, he is a Hebrew (1:9), the only one in this book, and he is the only character in the book (including the beasts of Nineveh!) who remains at the end unrepentant.

> Hence, Jonah is a Hebrew prophet disobedient and hypocritical, angered by God's will to save, yet claiming to affirm God's power to do so, having witnessed it in his own person. *Jonah* is thus an attack on Hebrew prophetic hypocrisy. Which group or groups the author has in mind cannot be identified specifically, but do not

all religions bring forth "hypocritical prophets" who claim great insight and unique callings, but who ultimately are found empty of substance, save their real anger at those who do not agree with them? Yea, their number is legion. For them, and their incessant fulminations, is Jonah written.[29]

Dove, son of faithfulness? A better title for this disgusting would-not-be prophet of the God of mercy would be "Vulture, son of wretchedness." Of all the prophets in the Hebrew Bible, he is the one most to be scorned and perhaps the most to be pitied.

A NARRATIVE SERMON ON THE BOOK OF JONAH

As I have reflected on my reading of the book of Jonah, I have decided that a frame narrative would be a helpful way to construct a narrative sermon on this book. I have made this decision because my reading uncovered several significant themes in the book, and I want to be certain that my hearers will be focusing with me on the theme that I found of central significance, namely, the hypocrisy of the prophet. Thus, I will frame my telling of the story with some introductory comments from a contemporary experience of Jonah-like characters I have encountered.

"Even the Cows!"

It was another Sunday night in another hotel room in another strange city. What else is there to do but flip through the cable channels to be found on the ever-present TV? Of some twenty-two channels, I counted ten that were showing programs related in some way to the subject of religion. Shouting there was, and some reasoning, and singing, and weeping, and speaking in unknown tongues. One man particularly caught my eye and ear. He sang pretty well, then strode to his clear plastic pulpit, and began to preach.

It took him exactly four minutes to send all Roman Catholics to hell. It was a stunning achievement, and all done with a sweet smile and barrels of sweat (in *four* minutes!). Then in just three more minutes (I timed him) all we Methodists joined our Roman friends in the lake of fire. I suddenly felt very uncomfortable and moved to turn the air conditioning down a notch. Had the room become hotter? In a forty-five-minute oration, my

29. Holbert, *Preaching Old Testament*, 75.

fellow Christian had sent approximately one billion of his fellow human beings to eternal torment. And all with a smile. Then the assembled crowd, and it was a large one, offered up thanks for the word received, and at least one hundred came forward to receive Jesus. And immediately Jonah came to mind, and I thought, "The old boy is not dead after all."

> My reading of the book of Jonah has focused on the prophet as hypocrite, and uncovered a man who knew the words of his religious tradition but offered them either grudgingly or scornfully, because his basic theological understanding was characterized by a narrow parochialism. That Jonah's God was indeed merciful, even for pagan sailors and Ninevites (and their beasts), was for him the very stumbling block that made his involvement with the work of that God finally disgusting and impossible. It was that theological stance that turned the word of God from a word of life into a word of hatred and death for Jonah and for all those to whom he spoke, however reluctantly and haltingly. The irony, as we saw, is that even that sort of speech from that sort of prophet can work the miracle of repentance and acceptance. As you can see, I believe that some evangelists of twenty-first-century America, particularly some found on television, are in my judgment latter-day Jonahs. This is tricky territory for preaching. One wants very much to avoid the very question that one is trying to raise, namely, the concern of a parochial bigotry disguised as "true religion." When I use such an illustration, how can I avoid being labeled a bigot in relationship to them and their very different ideas? I believe that one avoids the charge only if one admits one's own bigotry at the same time that one raises the question of the bigotry of others. I shall try to do that as the sermon progresses. I have tried to begin with a fairly light tone, because the reading has uncovered the fact that the Book of Jonah is written with humor as an important element, and I want to share that with my hearers. Why should they be deprived of that which made my reading so much fun for me? It would also be fair to say, however, that some may not find my gentle jibes either gentle or funny. So be it. Jonah was not written for the long-faced religionists among us. Or, maybe it was.

Once upon a time, the word of the Lord came to Dove, the son of faithfulness, and the word said, "Arise! Go to Nineveh, the great city, and cry out against it, because their evil has come up in my presence." Anyone with a name like Dove, the son of faithfulness, is bound to be a good choice for prophet. And Dove arose, all right, but he rose up only to "go down" to the port of Joppah, to buy a ticket on the first west-bound ship he could find, to go down into the ship, and to lie down, falling fast asleep. The call of God said, "Go East, young prophet," but the prophet has gone West. "Go to New York," God commands, and the prophet heads for Los Angeles. The dove has flown the coop, if you will pardon the expression, and we do not know why.

Now, it is hardly completely unique that a prophet in the Hebrew Bible is reluctant to do the bidding of God. Moses offered five increasingly lame excuses to his God, even when that God called him out of a flaming bush that somehow refused to burn up. I don't know about you, but a talking, flaming, unconsumable bush might be enough to convince me to act! But not Moses. Isaiah claimed that he was too sinful to help God, and just as importantly, the folk with whom he lived were not a whit better than he was. Under such circumstances, the work of prophecy is hardly a low-risk operation. Jeremiah said he was too young. But these three Israelite heroes all eventually did the work of God. But Jonah? He leaves without a word, running headlong from the presence of the Lord.

But Jonah soon discovers that escape from this God is not quite as easy as he thought. Like a divine baseball pitcher, God hurls a huge storm at the sea, and the tiny ship thought it was about to break up. The sailors on the ship begin to do whatever they can to save the vessel. First, they cry out to their many gods; they are pagans, but they know to cry for help to those forces who can offer help. In fact, they do the very thing Jonah was supposed to do, namely, cry out. Also, they throw some cargo overboard to lighten the ship. All their furious activity is quite different from the sleeping prophet, who says and does precisely nothing!

In great terror, the captain rushes into the hold of his ship to find the passenger who is not active with his sailors. "Why are you asleep?" he asks. "Arise! Call upon your God! Perhaps that God will give a thought to us so that we do not perish!" That is good religion. Call out to the source of help in expectation of help. One might have thought that the prophet would have thought of that, but not this prophet. Jonah remains silent.

Back on deck, the sailors have turned to a familiar way to find the will of the gods; they cast lots. Obviously, the lots were loaded. They point right to Jonah. And then begins a remarkable scene. In the midst of a raging storm, with giant waves battering the boat, the sailors demand information from the guilty one. I would have thought that a lynch mob might have been a more appropriate response to this silent, sleeping character who has put all of their lives at risk. But we will find that these sailors are altogether remarkable pagans. They shout, "Tell us whose fault this is?" They of course already know, but they want to hear Jonah say it. But they do not stop with that one question. They go on, "What do you do for a living? Where do you come from? What is your country? Who are your people?"

And Jonah answers—sort of. The great prophet of God finally speaks, not because of God's call, of course, but because he has been caught red-handed by a pack of floundering pagans. "I am a Hebrew," he intones, "and I fear YHWH, God of heaven, who made the sea and the dry land." It is a wonderfully well-phrased creed. And it is an answer to their questions, or at least a partial answer. And, if you look at it, it is quite an unusual answer. Jonah claims to fear YHWH, the God who made the sea, while he is running away from YHWH on the very sea YHWH supposedly made! It makes one wonder just how much Jonah really believes what he is saying.

Well, whether or not Jonah believes it very much, the sailors believe what he says immediately! The fear they felt at the storm is nothing compared to the fear they feel now when they hear Jonah announce to them that the maker of the sea is the God that he supposedly fears. They believe him, and they quickly guess that the storm is this YHWH's way of punishing an errant believer. How could he be so stupid to attempt to escape the God who made the sea—and on that very sea? This terrible predicament calls for action. Surely *now* it is time to get the rope, heat the tar, pluck the feathers, or most simply, weight the wretch down and drop him over the side.

But no! The sailors, of all things, *ask* the source of their imminent demise what they should do with him! They know as well as we do that he hardly thought of them when he boarded the ship and went silently off to dreamland. But these sailors are extraordinary; compared to Jonah they are laudable characters indeed. Jonah responds to their amazing question, "Take me up and throw me at the sea; then the sea will quiet down for you. I know it is because of me that this great storm has come upon you." Has Jonah suddenly gotten religion? Has he been converted by a well-timed Billy Graham rally floating by? I am suspicious. Why should he suddenly show concern for these sailors when he showed so little before? Could it be that he just wants to die, and therefore get away from God, the reason for his trip in the first place? He cannot seem to get away from God on land or on sea; perhaps *under* the sea will be a safe haven of death. And why not ask these sailors to do the deed? Then Jonah will have no responsibility at all either for his life or for his death.

But the sailors are as hard to escape as is God! They row hard to save the ship, as well as the jerk who is the cause of the entire mess. But they cannot, because the sea was growing more and more tempestuous. Finally, the once-pagan sailors pray a wonderful prayer to no one else but YHWH, that God Jonah has just introduced to them. "We beseech you, YHWH, do not let us perish for this man's life, laying on us innocent blood. You, O YHWH, have done exactly as you pleased!" They know that they have no choice but to throw Jonah overboard, but they are uncomfortable about it. They beg YHWH not to hold them guilty for his death; they did do their very best to try to save him. They close their prayer with a line worthy of Jesus in the garden of Gethsemane; YHWH has done whatever YHWH has decided to do. YHWH is sovereign.

And with that prayer uttered, they throw Jonah into the sea. Immediately, the sea is quiet. And the sailors' fear in the face of the entire episode is even greater than their fear of the storm and their fear at the disobedience of Jonah. They proceed to do what any true believers in YHWH do; they sacrifice to YHWH right on the deck of their ship and they make vows of loyalty and covenant. While the smoke of their sacrifice is rising into the sky, Jonah is dropping like a stone into the depths of the sea.

There is a certain breathless action to the first chapter of the story. As I indicated in my narrative reading, there are several gaps that invite readers to search for ways of closure. The biggest gap, of course, is the reason for Jonah's flight. I have tried very hard to fix that gap in the ears of the hearers so that they can feel the need to go on with the story in the same way that the reading urged that we go on. We want their surprise and pleasure to be as much like ours as it can be.

Nevertheless, in a telling like this, I must provide some teasing hints to the hearers to keep interest high. For example, I suggest a possible way to understand Jonah's request to be thrown into the sea, a way that I find consistent with the reading. I suggest that the sailors themselves concluded that Jonah was running from YHWH simply from his actions and his creed. This fact the reading uncovered, and I want my hearers to gain the pleasure from this incongruous event.

I included the modern references to New York and Los Angeles to make the East-West point clearly. The narratives of the Hebrew Bible offer many opportunities for this sort of modernizing, which, far from being merely cute, can be a necessary means of communication. The reader will note that I have attempted to include in the sermon many of the details discovered in the reading, things like the ascending-descending motif of call and response, the partial confession of Jonah, the changing meanings of the word "fear." As always, I do not, and would not want to, include all of the discoveries; I could detail my hearers to death. But it is these details that make the story truly memorable, and I want to share enough of them to make my own telling memorable.

But if Jonah thinks that escape from God will be found under the sea any more than on it, he is quickly corrected. For God appoints a special great fish to save the fleeing prophet by swallowing him down and keeping him in its fishy innards for three days and nights. And from the unlikely place of a fish belly, Jonah prays a very unlikely prayer.

He first thanks God for his rescue. "I called to YHWH out of my distress, who answered me." We might have expected an angry cry to God for saving him from his apparent desire to die in the sea. On the other hand, Jonah has now learned in the most painful of ways that escape from God and God's call is impossible. Perhaps Jonah's prayer is what Jonah thinks God *wants* to hear? Well, if that is his motivation for this prayer, it soon turns rather more ugly than he intended. "*You* cast me into the deep," Jonah prays. And we say, "*What?*" *God* did not cast Jonah into the deep; Jonah himself asked to be thrown into the deep by the sailors, and he only found himself in that predicament because he had run away from God in the first place. My suspicions about Jonah are once again aroused.

"All *your* waves and *your* billows passed over me," he says. He seems bent on accusing God of doing what he himself has done. "Then I said," as I went under your waves, "I am cast out from your presence." And again the reader says "No." He was not cast out from God's presence by God or anyone else. In fact, he *ran* from God's presence for reasons that we still do not fully understand. Jonah appears to have a very different understanding of the events of chapter one than we do.

He then describes his sinking from the top of the water, to deeper into the water, to weeds towards the bottom of the water, to the very roots of the mountains at the bottom of the world, to the shadowy land whose bars close forever, that is, the land of death. God brought him up, he says, "When my soul fainted from me, I remembered YHWH." One might call such a dramatic experience "fish-belly religion," but it could be at least a claim to a genuine relationship to the power of God.

But now Jonah reveals his true colors or at least partially reveals them. "Those who pay regard to vain idols forsake covenant loyalty." But the only folk in this story who have paid regard to vain idols, the pagan sailors, have certainly not forsaken loyalty. They have in several exemplary ways demonstrated true loyalty. And while Jonah is praying this prayer from his watery commuter car, those same sailors are worshiping YHWH. "I will sacrifice to you," Jonah promises. He never does, while the sailors are doing so even as he prays. "What I have vowed, I will complete." He never vows anything, and he never completes anything. The sailors again are doing what Jonah says he will do, but never does. In fact, the sailors consistently have done the work of the prophet in this story.

"Deliverance is YHWH's!" This pious-sounding shout concludes the prayer. And what does the prayer consist of? Jonah accuses God of doing him in, accuses the sailors of being idol worshippers devoid of loyalty, makes promises he never plans to keep, and concludes with an affirmation that he plainly believes refers only to himself. It is no wonder that after *that* prayer, the big fish throws up! My sentiments are with the fish.

> My way with the prayer attempts to follow the shape and discoveries of the reading itself. As the reading attempted to show, the prayer of chapter two is in all respects an illustration of the hypocrisy of Jonah. It is written precisely for the purpose of characterization, to help the reader focus on Jonah, and to begin to see that he is not a laudable character at all. However, the central reason for the actions of his character is not revealed yet.
>
> I might add that having the fish "throw up" at the end of Jonah's prayer is a wonderful way to seal the fact of the prayer's hypocrisy. Though I do not credit the original author with that delightful joke, it fits wonderfully well into this reading of the story.

Jonah finds himself back where he began, on dry ground, listening to the command of his God to "Arise! Go to Nineveh, the great city!" Two things, however, have changed. Jonah smells like fish guts and God calls him with rather different words. "Cry to Nineveh the crying that I tell you." There is no more open-ended request to the prophet, bidding him, "Cry out to the Ninevites." Now he is to speak precisely what God tells him to speak. God is apparently beginning to realize what we know, too. Jonah is hardly to be trusted with the word of God.

But at last Jonah "arises and goes to Nineveh, according to the word of YHWH." If he had done that in response to the first call, we would not have had all of this trouble. Now Nineveh was so big that it would have taken God three days' journey to walk across it. Jonah walks one rather slow human-day trip into the immense city, he stands on one street corner, and he utters a five-word sermon that comes out to seven words in English. "In forty days Nineveh will be overthrown."

Well, he finally did it; he cried out to the Ninevites. It was only five words, and it was only on one tiny corner in one suburb of the vast metropolis, but he did it. But the funny stuff starts immediately. The entire population of Nineveh is seized with a raging desire for repentance. Every last inhabitant tears off their clothes and dons the garment of extreme mourning, sackcloth. All begin a fast. The news soon reaches the king himself. He reacts by jumping off of his royal throne, tearing off his royal robes, and sitting down in ashes as his personal sign of penitence. He makes a royal decree that no one, whether human or beast, is to eat or drink anything at all. By so doing, the king hopes that the God announced by Jonah will relent, will change the divine mind so that they will not perish. It works. God takes one look at the fasting humans of Nineveh, and gets one earful of the mooing and baahing of the beasts of Nineveh, and God decides not to wipe them out for their evil after all.

> The continuation of the story of chapter three practically tells itself. I try to emphasize the ridiculous incongruity of the tiny sermon in one tiny place bringing about wholesale repentance in the world's most evil city. And the wonderful picture of all of human Nineveh crying to God and all of animal Nineveh mooing and baahing to God should not be missed in any setting.

This is a wonderful story, isn't it? If we could just stop here, we might read the headlines in the morning editions of the Jerusalem Post and the Ninevite News as follows, "RELUCTANT PROPHET MAKES GOOD: WORLD'S WORST CITY REPENTS!" But the story cannot stop there, because we still do not know something very important. Why did Jonah not go to Nineveh in the first place? And at last we are going to find out.

"But it was evil to Jonah, a great evil, and he was angry." What!? The world's worst city has repented after a five-word sermon, and the preacher is furious? What is going on here? Jonah tells us finally what is going on as he prays what surely is one of the worst prayers ever recorded. "I pray to you, O YHWH, is not this what I said while I was still in my own country? That is why I fled to Tarshish in the first place, because I knew that you were a gracious and merciful God, slow to anger and full of covenant loyalty, who is sorry for evil." So, that's been it all along! Jonah knew about the merciful tendencies of YHWH and tried to escape them, because he also knew that one word about this God, and repentance and forgiveness are likely to spring up anywhere—even in a disgusting place like Nineveh. And now Jonah's world is populated by repulsive Ninevites and their smelly beasts crying to God, not to mention pagan sailors sacrificing and vowing to God. Jonah's world is becoming altogether too inclusive! He'd rather be dead, and he concludes his prayer with a direct request to God to bump him off!

God, of course, is astonished, and thinks, "I finally got a successful prophet, and the guy is furious about the success." God turns to Jonah and says, "Is it good for you to be angry?" Jonah shuts up and leaves the presence of God for the second time, just as silent as he was before. He builds a little lean-to, just outside the city, to see what will happen. What is he waiting for? Well, he apparently thinks, if God changed the divine mind once, it could happen again, and a low-yield nuclear device might fall on the Ninevites. At least, one can always hope so. But God is not through with the prophet yet, and thank God, not through with us, either.

In a quick series of divine appointments, like the special appointment of the big fish, God creates a miraculous vine that grows up right over Jonah's head to shade him from the intense sun and to save him from his evil—that is to teach him that, in fact, *he* really *is* evil. Nineveh was nothing when compared to the evil of Jonah. And Jonah rejoiced over his plant with a great rejoicing. He loves his one-day plant, but hates everything else he sees. But God then appoints a magic worm to attack the plant so that the plant withers away. Then at daybreak, God appoints a ferocious east wind to beat on Jonah's head. Jonah about fainted, and once again he asked to die, although this time he did not ask God to do it; he spoke to his own spirit. The prophet of God has become a solitary figure, cut off from everyone and everything, including God.

But God speaks to him one last time. "Is it good for you to be angry because of the plant?" "Yes! I am angry enough to die!" shouts the prophet. And God springs the trap. "Oh, come off it, Jonah! You pity that plant, that little one-day wonder, for which you did absolutely nothing, which grew up one night and perished the next. Should I not pity Nineveh, the great city, where more than one hundred twenty thousand people do not know right from left, not to mention all of those beasts?"

And that is the end. And of course, the answer to God's question is Yes, Yes, Yes! God pities Nineveh, because they are creatures of God, both beasts and humans. And as the camera pans away from the scene, on the left we see the sailors joyfully sacrificing to God. On the right, we see Ninevites and their livestock sending up loud Hosannas to the skies. And in the middle, we see Jonah, sitting in the blazing sun, sucking his thumb, and hoping against hope for destruction. Dove, the son of faithfulness? No, I see no dove here. I see Vulture, son of Wretchedness instead. As this vulture sits, perhaps he hopes, too, that the whole scene will just go away.

And we Jonahs hope that it will go away, too. I mean, how can you live in a world where Ninevites might come sit in your pew? One can never be too careful. These modern-day Ninevites might include those weird religious kooks who speak in tongues or maybe those weird religious kooks who don't. There might be some homosexual Ninevites, always making their improper advances, not to mention all of those oversexed heterosexuals who can never confine their appetites to one person. There might be some Ninevites of a different color, different language, different smell, different dress, different customs. I mean the world is just full of Ninevites, and unless we Jonahs are on guard, they might sneak into where we are and join us in our worship of the one God. Why, even some of those TV preachers might slip in. Anything goes in a world ruled over by a God who is slow to anger, filled with love and compassion, and is graciously merciful.

Surely, it is better to stay outside with Jonah and stew silently in anger and disgust. No sense in joining a party where all are welcome. That is what finally troubles me, a twenty-first-century Jonah, about the cross of Jesus. You can't miss the fact that his arms are stretched out on that thing as wide as they will go. It is just like he wants to include everyone in sight in his loving embrace. It is better not to think too much like that. The next thing you know the Ninevites will be here with us, and we can hardly have that. Can we?

> I have tried to use the story's own shape and ideas, as I bring it to a close. I want my hearers to identify with Jonah, to see in him their own unnamed prejudices. And, also, I want them to see that I am a Jonah, too. Because I began the sermon with a swipe at TV evangelists, I wanted to be certain to get them back in the sermon at the end. The main idea of this telling is to highlight the hypocrisy of the prophet, and to begin to see the hypocrisy of those of us who claim religious allegiance to this God of mercy but whose willingness to practice that love and mercy with our fellow human beings falls short of our stated claims. I close with reference and quotation from the story of Jesus, because I want my hearers to see readily the overt connections between the ancient and lively

tale and the central story of Christianity. Jonah is far more than a delightful story about fish; it is a potent proclamation of the gospel and its inclusiveness. In my judgment, one of the best ways to get this story into the minds of our congregation is precisely to tell it, to release thereby its own detailed power so that modern hearers can see and hear themselves in all of their absurdity and need for forgiveness.

Is This an Effective Story Sermon?

I want to ask this question of each of the four sermons I offer in this book. By "effective," I am not simply asking: does it work as an event of communication? I have already suggested that these sorts of sermons have a built-in effectiveness, given the attractiveness of storytelling in our culture. In addition to its communicative effectiveness, does this sermon prove effective in answering the four general problems that Richard Lischer found with the narrative sermons of his experience: aesthetic, ontological, theological, and socio-political (see chapter 1 for details)? Of course, each listener to a sermon will react to the telling/preaching in different ways and will evaluate what I have done for themselves. However, I wish to suggest that my sermon on Jonah passes the tests set for narrative sermons by Lischer. He warns of a danger of moralism or universalism that can arise from these sorts of sermons, based as they often are on "transient expressions of grace." There is no moralism here, and the grace of YHWH, denied directly by the prophet, is front and center. Jonah's story is our story of bigotry and exclusiveness, both of which fly directly in the face of the story of God. Because I have rooted my sermon deeply in the text of the Bible, no congregation can be confused about whose story they are hearing; it is Jonah's story/my story sharply contrasted with the story of God.

Further, ontologically, this story is not neat or closed. Jonah remains on the outside of the party of God, refusing to join the repentant sailors and Ninevites. The story of Jonah challenges directly just who are Ninevites and who Jonahs in our time. For those who have no neat stories to tell or live, those who are on the margins of our society, God welcomes them. And for those who think they are God's chosen, their arrogant exclusivism comes in for assault from the story.

Theologically, the story is no mere meaningless repetition of general theological truths, nor does it merely retell the story without conceptualization built in. The narrative itself conceptualizes beyond a simple retelling of the story. In fact, I think it is finally impossible to tell a story from the Bible, or any story for that matter, without a measure of conceptualization. Stories are told to make a claim of one sort or another; it is a matter of the skill of the teller to determine whether that claim is clear and theologically astute or not.

Socio-politically, this story of Jonah is told precisely to effect change in thought and behavior. Jonah is lampooned in the story, because he is the classic religious bigot, steeped in the niceties of his tradition, fully conversant with its chief words and ideas, but finally untouched by its central demands for inclusiveness and grace. It could hardly be stated more powerfully or more memorably that God is impatient with those who refuse to receive and treasure those whom society judges Ninevites in their midst.

I claim that this sermon, faithful as it tries to be to the great story of Jonah, is in all respects an effective one, telling the story of God for all manner of listeners in such a way as to urge them to change both how they think of God and the way they respond to that God's demands.

FIVE

A Question of Interpretation

A Reading of 1 Samuel 15

Saul died due to his unfaithfulness in that he was unfaithful to YHWH concerning the word of YHWH which he did not keep; he also consulted a medium, seeking guidance, but did not seek the guidance of YHWH, who killed him and turned the kingdom over to David, the son of Jesse. (1 Chr 10:13–14)

IN NO UNCERTAIN TERMS, the Chronicler, that fourth-century BCE propagandist for right religion, describes the demise of Saul, the first king of Israel. He was, says the Chronicler, killed by YHWH for two clear-cut reasons. First, and perhaps foremost, he was "unfaithful to the word of YHWH." Second, he "consulted a medium," and though the Chronicler never footnotes his work, he certainly has the story of 1 Samuel 28 in mind as he indicts Saul for this second crime. As for the first accusation, the Chronicler must have 1 Samuel 13 and 15 in view, two encounters with the prophet Samuel wherein the old man of God rejects first Saul's dynasty and then Saul himself, both times with blazing prophetic rhetoric.

The influence of the chronicler's judgment of Saul has been profound. Readers of the story of Saul have regularly seen 1 Samuel 13 and 15 as those places where Saul was plainly disobedient to Samuel and to YHWH, and as a result was deposed from his kingship. At the top of the page of my copy of the Revised Standard Version of the Bible, where one finds the story of 1 Samuel 15, the editor's summary of the chapter reads, "Saul disobeys and spares Agag." More specific than the ancient Chronicler, these modern-day editors pinpoint precisely the root of Saul's disobedience, namely, the refusal to kill the Amalekite king, Agag, in apparent disobedience to the call from YHWH and Samuel to "utterly destroy" the Amalekite people and all that is theirs.

There is, of course, a certain neatness and finality to these clear cut judgments against Saul. If Saul has disobeyed, surely he *deserves* whatever punishment he receives at the hands of Samuel and YHWH. However, should one so blithely say that Saul "got what he deserved"? Of what more precisely does his disobedience consist? Does it strike any reader as incongruous that David, who breaks four of the ten commandments in one chapter (2 Samuel 11), is immediately forgiven (2 Sam 12:13) by the prophet Nathan as spokesperson for YHWH, while Saul is roundly condemned and rejected as king for what appear to be two technicalities of sacrifice? These haunting questions should drive us back to the text to see whether these simple judgments against Saul are justified.

As always, we must allow the text itself to have its fullest speech if we are to be enabled to discuss it with anything like completeness and understanding. In a superbly nuanced analysis of 1 Samuel 15, one with which, nevertheless, I cannot finally agree, Meir Sternberg warns us as readers about too readily accepting simple solutions from these biblical narratives.

> . . . as if to make things even more difficult for himself, the biblical narrator avoids the line of least resistance in presenting character, event, and the march of history. Unlike the didactic persuader, with whom he is so often confused, he will rarely stoop to the polarization of values and effects, with repulsive villains pitted against all-round paragons; nor to the wholesale evocation of stereotype and stock response; nor to homiletic address and lecturing.[1]

One might summarize Sternberg's important point in a single phrase; the Hebrew narrators were apparently incapable of telling a simple story. How easy it would have been to paint Saul as all evil, debauched, devious, and disgusting, all the better to set up his ultimate fall as a supremely satisfying and melodramatic dénouement. We could boo the villain and cheer the hero and return home satisfied that the strict moral order of the universe is still intact. But the biblical narrative regularly presents more than meets the eye. Rather than didacticism, we find subtlety of character and ambiguity of scene; rather than moralizing homiletics, we find nuanced dialogue and surprises of plot. And even in those narrations where it can be said that "the result is a foregone conclusion," that is, even if Saul *is* completely guilty of

---

1. Sternberg, *The Poetics of Biblical Narrative*, 483.

disobedience, as Sternberg thinks he is, "the means to its achievement or vindication," the ways in which the narrator persuades the reader to believe as he does, are by no means predictable or simple.[2] In that latter judgment I am in full agreement with Sternberg, but his certainty that Saul's guilt is a "foregone conclusion" I cannot share. But if our differences are to be adjudicated, I must read the text.

1 Samuel 15:1–3

> (1) *Samuel said to Saul, "Me YHWH sent to anoint you king over God's people, over Israel. Now, listen to the sound of the words of YHWH. (2) Thus says YHWH Sebaoth, 'I observed what Amalek did to Israel, how he stood against them on the road when they were coming up from Israel. (3) Now, go and strike Amalek! You (pl.) obliterate all that they have; do not spare them! Kill man and woman, weaned and nursing child, ox and sheep, camel and ass!'"*

Samuel's opening words to Saul are striking. Instead of announcing the prophetic command of YHWH immediately, the old prophet first refers to himself; the word order is unusual, hence my awkward translation. Is he simply increasing the import of the command to follow, or is he reaffirming his personal authority over the king of Israel? Or perhaps is the speech a mixture of prophetic power and egotistical dominance? Samuel creates a gap in our thinking as he utters his first word.

Peter Miscall notes that this is the first time in the entire story of Saul that it has been said that Saul was "anointed king" by Samuel. "Previously he was anointed *nagid* (prince?) and was 'set, given, or chosen' king or 'made king.' Saul is (here) anointed king, and the command is urgent."[3] Thus, the opening part of Samuel's address seems designed to emphasize the desperate urgency of the command about to be given to Saul. The prophet not only says that Saul was anointed king over "God's people," but he redundantly names the people "Israel." Saul and we hardly need to be told who the people of God are! Yet, the redundancy adds to the formality of the address, as does the line that follows. "Now, listen to the sound of the words of YHWH." Samuel might just as well have said, "the sound (voice) of YHWH" or simply "the words of YHWH." But he again engages in an

---

2. Sternberg, "The Bible's Art of Persuasion," 60.

3. Miscall, *I Samuel: A Literary Reading*, 99.

apparent redundancy as he said "the sound of the words of YHWH." We are reminded, however, that the first word of the speech called attention to Samuel, himself; "*me* YHWH sent." Samuel wants Saul to know that not only does the prophet represent YHWH; he wants Saul to know that the words he is about to hear are precisely the very sound of YHWH's words. Make no mistake, Saul, the prophet says. These words are not Samuel's; they are YHWH's. But also, the prophet implies, do not forget that I, Samuel, am the one chosen to make the sound of YHWH's words.

In verse 2, the prophet prefaces the sound of the words of YHWH with the formalized messenger formula of the prophets, "Thus says YHWH Sebaoth."[4] After that introduction, any hearer can be assured that the words to follow are none other than YHWH's words. "I noticed what Amalek did to Israel as he stood against them on the road when they were coming up out of Egypt." The word translated "noticed" often has the sense of "visit" or "punish"; this verse is often translated "I will punish what Amalek did" (See RSV, for example). Whichever translation is chosen, the sense of the verse is very clear. YHWH is enraged at the behavior of Amalek in relation to the chosen nation when they were escaping from Egypt. The initial narrative reference is Exod 17:8–16, while Deut 25:17–19 reiterates YHWH's desire to "blot out the memory of Amalek." The wording of Deuteronomy is reminiscent of the Samuel passage, although it is far more specific in its formulation of the accusation. "Remember what Amalek did to you when you were coming out of Egypt, how he attacked you in the road, when you were faint and weary, and cut off at your rear all who lagged behind you." The vocabulary is not identical, but the syntax of the sentence, and the general sense of the dastardly attack of the Amalekites, assures the reader that Samuel and YHWH are certainly referring to the same tradition. The facts of the Amalekite treachery are clear enough. The prophet now proceeds to announce the punishment, which is to be executed by the anointed king of Israel and his troops.

"Now, go! Strike Amalek, and obliterate all that is theirs." The word I have translated "obliterate" is the word *herem*. It means more specifically to "consecrate something or someone as a permanent and definitive offering for the sanctuary; in war, consecrate a city and its inhabitants to destruction; carry out this destruction; totally annihilate a population in war; kill."[5] What is significant to note in this broad but quite specific definition

---

4. See, above all, the classic discussion of the messenger formula in Westermann, *Basic Forms of Prophetic Speech*, 129ff.

5. Lohfink, "*herem*," in *Theological Dictionary of the Old Testament*, 5:188.

of *herem* is the inclusion of talk both of sanctuaries and of total annihilation. The argument between Samuel and Saul about the precise meaning of *herem* will turn on those two ideas and their relation to one another.

Later in this same article, Lohfink makes the following comment: "The Old Testament does not contain a single text from which we might derive trustworthy information about an Israelite *herem* for any period of Israel's history."[6] This statement implies that any assumptions about *exactly* what the word means or what anyone implies when it is used ought to be ruled out. Thus, what Samuel means when he announces *herem* may not necessarily be the same thing to the one to whom he announces it. Sternberg's assumptions then must not go unchallenged, when he states:

> Cast in blunt terms and symmetrical specifications, the decree leaves no room for misunderstanding and excuses, in regard to either enemy population or property; "both man and woman, both infant and suckling, both ox and sheep, both camel and ass."[7]

Sternberg assumes a common understanding of *herem*, whereas no such common understanding exists. We can only gauge the understandings of the term as we see the participants struggle in their attempts to carry out the command. There is, thus, "room for misunderstanding," or put positively, room for interpretation of the command given by YHWH through the mouth of the prophet.

We should note that Samuel includes Saul's troops in the demand to obliterate the Amalekites, because the word *herem* in vs. 3 is in the second-person plural. Thus, the command is not intended only for Saul as the king and anointed representative of Israel; the people are included from the very beginning. Samuel urges them "Do not spare them," but kill *all*, human and animal. There appears to be no doubt how Samuel understands the word *herem*; it means total annihilation and complete destruction without a shred of pity or remorse. The Amalekites had attempted to disrupt the passage of the Israelites from Egypt to the promised land, and for this deed they must be wiped off the face of the earth.

Four ideas from this introduction present themselves for further exploration.

1. The very ferociousness of this command is noteworthy. In no other place in the Hebrew Bible where the word *herem* occurs is the lack of pity singled

6. Ibid., 5:193.

7. Sternberg, *The Poetics of Biblical Narrative*, 487.

out as a part of the requirement for fulfillment of the demand.[8] It is true that in Deut 7:2 and Josh 11:20, the people in connection with the command for *herem* are demanded to "show no mercy" (both use a different Hebrew word than 1 Sam 15) to the enemy. However, the reasons are clearly expressed for this; Israel is "to make no covenant with them." The concern is that the enemy will become a snare for the chosen people, hence their obliteration is necessary to protect the people of Israel from their own weaknesses. In contrast, Samuel's demand appears to be particularly heartless and calloused. Is he thus putting the harshest interpretation on the demand for *herem* that he can? Why is his fury so pointed?

2. This dark fury raises the second concern. Is the total obliteration of the Amalekites just punishment for their confrontation with the Israelites, or is there a real sense of disproportion in YHWH's demand? The reason that this concern presents itself is the later punishment of Saul whose possible disproportion is a very real question. If Samuel had wanted to paint the Amalekites as monsters, fully deserving of annihilation, he could have chosen something like the more detailed description of their behavior presented in Deuteronomy 25, as noted above. On the contrary, he gives a bland phrase that I have read "how he stood against them on the road." It is extremely difficult to work up much righteous indignation against the Amalekites on the basis of such a vague charge. Thus, the question of justice and punishment is effectively raised.

3. The narrator very nicely masks his real interests by directing the attention of the reader to the sins of Amalekites.[9] Saul and his troops are supposedly singled out to be the instruments of God's justice. The narrator hopes that the reader will keep attention focused on the Amalekites, while his real interest in the difficulties between Saul and Samuel and YHWH remain hidden until the proper time. The narrator builds expectations and then proceeds to dash them, thus creating continual interest and surprise for the reader.

4. If Samuel is interpreting the command for *herem* in the very harshest of terms, is it not possible that other interpretations could be placed on the command? Could Saul be allowed to interpret the command in a rather different way? Or are Samuel's and YHWH's interpretations the only possible

8. Miscall, *1 Samuel: A Literary Reading*, 99.
9. Sternberg, *The Poetics of Biblical Narrative*, 485–86.

ones? This idea of the possibility of interpretation will be an important one for this particular reading of the story.

1 Samuel 15:4–9

> *(4) So Saul summoned the army, mustering them at Telaim—two hundred thousand foot soldiers and ten thousand men of Judah. (5) Saul came to the city of Amalek and lay in wait in the stream bed. (6) Saul said to the Kenites, "Go! Turn away! Go down from among the Amalekites, lest I gather you along with them; you showed devotion to all the people of Israel when they were coming up out of Egypt." So the Kenites turned away from the midst of the Amalekites. (7) Saul struck the Amalekites from Havilah to Shur on the border of Egypt. (8) He captured Agag, king of the Amalekites, alive, but all of the people he obliterated with the edge of the sword. (9) Saul and the army spared Agag as well as the best of the flock and the herd—the fat ones and the young ones—and every good thing. They were not willing to obliterate them; everything that was utterly worthless, they obliterated it.*

This is an immensely rich section, filled with several possible multiple meanings. On the surface, however, it seems quite clear. Saul has very obviously disobeyed the command of Samuel and YHWH. He was told "do not *spare*," while he and the army quite literally "*spared* Agag as well as the best of the flock and the herd." In fact, the narrator goes out of his way to demonstrate how Saul and the army were only willing to obliterate that which was "utterly worthless." It seems a miserable attempt to follow the command of YHWH.

The real interest of the narrator has thus surfaced; Saul is unwilling to follow the words of YHWH. His fate apparently is sealed. The reader can now see that the Amalekite punishment was only a smokescreen designed to reveal Saul's true colors as disobedient and hence unworthy to be king of Israel. But, the reader should beware and should not jump to final conclusions too soon. The narrator has tricked us once; is he above tricking us again?

Two interesting words occur in vs. 4. The word translated "summoned" is the same word read in vs. 1 as "listen," by far its more common meaning. Saul here "summoned the army." Later at vs. 24, he will say to Samuel that he had "listened to the voice of the army," using the same verb. That verb, shama', will be very important for this narrator, as we will continue to note. The second word that we should especially consider is the word translated "mustered." It is the same word used by Samuel to describe YHWH's "notice" of the deeds of the Amalekites, or YHWH's desire to "visit or punish" the Amalekites. By using both of these words, even with different meanings, so prominent in Samuel's command of vss. 1 and 2, the narrator calls attention to them and suggests that Saul is quick to respond to the words of YHWH. In response to Samuel's demand that Saul "hear," Saul immediately "summons," using the same verb. In response to YHWH's desire to "punish," Saul immediately "musters" (again using the same verb) a huge force designed to carry out the punishment called for. The narrator thus gives the reader every expectation that Saul is the right man for this job.

Saul, with his great army, goes directly to the Amalekite city, and secrets himself in a dry stream bed, apparently to await the most propitious time to attack. Then, the narrator delays the action with a brief tale about the Kenites. Using three rapid imperative verbs of motion, Saul commands that the Kenites, who "showed devotion to the Israelites when they came up out of Egypt," in obvious contrast to the odious Amalekites, should remove themselves from the scene of the slaughter-to-be. Just as YHWH's first command to Saul was "Go!" so Saul's first command to the helpful Kenites is "Go!" Saul here is portrayed as a man of strict justice; he will not destroy righteous along with wicked. The narrator thus builds Saul up in our eyes as a fair, compassionate, just, and discerning man. And further, by so acting, Saul has interpreted the command of YHWH in that he has not included the Kenites in the obliteration; in other words, he has made an exception of them. Does this warn the reader of the exceptions to come of king and cattle? Is this exception right and those wrong? On what grounds are we to make a judgment?

The Kenites obey Saul's command, and immediately Saul "strikes" the Amalekites "from Havilah to Shur on the border of Egypt." Saul was commanded in vs. 3 to "go and *strike* the Amalekites;" he has done precisely that. In fact, he has *struck* them from "Havilah to Shur," a huge distance, stretching possibly from the Western Arabian Peninsula to the very borders of Egypt.[10] After vs. 7, the reader can only assume that Saul has indeed performed the word of YHWH.

10. McCarter, *1 Samuel*, 261–62, provides a detailed attempt to change the text here, because the distance covered by Saul's victorious army is simply too great to be historically believable. However, the great distance may be the narrator's way of magnifying the enormity of Saul's obliteration of the Amalekites, making strict historical concerns unimportant.

Even vs. 8 might not be too much of a surprise. Saul's capture of the king alive is balanced by the complete destruction of every other Amalekite human at the edge of the sword. There is, too, an analogy in the biblical tradition for taking the king of a city given over to *herem* alive. Josh 8:23–29 records that the king of Ai was "captured alive" (the words are identical), while the rest of the people of Ai fell "at the edge of the sword." In the Joshua account, the king of Ai is brought to Joshua who promptly hangs him and buries the body under a huge heap of stones. Thus, we cannot at all assume that Saul's capture of Agag is in any sense a transgression of the command of Samuel. And, as Miscall rightly notes, "Saul is not denounced by Samuel for this exemption; it is not explicitly or implicitly stated, as so many commentaries assert, that this is a major violation of holy war rules by Saul. The issue of violation concerns what else is left alive."[11] Thus, through vs. 8, Saul's behavior seems exemplary. Verse 9, however, appears to change all that.

"Saul and the army spared Agag as well as the best of the flock and the herd—the fat ones and the young ones—and all the best. They were not willing to obliterate them; everything that was utterly worthless, they obliterated it." There is no question that this verse comes as a shock to the reader, who up to this point has watched an exemplary king follow the commands of the prophet and his God to the letter. He was called to "strike" the Amalekites in vs. 3, and he has "struck" them a great blow in vs. 7. He captured the king in vs. 8, but we were not offended by that since the complete obliteration of the Amalekites was accomplished at the end of the verse. But the fact that Saul and the army have more precisely "spared Agag" is an apparent direct violation of the demand of YHWH that stated clearly "do not spare." The narrator goes on to announce that they also spared the "best of the flock and herd," and continues by making even more specific precisely which ones the best are, namely the "fat ones and the young ones."

And if that were not enough, Saul and his army are willing to obliterate only those things that were "utterly worthless." I translate these two Hebrew nouns as a hendiadys, a structure where one of the nouns modifies the other, together making a much stronger formulation of the desired idea. The first of the nouns means "contempt," and as an adjective "despicable." The second means "blemish" or "defect," and is used almost exclusively in contexts where such defects disqualify people for priestly service (see Lev

11. Miscall, *1 Samuel: A Literary Reading*, 101. Thus, my RSV's editorial claim that Saul's sparing of Agag was the central problem of disobedience is called into question.

21:17, 18, 21, 23). Thus, it is clear that Saul and the army have saved the very best of the Amalekites' possessions, their king, the titular head of the people, and the finest of their animals. The narrator goes out of his way to say to the reader that all worthless animals and every other Amalekite person have been destroyed.

What are we to make of these facts at this point in the tale? In a detailed analysis of the verse, Sternberg concludes emphatically that the very point of the verse is to indict Saul beyond the shadow of a doubt; the verse, he says, "maneuvers the reader into concluding that Saul has seriously abused, if not betrayed, his office."[12] But can we be so certain as that? Let us examine some of the terms of the verse more closely.

1. *Hamol,* "to spare," vss. 3 and 9. As noted above, Saul and the army are said to "spare" Agag and the best of the animals in apparent contradiction of the command of YHWH. Sternberg notes that repetition and goes on to conclude that it demonstrates disobedience by "a direct conflict with the language of God's order." He further states that the narrator's use of this term offers to the reader the only "inside view of Saul throughout the narrative," showing us the "subjective motive for the omission which emerges together with its objective result."[13] However, these conclusions assume that the meaning of the word "spare" is exactly the same in both places. As Tsevat notes in *TDOT,* the verb does often mean "be sorry for" or "have pity"; however its semantic range also includes the more general "spare," which may or may not provide a clue to the emotional reasons for the action of sparing.[14] In other words, we only know from the actions of Saul and the army that one person and certain animals were spared from the battle; we cannot conclude from those facts that Saul did so for base reasons or that the picture presented to us produces "an impression of an orgy of looting," as Sternberg so imaginatively puts it. We know only that Saul and the army "saved them alive"; to jump to any conclusion about why they did so is to move beyond the bounds of the text as written.

2. Sternberg continues his indictment of Saul by discussing the word *abu,* "willing." Once again, he has built psychological foundations that are not automatically suggested by the text. Because Saul and the army "were not willing to destroy" the king and the good animals, Sternberg assumes that

12. Sternberg, *The Poetics of Biblical Narrative,* 492.

13. Ibid., 490.

14. Tsevat, "*chamal,*" In *Theological Dictionary of the Old Testament,* 4:471.

the narrator is painting for us a picture of greed. But why is it necessary to conclude that a lack of willingness can mean nothing else than greed, or "purely self-regarding?"[15] As Johnson says in *TDOT*, "The primary emphasis (in the use of the word 'willing') is not on the intention as a psychological factor in the inner man, but on the main behavioral patterns and actions in which the intention is manifested."[16] Once again, we can only say at this point in the story that they were "unwilling" to destroy them. The question "why" cannot be answered; on the contrary, we must allow the narrator to lead us to a possible answer, rather than assume that his intentions are immediately obvious. In my judgment, Sternberg has so loaded his reading with assumptions about Saul that it is impossible for him to hear any other information that might call into question what for him is the king's certain guilt.

For the sake of discussion, let me offer another series of possibilities to provide an explanation for the behavior of Saul and the army. They destroyed the "utterly worthless" to avoid the contamination of the sanctuary, where they intend to go with "the best of the animals" and the king to offer sacrifice there at the sacred site of Gilgal, and thus in a great holocaust to YHWH complete the obliteration of the Amalekites at the holy place. As noted, the word used to describe the "utterly worthless" is one often used to designate people and objects which were to be kept away from the sacred sanctuary. Further, the tradition often made it clear that only the very best was to be offered to God in the sanctuary. Given this possible reading of the facts at hand, why should Sternberg conclude, "There is not even a hint of the kind of extenuating circumstance later adduced by Saul: that the army was actuated by the desire to keep the best of the spoil for sacrifice. On the contrary, the narrative does its utmost to demolish any possible illusion about mistaken zeal and, instead, to bring home to us that their motives were pure only in the sense of being purely self-regarding."[17] On the contrary, I think the narrator has created a huge gap here in the text; we cannot know now why Saul and the army have acted as they have. We can only anticipate that the remainder of the story will provide clues that may help us to narrow the gap in our understanding.

15. Sternberg, *The Poetics of Biblical Narrative*, 491.

16. Johnson, "*abhah*," In *Theological Dictionary of the Old Testament*, 1:24.

17. Sternberg, *The Poetics of Biblical Narrative*, 491.

1 Samuel 15:10–12

> *(10) An so the word of YHWH came to Samuel. (11) "I am sorry that I crowned Saul king, because he has turned away from following me, and my words he does not establish." Samuel was furious and cried to YHWH all night. (12) And Samuel rose early to meet Saul in the morning, and it was told to Samuel, "Saul went to Carmel, and behold he established a monument to himself and turned and went down to Gilgal."*

There is a rapid change of scene between vss. 9 and 10. We leave Saul at Gilgal with his army, Agag, and the finest flocks and herds of the Amalekites, and move back to the prophet who is at some undetermined location. YHWH has interpreted the scene we have just witnessed at Gilgal in one possible way. Saul is in effect deposed with the words "I am sorry that I made Saul king." The verbs "sorry" and "made" are both used in Gen 6:7 where YHWH also announced the divine sorrow, in that text sorrow for the creation of human beings. The result is the universal flood. The reader can only anticipate that Saul will soon be swept away in some new divine cataclysm.

The word rendered "sorry" is often translated "repent," as in "to change one's mind." There seems to be an element of pathos in its use. For example, Job's famous speech of 42:6, "I am sorry on dust and ashes," carries the sense of some sort of recantation of prior words and actions, but also includes a sense of tragedy that things have come to such a terrible pass that Job sits on an ashheap, holding only a broken piece of pottery. Job's sorrow, then, is for far more than any one thing; he wishes things were different with God, with himself and with the relationship between the two of them. Thus, YHWH's sorrow over making Saul king includes the same combination of anger, sadness, and pathos.

And the reasons for YHWH's "sorrow" are two. First, Saul has "turned away from following me." Whatever Saul has done or not done at Gilgal is seen by YHWH to be nothing less than disobedience. Second, with a sweeping judgment on Saul's behavior, YHWH accuses him of "not establishing my word." In YHWH's speech, the reader can see that the gap created by the possible readings of vs. 9 has been closed, at least from the divine side. Yet, it remains important for the reader not to take YHWH's side so quickly. YHWH, like Saul and Samuel, is another character in the story, and may or may not represent the final word of that story. All evidence is not in with the speech of YHWH; we must read on. What we do know is that YHWH has found Saul wanting, precisely because he has been disobedient to the word of YHWH, that word which Samuel announced to Saul in vs. 1. It may sound most peculiar to say that YHWH is "merely" one character, but if we automatically lend greater weight to the addresses of YHWH we forget that those speeches were written by the narrator just as were those of Saul or Samuel. The narrator may finally be presenting YHWH's viewpoint as the crucial one, but the reader cannot so conclude on the too-simple basis that "YHWH said it." Again, we must always read on and resist the temptation to close down the meaning of the story too soon.

Samuel's reaction to the sorrow of YHWH is fascinating. He "was furious and cried to YHWH all night." Why is Samuel angry at YHWH's change of mind? Sternberg assumes that Samuel is angry at YHWH because he (Samuel) does not believe that Saul has done anything quite deserving of total rejection. Sternberg implies by this reading that Samuel has some sort of sympathy for Saul and his plight.[18] In the last verse of the chapter, the text appears to say that Samuel "grieved for Saul." We shall examine that phrase more closely later. When Samuel confronts Saul in the verses to follow, one would be hard-pressed to find in the prophet's words any sense of sympathy for Saul.

If Samuel is not in sympathy with Saul, then what might be the source of his fury? We noted that Samuel was very concerned with his own position as prophet in his first word to Saul in vs. 1. If YHWH deposes Saul so readily, will not Samuel's role as king-maker be called in serious question? Would the impression of his great power before the people not suffer a serious setback? Again, the gap in the text is a wide one. Thus, his all-night crying to YHWH could be the result of fury at YHWH for rejection of Saul or fury at YHWH for making Samuel out to be the fool because of that rejection.[19]

After his sleepless night of rage, Samuel rises early to meet Saul in the morning. Everything in the text suggests Samuel's haste; there is no delay once the decision is made to confront Saul, who has been judged disobedient by YHWH. One gets the impression that Samuel has accepted the prophetic role to announce YHWH's inexorable decision to Saul that his kingship has come to an end.

18. Sternberg, *The Poetics of Biblical Narrative*, 492.
19. Miscall, *1 Samuel: A Literary Reading*, 103.

A rather curious event occurs while Samuel is rushing to meet Saul. An unnamed person comes up to the enraged prophet and tells him that Saul has gone to Carmel and erected a monument for himself there, just before moving on to Gilgal. We hear nothing of this monument either before or after its brief mention here. The effect of this news is palpable; Samuel, already boiling with anger, can only be reinforced in his desire to announce to Saul YHWH's harsh decision. A more suspicious reader might wonder whether this event occurred at all; the narrator only *reports* to us that someone *said* Saul set up a monument. The word used for "monument" is a very common Hebrew word meaning "hand," or figuratively "power." However, this meaning of a physical monument occurs only in two other places in the Bible, 2 Sam 18:18, with the reference to Absalom's tomb, and possibly 1 Chron 18:3, although there the text may be referring to military power rather than to some monument. Whether or not Saul actually did what the stranger reported, the effect of the report is to infuriate Samuel all the more and to make him even more ready to besmirch Saul's name as an arrogant megalomaniac. Note that the narrator does not report the event, but has another character do it. Thus, the narrator dissociates himself from the event that becomes simply another piece of possible information for the story, rather than an established fact of the narration.

However we understand that little event, the confrontation between Samuel and Saul promises to be a titanic struggle, pitting the already-judged disobedient Saul, possibly swollen with power by his victory and monument, surrounded by stolen Amalekite booty on the one hand, and Samuel, the infuriated prophet, called to announce YHWH's rejection of the king, on the other. At this place in the story, the reader has an astonishing number of questions that cry out for answers. And because we are consumed by questions, the narrator thus insists that we read further in his masterful tale.

1 Samuel 15:13–21

> *(13) Samuel came to Saul, and Saul said to him, "May you be blessed by YHWH! I have established the word of YHWH!" (14) Samuel said, "And what is the sound of this flock in my ears, and the sound of the cattle that I hear?" (15) Saul said, "From the Amalekites they have brought them, for the army spared the best of the flocks and herds in order to sacrifice to YHWH your God. The rest we have obliterated."*

> (16) *Samuel said to Saul, "Silence! Let me tell you what YHWH said to me this night." They said to him, "Speak!" (17) Samuel said, "Though you are little in your own eyes, you are head of the tribes of Israel. YHWH anointed you king over Israel. (18) YHWH sent you on the way, and said to you, "Obliterate the sinners, the Amalekites, and fight against them until they are consumed, all of them. (19) Why did you not listen to the voice of YHWH and swoop on the spoil, and do evil in the eyes of YHWH?" (20) Saul said to Samuel, "I have certainly listened to the voice of YHWH. I have gone on the way that YHWH sent me. I have brought Agag, king of Amalek, but Amalek I have obliterated. (21) The army took from the spoil, the best of the flocks and herds to be obliterated in order to sacrifice to YHWH your God at Gilgal."*

This section brings us to the crux of the debate between Saul and Samuel. The narrator offers to us the point of view of Samuel as he marches in fury to meet the one he thinks is a completely disobedient king. We have no reason to disagree with that judgment, because we have witnessed the behavior of Saul and his army in vs. 9, and we have heard the anger and sorrow of YHWH and Samuel in response. We are set up by the narrator to be convinced that Saul has indeed disobeyed, and as Samuel approaches the king, we anticipate either abject admission of guilt or perhaps defiance in the face of Samuel's certain rage. We receive neither.

"May YHWH bless you, Samuel! I have established the word of YHWH!" The last thing one would expect from Saul is this breezy and open-faced response. He begins with a sunny, traditional religious greeting, and follows it with a crystal-clear announcement that he has precisely done his duty. We note that YHWH's decision to change the divine mind about the kingship of Saul in vs. 10 was based primarily on YHWH's belief that Saul "has not *established* my word." In direct contradiction of that claim, Saul says, "I have *established* the word of YHWH." Is Saul a dolt or a liar? How can he say such a thing given all of the evidence compiled in vss. 9–12? But, the reader must recognize that all of that evidence came from the point of view of Samuel and YHWH. We have not, before vs. 13, heard Saul's interpretation of the events. We must now listen with open minds to his reading of the events described especially in vs. 9.

But Samuel is in no listening mood; his mind, and apparently the mind of YHWH as well, are already made up. Though Sternberg calls Samuel's question of vs. 14 a "mild query,"[20] it could also be a sarcastic rejection of

20. Sternberg, *The Poetics of Biblical Narrative*, 500.

Saul's claim for obedience. One might paraphrase as follows: "So, you have obeyed, have you? Well, then what are all these bleating sheep and lowing cattle doing here?" Rather than confront Saul directly, Samuel snidely insinuates that he is a bold-faced liar. When confronted by a puddle of Coke on the kitchen floor, a parent will often say to a child with a glass in her hand and a mouthful of Coke, "What is this puddle doing here?" It is a request for confession, but it is a deviously nasty way to get one. Also Samuel formulates his question around the two words which were prominent in the first command of YHWH to Saul back in vs. 2, namely, "sound/voice" and "hear/obey." In fact, for Samuel, the "sounds" which he "hears" from the livestock are proof positive that Saul has not really "obeyed" the "voice" of YHWH at all.

But, of course, Samuel's question is based on *his* interpretation of YHWH's command to "obliterate"; he clearly thinks that such obliteration must be done on the field of battle. He will make this position clear in vs. 18. Saul has just indicated that he and the army have spared Agag and these superb livestock in order to sacrifice them in a great holocaust to YHWH at the sacred sanctuary of Gilgal. Saul thus has interpreted the command rather differently; nevertheless, he is convinced that his interpretation is still well within the bounds of the demand for obliteration. Samuel's snide question indicates that he does not think that Saul's interpretation is acceptable at all. Or, it could also be that the rigid old prophet is incapable of hearing another interpretation. Saul apparently so thinks, because he offers in vs. 15 a further explanation of his assertion of obedience in vs. 13. In fact, Saul takes Samuel's devious query as a straightforward request for information and proceeds to supply it. "From the Amalekites they have brought them (sheep and cattle); the army spared the best of the sheep and cattle in order to sacrifice to YHWH your God. The rest we have obliterated."

Sternberg finds in this response further evidence that Saul "is meant to condemn himself by his incessant shifts and turns."[21] He claims that Saul's announcement that the "army" did the sparing while he, Saul, joined them in the obliteration tends to blame them and exonerate him. However, the narrator, who offers to the reader the facts of the events in vs. 9, has no such sharp differentiation between Saul and his army. He told us that "Saul *and* the army spared Agag" and the rest, and that *both* Saul and the army obliterated the despised and worthless spoil. Thus, Saul's statement of vs. 15 could be seen as a strictly factual one; the army *did* spare the flocks, and

21. Ibid., 501.

they all did obliterate the rest. There is no necessary "shift and turn" here on the part of Saul. He straightforwardly says to Samuel that the flocks have been saved for sacrifice. For Saul, there was no demand made in the call for obliteration that all had to be slaughtered on the field of battle. Is Saul's different interpretation of the command to be discounted completely? If so, on what grounds?

Samuel has heard enough of this, and commands Saul to be silent; he announces to the assembled army what YHWH said to him the previous night. The written Hebrew text has *both* army and Saul respond that they are ready to hear what Samuel has to say; RSV and many others suggest that only Saul responds to Samuel in vs. 16. The narrator, by including both army and Saul, further binds them together in the events of vs. 9 which have precipitated the apparent crisis at hand. Yet, to this point, neither Saul nor his troops have any notion that there is a crisis. They will soon be disaffected of that notion by an enraged prophet.

Samuel begins his speech of vs. 17 with a reference to Saul's initial protestations to the prophet just before Samuel anointed him as "prince over Israel" (1 Sam 9:21). There, Saul spoke of being from the "least of the tribes" and from the "humblest of the families" of that tribe. The obvious irony for the story is that Saul is in physical stature "taller than any of the people" (1 Sam 9:2).[22] Samuel harks back to Saul's initial reluctance to become king (note, for example, Saul's attempts to hide on the day of his public coronation in 1 Sam 10:17–27), and accuses him of being inadequate for the great task of the leadership of YHWH's people. He then reminds him that it was no other than YHWH who anointed him king. Further, this same YHWH sent "you" (all the verbs in this speech are in the second-person singular; Samuel has no interest in the actions of the army here) "on the way to obliterate the sinners," "to fight against them until you have consumed them, all of them." The Hebrew text repeats the pronoun "them," unnecessary grammatically, but surely designed to emphasize the prophet's main point; the command of YHWH implied that Saul was to *fight* until all were consumed. Of course, Samuel is once again interpreting the initial command. That command of vs. 3 said only "strike" and "obliterate." Saul claims to have done both. Samuel, after the fact, says that the command said to "fight until they are consumed." The command plainly did *not* say that.

22. Good offers a psychological reading of this claim of Saul's "littleness in his own eyes" over against his enormous physical stature. This incongruity in Saul's self-perception is the key, according to Good, to Saul's central problem, and why he is eventually deposed as king (*Irony in the Old Testament*, 70–72).

Samuel continues to wrap his interpretation in the cloak of YHWH by claiming directly that *his* interpretation is YHWH's, and that by not adhering to that interpretation of the initial command, Saul has precisely *not* "obeyed the voice of YHWH." Samuel then accuses Saul himself of "swooping on the spoil," clearly an attempt to picture the king as hungry for booty and wealth. By portraying Saul in this way, Samuel reminds the reader of the previous chapter where the starving Israelite warriors, forbidden to eat food because of a religious vow uttered by Saul, fall on "the spoil" of the defeated Philistines and eat the meat with the blood still in it, a transgression of dietary laws. Samuel thus classes Saul with the unrestrained gluttony of that event. For Samuel, Saul is weak yet rapacious for goods; he is unfit to rule the people of YHWH.

How will Saul respond to this very personal attack from the powerful Samuel? It is a remarkable display of courage and truth telling. "I have surely obeyed the voice of YHWH," he begins. None of the things that Samuel has said have convinced Saul that his actions have in any way transgressed YHWH's command. "I have gone on the way which YHWH sent me." Samuel said that YHWH "sent him on the way," (vs 18) and Saul says directly that he has gone on that way and no other. "I have brought Agag, king of Amalek, while the Amalekites I have obliterated." These two statements are fully consonant with the facts of vs. 9. Sternberg claims that the sparing of Agag is "the heaviest sin of all"[23] but Saul's major antagonist in the story, Samuel, shows no overt interest in the Amalekite king until the very end of the tale. Samuel plainly does not use Agag as the reason for Saul's rejection.

Verse 21 is especially important to our understanding. "The army took from the spoil the best of the sheep and cattle to be obliterated to sacrifice to YHWH your God in Gilgal." Listen to David Gunn's comments about this speech.

> This is a splendidly forthright reply . . . Saul freely acknowledges that Agag is present at Gilgal and that the people have brought the best of the spoil to Gilgal. Saul asserts, however, that these facts are consonant with the fulfillment of the prophet's instruction. Now had they been so patently in contravention of the instruction we might have expected the king to veil them in some way (by claiming, perhaps, that the livestock were captured elsewhere, and so on). On the contrary, Saul's response makes clear (what the first

---

23. Sternberg, *The Poetics of Biblical Narrative*, 506.

response suggested) that it is not the "facts" that are in dispute, but their interpretation vis-à-vis the instructions.[24]

Saul reiterates in rather more detail his reply to Samuel's assaults first made in vs. 15. There is no dissimulation here. He even picks up Samuel's word, "spoil," used to attack Saul as a thief, and suggests again that the army took the very best of that spoil precisely to honor Samuel's God in the holy place. As Miscall points out, Samuel had accused Saul of three transgressions.[25] First, he claims that Saul did not listen to the voice of YHWH. Saul flatly says that he has so listened. Second, he says that Saul swooped on the spoil. Saul says that the best of the spoil have been taken to honor YHWH with sacrifice. Third, Samuel says that Saul has done that which is evil in YHWH's sight. Though Saul does not specifically answer that charge, his rejection of the first two accusations implies that the third is in fact meaningless. At the end of vs. 21, the reader is confronted not with different facts but with two different interpretations of those facts. Saul claims to have obeyed in full the commands of YHWH. Samuel is just as convinced that Saul has completely disobeyed. How is the reader to adjudicate this impasse? Or one might also ask, is the reader to adjudicate the impasse? Are other issues at stake for the narrator?

1 Samuel 15:22–29

> (22) Samuel said,
> "Does YHWH enjoy burnt offerings and sacrifices as much as obeying the voice of YHWH? Look! Obeying is better than sacrificing, paying attention better than the fat of rams!
>
> (23) Surely, rebellion is the sin of divination, and presumption is wicked idolatry. Because you have rejected the word of YHWH, YHWH has rejected you from being king!"
>
> (24) Saul said to Samuel, "I have sinned, because I moved beyond the mouth of YHWH and your words. Surely, I have honored the army and obeyed their voice. (25) So, now, please forgive my sin, and return with me, in order that I may worship YHWH." (26) Samuel said to Saul, "I will not return with you, because you have rejected the word of YHWH, and YHWH has rejected you from being king

24. Gunn, *The Fate of King Saul*, 48.

25. Miscall, *1 Samuel: A Literary Reading*, 105.

> over Israel." (27) Samuel turned to leave, and he (Saul) grabbed the
> hem of his robe so that it was torn. (28) So Samuel said to him,
> "YHWH has torn the kingdom of Israel from you today and has
> given it to your neighbor who is better than you. (29) Also, the Glory
> of Israel does not lie or repent. (The Divine One) is no human being
> who repents!"

In response to Saul's attempts to explain his actions and the actions of his
army, Samuel utters a withering prophetic indictment that has become
justly famous. The essence of his poem is the sharp distinction between
sacrifice and obedience. Saul has claimed twice that he and the army intended to complete the obliteration of the Amalekites with a huge sacrifice
at Gilgal, the sacred sanctuary. As I have noted several times above, this
interpretation for the call for obliteration differs from the one proposed
by Samuel. For Samuel, obliteration means *fighting* until the ones to be destroyed are completely consumed (vs. 18). Hence, Samuel's poetic distinction between obedience and sacrifice is based solely on his interpretation
of the command for obliteration. For Samuel, Saul has disobeyed the "voice
of YHWH." But for Saul, and his different interpretation of the command,
Samuel's powerful poetic couplets must appear to be completely beside
the point, because he assumes that his intention to sacrifice the best of the
Amalekite livestock at Gilgal is *precisely* to obey the voice of YHWH. While
Samuel might think that his memorable lines of vs. 22 are devastating in
their effect, Saul must only wonder why the old prophet is so worked up.

In vs. 23, Samuel extends the consequences of Saul's disobedience by
calling it "rebellion," a word used often as a sign of the stubbornness of the
people of Israel against their God. And this rebellion, continues Samuel, is
just as bad as "divination," that evil practice of consulting magicians and
wizards rather than YHWH, the source of all truth. Surely, our narrator
here offers to us a foreshadowing of the story found in 1 Sam 28, where Saul,
after piously expelling all necromancers from Israel, is forced by the silence
of YHWH to consult a female medium at Endor in a tragic attempt to discern his future. Saul's disobedience is rebellion, says Samuel, a rebellion
against YHWH fully as odious as consulting witches and wizards, a crime
punishable by death in the late law codes (see Deut 18:10–11; Lev 20:27).
In the parallel line, Samuel accuses Saul of "presumption," or perhaps "ar-
rogance" and calls it "wicked idolatry," again classing Saul's disobedience
with crimes of a cultic nature, crimes which are fully worthy of being cut off
from Israel and killed. Saul, according to Samuel, is a dark and evil force, a

rebellious and wicked idolater, who deserves the fate of any such creature, a fate the prophet delivers in ringing words. Because Saul has rejected the word of YHWH, YHWH has rejected him from being king. Given Samuel's understanding of what Saul's disobedience really means, there can be little alternative. Note, too, how cleverly the prophet rings his poetic denunciation with those two key terms of vs. 1, "voice" and "word." In vs. 22, Samuel says that "obeying the voice of YHWH" is better than sacrifice, while at the final line of vs. 23, Saul is said to have rejected the "word of YHWH." In vs. 1, before Samuel announced what God had called Saul to do, he said, "Obey the voice of the words of YHWH." Saul has obviously and completely failed to do so, according to the interpretation of Samuel.

Saul's reaction in vs. 24 to Samuel's prophetic denunciation may be read in at least three ways.

1. Saul finally admits that he has sinned and transgressed, indicating that he knew all along that what he had done was wrong. Thus, his earlier claims about intentions to sacrifice were all lies, attempts to cover his deep sense of wrongdoing.[26] And, further, he now tries to blame the army for his failings by suggesting that he listened to *their* voice because he "feared" them. The fact that there is no reference to Saul's fear of the people before in the story again shows that the king is in fact a weaseling liar. This is a possible reading, but is not congruent with the reading I am developing here. There are other possibilities.

2. Saul mentally snaps in the face of Samuel's onslaught. Earlier he was indeed convinced that he had obeyed YHWH and Samuel, but the prophet has finally broken him, has forced him against his better judgment to confess a sin he did not commit and to blame the people for this imagined sin in the bargain. Perhaps the scene that follows, where Saul desperately grasps the robe of the departing Samuel, is an indication that the dignity of the king has dissolved into powerlessness and sniveling. That scene is consistent with the portrait of a man close to madness, a madness that will erupt later against his rival, David. Thus, vs. 24 represents a radical break from the Saul of the earlier part of the story; Saul moves from certainty about his obedience to a confused and pathetic supplicant, reduced to groveling and passing the buck. I think that that is a possible reading as well. But there is a third possibility.

26. Sternberg, *The Poetics of Biblical Narrative*, 513.

3. David Gunn has articulated this last possible reading of the verse. If we accept the fact that the entire drama of the scene has revolved around two interpretations of the command to obliterate the Amalekites, then Saul must realize at vs. 24 that his interpretation has been thoroughly discounted by Samuel, if indeed it has been heard at all. "Saul therefore has little choice but to acknowledge that as it now appears he has, after all, sinned, broken the strict terms of the command."[27] Of course, the "strict terms of the command" have been so interpreted by Samuel.

Two particular words used by Saul in this admission of guilt further indicate that he is hardly submitting to Samuel in abject contrition. I have read the verb he uses as "moved beyond," though the more common reading is "transgress." By using this verb to describe his relationship to the command of YHWH, Saul implies that he has given that command another meaning than the one that Samuel insists is the only correct one. He thus carefully circumscribes his admission of "sin" by his insistence that what he has done can only be called sin within the interpretation of the command offered by Samuel. Samuel is in control of the scene, and within that control Saul is a sinner. He admits that "fact." Secondly, Saul does not say that he has "moved beyond the 'word' of YHWH" or the "voice of YHWH"; he says that he has moved beyond the "mouth of YHWH." By carefully avoiding those two familiar words, "word" and "voice," Saul again limits his admission of sin to his different interpretation of the "word" of command. "To move beyond the mouth" is rather different than "disobeying the word." Even after vs. 24, Saul could still say, and with no sense of dissimulation, that he had indeed obeyed the command of YHWH, as he had interpreted it.

Saul goes on to say that in addition to "moving beyond the mouth of YHWH," that is, to interpret the command rather differently, he "moved beyond your (Samuel's) words." Now, and only now, Saul says that he went beyond the "word," but the word he went beyond was Samuel's not YHWH's. Saul seems here to recognize that Samuel may be God's prophet, but he is also a human being, interpreting the word of God for the world in which he lives. We saw above how the narrator showed that Samuel is indeed an interpreter of YHWH's word and not merely a neutral channel of it. Hence, Saul seems to recognize that he is locked in an interpretive debate with Samuel, and that the old prophet is hardly likely to deviate from his understanding.

27. Gunn, *The Fate of King Saul*, 53.

Saul concludes his response to Samuel by saying, "I honored the people and listened to their voice." Rather than assume immediately that Saul is here blaming the people, Gunn offers another reading. "By speaking of the initiative of the people he is not weakly passing the blame but freely acknowledging his own error."[28] Saul realizes that his actions with the proposed sacrifice of the Amalekites' best flocks have been misconstrued by Samuel as an honoring of the people above honoring YHWH. He admits that *he* has done it, and he obviously expects the prophet to accept his admission with thanks and forgiveness. "Saul is not 'wriggling' but expressing the deepest contrition possible in the circumstances."[29] Saul remains calm as he admits that, under the ground-rules laid down by Samuel, his actions could be misunderstood. The prophet, however, remains adamant, even though Saul asks him to "return with me that I might worship YHWH." His immediate request that he might worship YHWH demonstrates all the more clearly that Saul wants reconciliation with YHWH and Samuel; what better way to achieve that reconciliation than with a public act of worship in the presence of the prophet. Saul does not utter vs. 24 with desperation in his voice and tears in his eyes. He speaks as one who feels that he has been misunderstood and who then goes out of his way to effect reconciliation with the one who has misunderstood him. The naïve Saul imagines that cooler heads will prevail. He is desperately wrong.

"I will not return with you"; the prophet thunders, "because you have rejected the word of YHWH, YHWH has rejected you from being king over Israel." Samuel will accept no deviation from his interpretation of the command. Saul said in vs. 24 that he had "moved beyond the mouth of YHWH and your (Samuel's) words," suggesting that there might be possible room for discussion about the meaning of the original command. Samuel rejects all such discussion; "you have *rejected* the *word* of *YHWH*," he says, not merely interpreted *my* words and YHWH's *mouth*. "Tit for tat," says Samuel. A rejection of YHWH's word has earned you YHWH's rejection of your kingship over Israel. And with that final statement, the rigid prophet turns his back on the king and prepares to leave. The discussion, as far as he is concerned, is at an end.

Saul, now realizing that Samuel is not going to worship with him, is not willing to discuss reconciliation with him, and has in fact delivered the divine word of absolute rejection to him, grabs the retreating prophet

28. Ibid.
29. Ibid.

154

to prevent his leaving. This action could be construed as one of proud anger or abject desperation. Perhaps both are involved, as Saul begins to see that his actions with the Amalekites have not earned him the rewards he anticipated but rather complete and total condemnation. As Saul grabs the prophet's robe while the prophet is still moving away from him, the robe is torn. No self-respecting prophet in the mood of condemnation would miss such an opportunity as that! Perhaps with a grand gesture and a withering stare, Samuel takes the torn robe as still another indication that YHWH has "torn" the kingdom from Saul, but this time he adds the new fact that YHWH has given the kingdom "to your neighbor who is better than you." With the introduction of a replacement for Saul, apparently already chosen by YHWH, Saul's demise is complete; he can never again truly be the king of Israel. The fact that David is introduced to us in the next chapter suggests that the narrator is once again foreshadowing the future movement of the story.

Yet, there is here as well another possible reading. YHWH has said nothing about a replacement for Saul; YHWH only to date regrets the crowning of Saul to be king. Is Samuel here announcing divine words without the benefit of having heard any? Is he delivering to Saul what is in fact an empty threat of a replacement for him when one has not yet been chosen? That this reading is at least one to consider is affirmed by the next verse. In an apparent attempt to seal the threat just made, Samuel proclaims a theological axiom about YHWH. "The Glory of Israel does not lie (perhaps with the implication that Saul has lied over and over). Nor does that One repent (change the divine mind). The Divine one is not a human being who repents." Samuel says that whatever YHWH says is irrevocable, because YHWH does *not* repent. Thus, we are to conclude from this statement that YHWH's rejection of Saul and choice of another are fixed actions and not to be altered.

The irony is, of course, that in this very story YHWH has "repented." In vs. 10, YHWH announces that the divine mind has changed concerning the kingship of Saul due to Saul's refusal to "establish my word." YHWH can indeed repent; thus Samuel's theological axiom is called into question by no one other than YHWH. Does this fact not then call into serious question the role of Samuel as absolute messenger of the word of YHWH? All along in the story we have noted hints that Samuel has gone beyond the role of simple conduit for YHWH's word, and has on occasion injected his own interpretations of those words. These occasions raise again the basic problem of the confrontation between Samuel and Saul: who has the right to interpret the will of God? Is there any room for discussion or disagreement? Thus, we must ask in this particular instance, has Saul been treated justly? Was the removal of his kingship a just act? Is the question of justice an important one for the story? We must continue to ask questions like these as we conclude our reading.

1 Samuel 15:30–35

> *(30) He (Saul) said, "I have sinned. You honor me, please, in the presence of the elders of my people, and in the presence of Israel. Return with me that I might worship YHWH, your God." (31) Samuel returned after Saul, and Saul worshipped YHWH. (32) Then Samuel said, "Bring me Agag, king of the Amalekites." Agag came to him bound, and said, "Surely, the bitterness of death has turned aside!" (33) Samuel said, "Just as your sword made women childless, so shall your mother be childless among women!" So Samuel killed Agag before YHWH at Gilgal. (34) Samuel went to Ramah, while Saul went up to his house at Gibeah of Saul. (35) Samuel never again saw Saul until the day of his death. But Samuel mourned because of Saul, and YHWH repented that "he" had crowned Saul king over Israel.*

Saul's attempts at reconciliation with Samuel have obviously failed. Though he proclaimed his sin in vs. 24, we noted that his confession was carefully worded so as to imply that his actions could only be considered sinful in the very specific context created by the narrow interpretation of the initial command of YHWH provided by Samuel. But the events and words of vss. 25–29 have made it abundantly clear that Samuel is not a man given to discussion or compromise. Hence, Saul does the only thing he can now do; he confesses sin to the prophet, and begs him to show the king honor before the elders of Israel. He pleads once again that Samuel accompany him to worship in order that the people might see at least an outward display of reconciliation between king and prophet. Samuel now goes; after all, he has won the day. Saul's interpretation of the command has been called apostasy and disobedience; there is no doubt of that in the mind of the people. For Samuel to join Saul in worship would not now imply that Saul is either forgiven or reconciled in fact. It is only a political act, designed to save at least a modicum of peace in the kingdom. The facts have not changed; Saul has been rejected, and Samuel has announced his replacement. We should note in this regard that though Samuel accompanies Saul to worship, we are told that Saul worships alone (vs. 31) and is not joined by Samuel in that act.

At last, our attention is turned to Agag. The Amalekite king has played no role whatever in Saul's demise, hence any attempt to claim that Saul's sparing of Agag was a fatal mistake is belied by the text itself. In fact, Samuel's treatment of Agag suggests an interesting irony with respect to Saul's proclaimed intention to sacrifice the "best" of the Amalekite residue. The prophet first has Agag brought to him. What the Amalekite leader says, apparently to himself, has been the source of considerable debate.[30] The Hebrew text reads literally, "Surely, the bitterness of death has turned aside." This perhaps means that Agag is convinced that his life is about to be spared by Samuel. However, it could also mean that his death, which he sees now fast approaching at the hands of the old prophet, has lost its bitterness. In short, he is ready to die. As often in this story, the narrator leaves us uncertain about the full meaning of the phrase.

Samuel, always full of poetic couplets, announces Agag's fate with a clever rhyme that plays on the words "women" and "childless." Given the structure of the whole story, I am inclined to think that the first meaning of Agag's muttered phrase may be the intended one. If so, his fate rather closely mirrors that of the other king in the story. Agag, like Saul, comes expecting a word of release/reward from the prophet. What both get instead is a stinging denunciation in poetry, which leads to the death of one and the rejection of the other. Further, Agag's immediate death is merely a foreshadowing of the death of Saul, after a downward spiral of rejections by his would-be friend and rival, David, by his son and daughter, Jonathan and Michal, and even another rejection by Samuel, this one offered after the prophet's death. In the death of Agag, the reader can see the fate of Saul, delayed but certain.

But note where Agag is killed by Samuel—"in the presence of YHWH at Gilgal." Saul's intention to sacrifice the Amalekite flocks "in the presence of YHWH at Gilgal," an intention not believed or perhaps even not heard by Samuel, is now ironically carried out by that same Samuel. Is it the case that Samuel may ritually slaughter the enemy king at the sanctuary, while Saul cannot? Does this scene not again raise the question of just who has the right of interpretation? It is clear to the reader by now that Saul has no such right.

---

30. See, for example, McCarter, *1 Samuel*, 265 and Klein, *1 Samuel*, 146.

Saul and Samuel now go their separate ways, and the narrator tells us that they never meet again at least while both were still alive (1 Sam 19:24 seems to offer a slight discrepancy to that claim). Then we are told that Samuel "grieved because of Saul." This phrase causes Sternberg again to claim that Samuel was still somehow on the side of the fallen king, was in fact "moved" by his final admission of sin.[31] He connects this "grieving" with Samuel's earlier all night crying to God (vs. 11), a crying that he assumed meant that the prophet was sorry for Saul's rejection by YHWH. As I noted in the discussion of that earlier passage, Samuel's grieving and crying do not necessarily mean that he is sad for Saul's fate. The text says that he was grieving "because of Saul." That could mean any number of things. This word is regularly used when persons have died. It may be that Samuel is merely going through the prescribed rites of mourning for a king who is in reality dead, though his body is still animated by breath. In truth, we can know nothing of the inner feelings of Samuel. We can know that he has deposed a king and done it with prophetic power and fury. At no time did the story ever indicate that Samuel had the slightest hesitation in doing so. Surely, the prophet is not sad to see the disobedient apostate go; he thus grieves because Saul is dead to him, to the kingdom, and to YHWH. There is no emotion in the grieving. It is just custom.

And while Samuel is grieved, the narrator reiterates that YHWH changed the divine mind about having made Saul king. Thus, the story ends with a grieving Samuel and perhaps a chastened YHWH who feels that the choice of this king was a poor one, after all. Saul, the deposed king, meanwhile, has gone home, from whence he started some years before, searching for some lost donkeys. Instead of finding donkeys, however, he wound up with a kingdom.

This story is about the right to interpret the will of God. Unlike Sternberg, I do not think that the goal of the narration is to "bring the audience's viewpoint into alignment with his (the narrator's) own,"[32] a viewpoint he later describes as the conviction of Saul's certain guilt and just punishment. For me, the story is rife with ambiguity and questions. I find no place in my reading where Saul could be judged to be guilty of disobedience to YHWH, if it be granted that there may be different ways to interpret the command of YHWH. Of course, to Samuel, Saul is guilty of the most heinous of crimes, the "rejection of the word of YHWH." But, my reading has indicated that

31. Sternberg, *The Poetics of Biblical Narrative*, 513.
32. Ibid., 482.

the narrator may not be using Samuel as his spokesperson. On the contrary, the fact that the narration leaves me with these questions and this ambiguity makes me wonder whether the narrator does not have great sympathy for Saul as a man caught up in forces over which he has no control. YHWH regrets making Saul king, and Samuel, YHWH's spokesperson, carried out the divine will for rejection with a vengeance, albeit adding numerous nuances of his own in the process.

But is there a right and wrong here? Was Saul justly judged and deposed? If one believes as Samuel, the answer can only be yes. Yet, the portrait of a naïve but truthful Saul is haunting. As I watch him trudge home from Gilgal, with Samuel's stinging rebukes in his ears, the question of fairness arises. Did Saul deserve all this? Listen to Gunn raise the question in a rather different way.

> . . . Saul operates not in some theological vacuum where simple and abstract questions may be met with simple and abstract answers, but in "real-life" situations of moral complexity and theological obscurity.[33]

To ask the question of "deserving" or simple "fairness" is to miss the point of this tale. Saul is involved in a situation of "moral complexity and theological obscurity," and precisely there the preacher can enter the story. For those two phrases summarize the position of us all in the twenty-first century. Like Saul, we strive to understand and to perform the will of God in an immensely complex and confusing world. And, of course, like Samuel, there are those who would offer clear, direct, and unimpeachable explanations of God's will, interpretations that will brook no arguments. Who is to determine whether the Sauls or the Samuels are correct? Are we not all left, at least much of the time, to grope toward the truth, never fully certain that we are in possession of that truth? We cannot adjudicate this story of Saul and Samuel on the basis of justice or fairness. At the end, we can only say that we are all called to interpret the word of God for our time, but no one of us may ever claim that our interpretation is the only one. Down that road, one finds anger, rejection, and death.

33. Gunn, *The Fate of King Saul*, 123.

A STORY SERMON BASED ON 1 SAMUEL 15

The following narrative sermon is an example of the type I call "fictional narrative." I have determined, after my reading of 1 Samuel 15, that one of the ways I can best present the important, and particularly difficult, theme of the chapter is by creating a fictional story in modern dress. Instead of retelling the ancient story, I have decided that the theme of choosing to interpret the will of God in a modern context of enormous complexity may better be expressed in a contemporary story of my own creation. I have made this choice for the following reasons.

1. The fact that those who know the story of Saul and Samuel (unfortunately not a very large number to be sure!) will probably know it only as a story of Saul's disobedience to Samuel and God makes a very high hurdle that the preacher must jump before a new and fresh word can be heard. By writing my own story, I remove the hurdle, or at least lower it a bit, to hearing the theme I intend to proclaim. The theme may be thus heard without biblical preconceptions. Though I realize that such preconceptions are always a problem when dealing with the Bible, they seemed particularly acute to me in this case.

2. The biblical narrator was especially subtle in this narrative, spicing the tale with any number of similar words with different meanings, and offering to the reader numerous occasions where multiple understandings were clearly possible. By telling my own story, I can more directly point the theme, thus making its appropriation and understanding more possible for the hearer.

3. To write a contemporary fictional story, based on a very careful narrative reading, is a helpful test to see whether or not I can well articulate the significance of the ancient story for modern people. If my story effectively translates the theme of the reading in such a way that it can be heard, then the infamous gap between ancient book and modern life will have found another kind of bridge over which the Bible's story can pass in order to meet us moderns as we walk onto the bridge from the other end.

4. There is intrinsic value for the preacher to try a hand at what our schools are fond of calling "creative writing." Because words are the main tools of our craft, we may find that our imaginations are energized and set free in new ways when we attempt to recreate the Bible's great themes in our own

imaginative language. Not only should we read great imaginative fiction, we should also write some fiction, though it may be less than great and somehow not quite as imaginative as we would like. As the following example will readily prove, I am no new Flannery O'Connor waiting to be discovered. Still, as I wrote the story, parts of my mind were used that I do not often use, not to mention parts of my store of knowledge. Though you may be completely resistant to such an idea, and are even now thinking that such stuff is not for you, I suggest you try it before you decide to reject the possibility out of hand. You may be surprised by the results.

There are, of course, significant risks that accompany this kind of sermon.

1. What if no one sees the connection between the biblical reading and the story you have created? However, we can hardly assume that our hearers always find the connections between our sermons and the biblical text even when they are overtly and continuously mentioned! I have tried to lessen this problem by using names in my story that are directly reminiscent of the characters in the Bible story. One of the major reasons for exploring the possibility of narrative preaching is to be more responsive to the biblical text. In a fictional narrative sermon, the text is quite obviously not used directly. However, I hasten to add, that without the careful narrative *reading* of the text this fictional narrative, and its particular form, would have been impossible.

2. To cut oneself away from any direct references to the biblical story is to run the risk of losing authority for the sermon. Clearly, no preacher will want to use a fictional narrative on his/her first Sunday in the pulpit. After the congregation has been convinced over some time that you are dedicated to the Bible's word and authority, using it as the central foundation for your preaching, then this innovative approach will not be viewed as a personal deviation from that basic commitment. They will hear it as biblical, because they trust that you have wrestled with the Bible to arrive at the sermon, though the Bible itself is not mentioned.

3. The basic danger is to write a story that does not in fact well illustrate the theme, thus defeating the purpose of the story in the first place. And the story itself might be so poor as to be unhearable, and unbearable, for the congregation, who have come hungry for the gospel and have been sent empty away. But this risk, as always, must be weighed against the gain

of freshness and newness, the possibility that the word might fall on ears drugged with familiarity in ways that unclog and unstop. Story preaching has that possibility.

"Come, Behold the Works of the Lord"

Senator Gibson "Gib" Saul had heard all this before. He squirmed slightly in the pew in a vain attempt to get comfortable. He remembered a book title he had seen not long before—*The Comfortable Pew*—Whoever wrote that, he thought, had never sat in one. A wry smile curled his lips, a smile made famous by a thousand magazine covers. "Senator Saul—Courageous Champion of the Poor!" "Gib Saul Lectures the President on Civil Rights." "One for the 'Gibber': Saul Leads the Fight Against Bloated Defense Bill." From *Time* to *Life* to *People* to *The National Inquirer*, "Gib" Saul's handsome face was never long out of the public eye. After three terms in the U.S. Senate, Gibson Saul was one of the most powerful people in the country. Whispers of the White House had circulated for several years.

Saul forced his wondering mind to refocus on the figure in the pulpit not twenty feet from his too-hard pew. Bishop Franklin Samuels was on the platform today. His sonorous voice filled the vast gothic vault. Saul knew the bishop well. They had been on many a committee together. They had struggled to help those millions who had not made it in the ways that the senator and the bishop had. Saul liked the bishop. Oh, he was a bit too rigid, as religious bureaucrats tended to be. But his heart was in the right place. He did what he could within the carefully defined limits of the world's oldest political party—the Christian church.

> The first two paragraphs are designed purely to introduce the protagonists. This must be done quickly, because the 15–18 minutes of a sermon do not allow much time to linger over details. Saul is ambitious, prominent, committed to a liberal social agenda. The fact that he is in church suggests his religious interest. Samuels is powerful, a leader in his church, also concerned about progressive social causes. I try not to so type the two that they become figures of cardboard. These are men of conviction and commitment, and they both have the authority to act on those convictions in significant ways.
>
> As you can see, the two are not exact mirror images of Saul and Samuel in the Bible, but their respective biographies are quite similar in their peculiarly modern ways.

The text for the day was Psalm 46. The hymn preceding the sermon was Martin Luther's wonderful "A Mighty Fortress is Our God." Saul loved that hymn; old Luther was a tough and rebellious man after his own heart. We need more like him, Saul thought. I wish Luther were preaching today. But the preacher was Bishop Samuels after all. Saul forced himself to listen.

"Hear vs. 8. God's works in the earth, God's desolations in the earth, are nothing else than God's actions described in vs. 9. God stops wars by breaking the bow, by shattering the spear, by burning the shields with fire! God's acts of desolation are far different than ours, my friends." The bishop was winding up for a flashy end; Saul had heard him before. "Whereas we would desolate the earth with our modern bows and spears and shields, all now shaped like mushroom clouds, God would desolate not the good earth that God made. No, God's will is that the weapons themselves would be desolated, that they would be destroyed! 'Be still and know that I am God!' If we would truly hear that, my sisters and brothers in Christ, we will follow God by destroying those engines of death that threaten us all and blaspheme the Lord of Hosts. It is our God who is exalted in the earth, not Titan, or Minuteman, or SS-20!"

Saul had heard it all before. The bishop was well known for his outspoken criticism of nuclear weapons, although Saul could not remember ever seeing him at a rally or march. Saul, of course, did not miss any of them. He would speak, and the crowds would listen. Then, he would leave in his limousine, while some of the more radical ones would be arrested for trespassing or damaging government property. "Be still and know that I am God." Somehow the words so familiar did not sound quite the same today.

Saul reached quickly for his Bible and turned to the Psalm for himself. "God is our refuge and our strength, a very present help in trouble. Therefore we will not fear though the earth should change. Come, behold the works of the Lord." The bishop's words came again to Saul's mind. "If we would follow God, we will destroy the engines of death," he had said.

As Saul went deeper into himself, consumed by the Psalm, the service ended. He was not aware of its end. Suddenly, the bishop's huge voice broke into his ears. "Gib, Gib, where are you? Earth to Gib! My, my, I thought you were here, not somewhere else. Was my sermon that hard to understand?" Bishop Samuels was his usual jovial self, and especially after hundreds of parishioners had rushed up to him with admiration plastered all over their faces. "Did you mean all that, Frank? I mean, all that stuff about God destroying the weapons?" Saul's question was so direct as to be shocking.

Several members of the congregation shuffled nervously. "Well," said Samuels, "I certainly meant that God's will was to get rid of our weapons; of course, how they should be gotten rid of is a decision each of us must make for ourselves." Without a word, Senator Saul turned and hurried out of the church.

> In a story this brief, I must hurry the action along. Saul is now moved by the psalm in a way he has never been before. The bishop has moved him even with words he has spoken before. Saul will now act in ways that the bishop cannot accept. The command has been given, but the interpretations of the command will not be the same. You can begin to see the relationship between my story and my reading of the biblical text.

In the next twenty-four hours, events happened very fast. Senator Saul went to the Sunday rally and march as planned, but after his speech, which was remembered by those present as especially impassioned, he did not leave in his limo. When the radical few chained themselves to the high iron fence around the White House, Saul joined them. When the police came to take them to jail, Saul went with them. Though he was quickly released, he that same evening joined a march to the Pentagon. Once there, he proceeded to pour animal blood all over some missiles which were being displayed in the main lobby. He went back to jail, and this time he did not bail himself out.

The papers screamed their headlines. "Gib Saul Jailed!" "Popular Senator Defaces Pentagon!" "Saul Vows to Destroy Weapons." "Psychiatrist Called in to Examine Gib." In jail, Saul wanted only one thing—his Bible, and he wanted to see only one man—Bishop Samuels. The bishop was already on his way to the jail. It was late evening on a Monday.

Impeccably dressed as always, the bishop was led to the cell where his friend was being held. Saul was a mess. He smelled bad and looked worse. The famous smile was not to be found. It had been replaced by a look of rock-hard determination. "You look awful," said Samuels. "I feel wonderful, really alive for the first time in my life—thanks to you, Frank." "Me?!" The bishop sounded horrified. "What earthly relationship could I possibly have to this person I see before me, a person I thought I knew, a person I respected more than I can ever say?" "But Frank," the smile returned, "you said it yesterday. God's works are to destroy the weapons. If I am to be a child of God, I must destroy the weapons. You said that, did you not?"

"Gib." The bishop put on his pastoral voice. "What about your career, and your family? You have spent nearly twenty years in the senate. You have been a voice of compassion and courage for millions in this country. Will you now throw it all away? Be reasonable."

"Frank, I am being reasonable. I had heard the forty-sixth Psalm a thousand times, some of those from your own lips. But yesterday I finally heard it, really heard it. 'God destroys weapons,' it says. Then you said, 'We must destroy weapons, if we are to follow God.' I *will* follow God, Frank. I will destroy weapons. All of my speeches and writings have implied this for a long time. I am finally putting my money where my mouth is. Surely you can see that, Frank. I don't want your blessing, but I do want your understanding."

"But I don't understand, Gib. I don't understand! I do understand the forty-sixth Psalm. After all, I do have a PhD in the Old Testament. Yes, it says that God destroys weapons, but for heaven's sake, Gib, that is *God's* business. We can't just go out and destroy weapons. It is, after all, against the laws of this country. Without those laws, we would all return to chaos, to barbarism! You are a leader in the free world. Think of your influence, your enormous opportunities to bring change to the world. *Some* people may feel called to perform radical acts, but not people like you. Let some of the long hairs get tossed in jail; they mostly do it to massage their own egos anyway. But, Gib, the world needs reasonable people of integrity, courage, and good will to bring change through the channels of negotiation and compromise. Don't fail them and me by doing something stupid! Maybe some rest would help. How about the Bahamas? You love it there. Take your wife and go; it can easily be arranged. A couple of weeks and you will be a new man, and all of this will have blown over. What do you say?"

Senator Saul looked at Samuels for a long time. Then he said, "But I am doing what you said, what God said. Why should I go back to that compromising half-hearted activity? I think I am fulfilling the command of God, Frank. Are you going to tell me that I am not, you of all people, the representative of God on earth? Can you look me in the face and say *that?*"

The pastoral voice of Bishop Samuels had disappeared. "You are a naïve fool, Saul, a fool! The world does not need any more way-out radical nincompoops with stars in their eyes and bottles of animal blood in their hands! Not only are the poor always with us, so are fools like you! If you cannot see that, then I cannot open your eyes. I leave you to your fate! I hope you know what this means. Your career is ruined, the presidency is lost, and I imagine whatever family life you may have had will soon be gone. And don't blame me for it, oh no, don't you dare blame me! Psalm 46 is not the only part of the Bible. Jesus said, 'Be wise as serpents, but gentle as doves.' Do you remember that one? Oh, Gib, Gib, wake up. It's the real world, not some pie in the sky cloud cuckooland. Sure, God will someday destroy the weapons, but we have to live in a world with them now, and that means compromise, talk, negotiation!" Samuels paused for a breath; his face flushed.

"I can see that you are not listening! Very well; I have done what I could to make you see the truth. My conscience is clear! Goodbye, Gib. May God protect you; God's all you've got now!" And the bishop left; Gib never saw him again. The bishop died some five years later.

And Gib? Oh, the bishop was right in more ways than even he knew. Gib left the senate, his wife divorced him, and he spent the rest of his days in and out of jail, in and out of munitions factories, in and out of submarine bases. Yes, Bishop Samuels was right. All he did have left was God, and the words the bishop had said in that sermon so long ago. "Brothers and sisters in Christ, if we would follow God, we will destroy the engines of death." Saul died alone, and essentially forgotten by those powerful ones who were once his friends. At his funeral, the forty-sixth Psalm was sung and spoken. And a preacher, one who had been ordained by Bishop Samuels, said a few words. "My friends, the life we celebrate today tried to live out the words of this great Psalm. Though many of us would disagree with the ways he went about that, none of us can deny that he tried." They laid Saul to rest in a place not far from the large monument that heralded the grave of Bishop Samuels. Ironically, the same words can be found on both their stones, even though the bishop's is a good deal more impressive. And the words are from the forty-sixth Psalm. "Come, behold the works of the Lord."

> I wanted to end my story with the same sense of ambiguity that I found in my reading of 1 Samuel 15. Both Samuels and Saul did in their minds what were the works of the Lord. The final uncertainty about who was "right" is left for the hearer to ponder as she/he hears the brief funeral speech at Saul's death which notes disagreement with and confusion about his actions, and as the grave markers bear the same citation from the forty-sixth Psalm. Even as I wrote the story, my identity moved back and forth between Saul and Samuels. I am far more like Samuels in my own life, as are most of us religious professionals, but I felt great sympathy for Saul as he attempted to live out his understanding of the Psalm, which was his command from God.

> I believe that my fictional narrative did what I hoped it would do, namely, emphasize and make especially real and poignant the theme as it was uncovered in the reading of the text. Who can rightly interpret the will of God for our time, or for any time? First Samuel 15 does not answer that question; it rather raises it in an especially memorable way. I offer my story as another way to bring that theme into the life of a congregation.

As I finished my fictional narrative, I was both exhilarated and disappointed. I very much enjoyed the play of imagination that gave birth to the story. But, as I read it again, I was less than satisfied with its literary quality. And the closing ambiguity is not fully satisfactory. It is clear that other elements of the worship service in which such a sermon is preached will need to sound the chords of the gospel. God is with us even in the midst of our ambiguities and doubts. Perhaps it is simply not good enough to present the theme of the biblical text. I suppose only my hearers can be the final judge of that. However, I do hope that this example of a fictional narrative sermon can serve as an impetus for you to try that rather different way to proclaim the word you have been called to proclaim.

Is This an Effective Story Sermon?

I am less sanguine about this sermon than I was about the previous chapter's sermon on Jonah. That is primarily because of the radically different nature of the two texts at hand. Jonah is unambiguously the gospel of God, and a careful and faithful retelling of the story will express that fact. But 1 Samuel 15 is altogether different. In my reading of it, we found no unambiguous truth, save the struggle of interpretative rights; who finally has the right to interpret the word of God? My reading revealed that the world often chooses the easily acceptable way of hearing God as that way is interpreted by those the community lauds as interpreters, those with powerful platforms and comfortable positions. When I raise Lischer's four problems for narrative sermons, my responses are rather less certain.

Genuine ambiguity does not yield moralism or transient experiences of grace, but it does yield questioning, a kind of tentativeness, that throws the certainties of the gospel somewhat in the shade. That is why I stated in my comments immediately after the sermon that other elements of the service of worship will need to address this ambiguity and offer the broader contexts of biblical and theological realities. The story is hardly a closed one, and thus could speak well to those listeners who live with a lack of certainty and neat closures in their lives. The story attempts to take a common biblical text, Psalm 46, and show how differently the words can be heard and acted upon. By its very nature, this is conceptualizing the Bible, not simply repeating it without theological reflection. Does it call for sociopolitical change? By implication, each listener is asked to reflect on God's demand for destruction of the weapons of war. Is the senator right to act as he does? Is the bishop right to read and act as he does? Will listeners actually make these judgments as they listen, or will the story remain for them only a distant story, interesting but finally not a demand of the gospel of God? I believe this fictional story sermon can be effective as a sermon, but I am less convinced of that effectiveness as I was with my Jonah sermon. I think it communicates, but may be too subtle in that communication fully to be effective in the ways in which I am defining effectiveness.

SIX

"Things are Seldom What They Seem"[1]

A Reading of Judges 4

A FTER PARTICIPATING IN THREE narrative readings of biblical texts, I hope that it is becoming ever more clear that the Bible presents more than initially meets the eye. The rich resources of the narratives of the Hebrew Bible have begun to appear to us as we have searched with care the details of three discreet stories. However, the texts that we have read so far have long been judged to be superior examples of the narrator's art. Other analyses of Jonah, Gen 2:4b—3:24, and 1 Samuel 15, even when they have not been read for character, plot, point of view, word play, and other kinds of detailed nuances at the level of word, sentence, or larger structure, have still been seen as examples of excellent narrative literature. The surprise of just how good they are is perhaps somewhat blunted by these prior expectations.

I turn now in this chapter to what appears to be a far less promising story, namely, the prose account of the events surrounding the defeat of Sisera, the general of King Jabin's Canaanite army, by the alliance of Deborah, Barak, and Jael. The apparent lack of promise in this story for a rich narrative reading is the result of at least three factors. First, the vast bulk of scholarly attention has been focused on the related poetic account of these events in Judges 5. That account has long been assumed to be far older than the prose account of chapter 4, which has been described as a prosaic, more pedantic telling of the tale, a tale said to have been brought more vividly to life by the wonderful, very ancient poem. Also, the poem is riddled with

1. I have borrowed the title of this reading from a song found in the operetta, "H. M. S. Pinafore," by Gilbert and Sullivan.

numerous puzzles of grammar and philology, more than enough to tax the acumen of doctoral candidates, not to mention a large number of seasoned scholars.

Second, the major interest of scholarship has long been the history of the events that lies behind these chapters of Judges and that played some role in calling them forth. Because the poem is said to be older, indeed often said to be not far removed in time from the events enshrined in it, scholars have been far more ready to plumb the poem's depths in an attempt to extract historical nuggets. Because the prose account is fully dependent on the poem, as most agree, its historical value has been seen to be considerably less than that of its older master.

Third, the prose tale is embedded within the rigid framework established in the early chapters of the book of Judges. The collector of the stories of the Judges is convinced that the history of the people of God in this period followed a tragic and ever-repeated four-step cycle. They sin, usually through some kind of idolatry. Then, God punishes them for their sin by handing them over to a named enemy who oppresses them cruelly for a designated number of years, often forty, the Bible's round number representing a generation. They then cry out to be released from their oppression. The cry comes to God who sends to them some kind of deliverer to bring them freedom. With the death of the deliverer, they sin again, and the terrible cycle starts all over. Such a tight ideological straitjacket ought to be poor ground for the rich inventions of narrative. Tales fitted to this mold would seem to be little better than propaganda, illustrating in lockstep the simplistic concerns of the religious collector of the stories.[2]

For these three reasons, then, one might not expect to find much to enjoy in the way of narrative delights in Judges 4. However, since the concern in a narrative reading is not primarily a historical one, our time will not be spent ranging over the topography of Israel or attempting to identify modern counterparts to certain named cities and other places in the story. We will focus on the details of the story as a story, leaving history to others. It may be that this excessive concern with history has not allowed the story to be heard clearly; that is at least one presupposition with which I begin the reading.

2. I am grateful to D. F. Murray, "Narrative Structure and Technique in the Deborah-Barak Story (Judges IV 4–22)," 155 for many helpful suggestions for my reading. My large debt to him is explicit in the notes to follow. However, my work deviates from his at many significant points.

A second presupposition is my conviction that Hebrew narrators are in the main very good at narration. Thus, I want to hear them out, on their terms, so that I can fairly judge what it is they were trying to do. It may be that this story is no more than a piece of propaganda for a simple religious ideologue, but I will not assume that before I have the chance to read the story. It just *could* be that even propaganda in the hands of superior narrators may rise above the pedestrian level; it may, in fact, rise so far as no longer even to appear to *be* propaganda. We can only make such claims after we have read the text.

Simple propaganda for a simple, clear-cut cause does not easily lend itself to rich preaching. What usually results from such material is a moralistic harangue, which is, of course, itself propaganda. I am attempting in this book to deepen the insights that the Bible can yield to preachers in order that their preaching may take on the qualities of that deepened insight. I shall attempt to demonstrate in the following reading that there really is more than meets the eye in our Bible. Things really are "seldom what they seem!"

Judges 4:1–3

(1) *The Children of Israel again did what was evil in the eyes of YHWH when Ehud died. (2) So, YHWH sold them into the hand of Jabin, king of Canaan, who was king in Hazor. Now the leader of his army was Sisera, and he sat in Harosheth of the Gentiles. (3) The children of Israel cried out to YHWH, because he had nine hundred iron chariots and he oppressed the children of Israel terribly for twenty years.*

As the story commences, it appears that our worst fears are confirmed; the author provides a clear example of the ideological pattern that was enumerated above. A previous judge, Ehud, has died, and immediately the people of Israel have fallen into sin. The author does not even bother to tell us the nature of their evil, but it is bad enough to trigger the second step of the pattern; YHWH sells them into the hand of Jabin, the king of Canaan. Though Jabin is king, the real man with whom the people of Israel must reckon is Sisera, the commander of Jabin's army. What makes Sisera so formidable a foe is his huge force of nine hundred iron chariots, a veritable phalanx of unbeatable machines, that would be to Israelite spears as were Italian tanks to Ethiopian shields in 1935. It is little wonder that he was able to oppress Israel terribly for a long twenty years.

Yet, within this very formulaic portrayal of the situation of Israelite oppression, the narrator presents two possible anomalies. First, the cruel and powerful Sisera is described as "sitting" in his hometown. The Hebrew word can also mean "living" or "dwelling," and one might imagine that one of those would be the best translation at this point. However, the text also says that he merely "had" nine hundred iron chariots; it says nothing about his use of them. Indeed, the picture could be that Sisera is fixed in his city surrounded only by a potentially powerful force of chariots. There is no movement in the scene at all. Could it be that the Israelites have been oppressed by a "paper tiger," a potential power only who is in fact little inclined to act?

Two more insights are provided by the immediate context of our story. Because the narrator uses a familiar frame to launch his story, he urges us to remember that this story is only part of a larger one, the book of Judges. The stories of the two judges that precede this story shed possible light on the beginning we are examining. Ehud, the left-handed Benjamite, was described in the previous chapter as dispatching the obese, relatively immovable Eglon, the king of Moab. In fact, the deed was done when Eglon arose from his seated position to receive what he thought was a divine message (Judg 3:20), but what turned out to be the point of Ehud's concealed sword. Cruel enemies who are found sitting can certainly be defeated (Judg 3:15–30).

The judge who more immediately preceded this story is Shamgar about whom we know only one thing; "he killed 600 Philistines with an ox goad" (3:31). Now an ox goad is a most unlikely weapon, but Shamgar was enormously successful with it. Could it be that 900 iron chariots, the expected means of military victory, might not achieve the expected victory after all?[3] In two subtle ways, then, the narrator warns the reader that "sitting" tyrants are not always safe from defeat and death, and that traditional weapons, no matter how terrifying, may not gain their users the victory. With these possibilities in mind, we now can read the story to come with eyes and ears a bit more alert.

3. Sternberg, *The Poetics of Biblical Narrative*, 273.

Judges 4:4–10

> *(4) Now Deborah, a woman, a female prophet, the wife of Lappidoth, she was judging Israel in that time. (5) She was sitting under the palm of Deborah between Ramah and Bethel near Mount Ephraim. The children of Israel came to her for judgment. (6) She sent word and called for Barak, son of Abinoam from Kedesh in Naphtali, and she said to him, "Has not YHWH, God of Israel, commanded, 'Move! Gather at Mount Tabor, and take with you 10,000 men from Naphtali and from Zebulon?' (7) And I will gather to you at the stream Kishon Sisera, the leader of the army of Jabin, along with his chariots and troops, and I will give him into your hand." (8) But Barak said to her, "If you will go with me, then I will go; but if you will not go with me, then I will not go." (9) So she said, "There will be no glory for you on the road you are going, because into the hand of a woman YHWH will sell Sisera." So Deborah arose and went with Barak to Kedesh. (10) Barak summoned Zebulon and Naphtali to Kedesh; and there went up at his heels ten thousand men. And Deborah went up with him.*

The prologue to the story (vss. 1–3) contained the first three steps of the familiar pattern: sin, punishment, and outcry to YHWH. Thus, we are prepared to hear word of a deliverer.[4] And the word that we get is quite a surprise. "Deborah (the name is in the emphatic first position in the sentence), woman, female prophet, wife of Lappidoth, she" is introduced to the reader. The narrator indicates her gender in five cascading ways. Her name has an obvious Hebrew feminine ending; she is then said to be a woman; she is also a female prophet, using the feminine form of the Hebrew word for "prophet"; she is a wife; the feminine pronoun is included, quite unnecessarily, before the verb. (Even the name of her husband, Lappidoth, has an obvious Hebrew feminine plural ending!) The deliverer of Israel is to be a woman this time! We need not have detailed information about the status of women in ancient Israel to feel the surprise built into the introduction of Deborah. Quite suddenly, the rigid pattern of the book has been made much more interesting by the gender of the deliverer. If we may paraphrase the enemies of Saul, we might at this point ask, "How can this woman save us?" (See 1 Sam 10:27).

Not only is Deborah a rather unlikely candidate to save Israel from Sisera and his nine hundred iron chariots because of her gender; her

4. Ibid., 271.

occupation and practice hardly seem conducive to military struggle either. She is described as "judging" Israel, but her activity at this stage does not at all refer to military conflict. The reader needs to be reminded that the first judge of Israel, Othniel, was described in 3:10 as follows: "he *judged* Israel and went out to war." Deborah is described using the same word, but the result of her "judging" is far different than that of Othniel. "She was sitting under the palm of Deborah between Ramah and Bethel near Mount Ephraim, and the children of Israel went up to her for judgment." Deborah is, in effect, an attorney, quietly adjudicating legal matters under a tree that bears her name. The implication is that she is a famous legal master, so famous and familiar that her outdoor office is known by the title "Deborah's palm tree."

The reader should also note that the narrator describes her as "sitting" under her tree. By so doing, he reminds us of Sisera, who was "sitting" in his hometown in vs. 2. In fact, the structures of the two sentences are identical, thus drawing the two of them together in the reader's mind. But how will these two sedentary individuals be engaged in the struggle that is needed to throw off the Canaanite yoke? We can begin to see that the story presents us with a case of dramatic irony; we know the general outcome of the story thanks to the familiar frame that the author has used to envelope it, but within that frame we see the free play of the imagination of the author as the story moves to its inevitable end. We derive pleasure from our knowledge, and may watch with fascination as we attempt to discover how the determined end will be worked out.

Through five verses we have been introduced to four characters, none who has moved anywhere! Both Sisera and Deborah are sitting, while Jabin and Lappidoth are merely ciphers, only names in the story. Yet, there may be more. Jabin is king, indeed the king of all Canaan, and we expect him to be a major protagonist in the story. After all, in the preceding story of Ehud, Eglon, the king, was the principle antagonist of the hero. But Jabin does nothing, while his underling, Sisera, is at the center of the plot. Lappidoth, husband of Deborah, would be expected as a man to be centrally involved. He is never mentioned again, while his wife is vitally active in the plot. Even at the very beginning of the story, reversal of expectation appears to be a central feature of the tale. We will need to see whether that feature remains prominent as the story progresses.

The activity of the story picks up in vs. 6, as Deborah moves into action. But the action she takes can only be disappointing to a reader who looks for the unexpected deliverer to engage the enemy and defeat him, thus winning freedom for her people. Instead she summons a man to perform the deed. The plot seems to have fallen back to the ordinary.[5] Two men will now fight for control of the land. Instead of an act of deliverance, the reader hears a prophetic summons to "Barak, son of Abinoam from Kedesh in Naphtali." Our interesting and surprising deliverer, a woman, has now become only the instigator of deliverance; the man will do the real work of fighting the foe. And the man summoned is drab at best; we are told he is someone's son and that he lives in Kedesh, no more. The thrill of anticipation that accompanied the elaborate introduction of Deborah is hardly matched by this colorless Barak.

And the divine word to him is also fairly standard. He is told to "gather" *(mashak)* at Mount Tabor and take ten thousand troops from two tribes, one his own and another nearby. But lest he think that he is in control of the battle to come, YHWH, through the mouth of Deborah, announces, "I will gather *(mashak)* to you at the stream of Kishon Sisera, leader of the army of Jabin, and his chariots and troops." Barak is not at all in control of the event about to occur. Deborah proclaims that YHWH commands that Barak gather at Tabor where he will await Sisera who has himself been gathered at the express command of YHWH. The prophetic word concludes with "I will give him into your hand." The battle will be won, but the victory will be YHWH's "gift," not the result of the military prowess of Barak.

All of this language is quite familiar and traditional. The prophet, though female in this case, proclaims the word of God to a chosen leader who is commanded to work for God, but who is also warned not to assume that the human activity is in any way independent of God's gift of victory. Still, God, through Deborah, does promise that Sisera will be given directly into the hand of Barak; he is promised at least a measure of earthly glory. Perhaps on that promise the would-be hero can go out to battle.

If Barak had now gone out to fight, the story would be quite traditional. Instead, he says, "If you will go with me, then I will go; but if you will not go with me, then I will not go." The first word from God was "Go!" or "Leave!" As if Barak has missed all of the commands that followed that single imperative, he uses that verb four times as he flatly refuses to move unless Deborah goes with him. It is a most ignominious way for a hero to begin! By this surprising reaction, the narrator has once again energized the story. Deborah is again thoroughly entangled in the struggle to come,

5. Ibid., 273.

and Barak is not only bland in his introduction but is apparently a coward to boot. If the Israelites are to prevail over the Canaanites and their menacing iron chariots, the victory may not be as simple as we were first led to believe. To face the awesome war machine of Sisera, the Israelites are led by a female court judge and a most reluctant man; the odds against victory seem to be growing by the moment.

Now the prophet, Deborah, becomes the mother Deborah, called upon to reassure the insecure man she has just called to fight. (The reader should note that the poem refers to Deborah as a "mother in Israel" in 5:7.) "I will certainly go with you," she says. Thus, she restores the confidence of the faltering Barak. But she goes on to offer another surprise to the chosen one, a surprise both disconcerting and mysterious. "Nevertheless, there will be no glory for you on the road you are going, for into the hand of a woman YHWH will sell Sisera." What are we and Barak to make of this statement? In vs. 7, in the midst of a prophetic word from YHWH, Deborah, speaking for YHWH, announces that, "I will give him into your hand." Deborah has just assured the uncertain Barak that she will certainly accompany him to the site of the battle. With this assurance Barak may take heart that at least part of the coming victory will be as a result of his risks. But now Deborah takes even that small hope away. Sisera will not be given into Barak's hand after all, but instead will be "sold" by YHWH into the hand of a woman in the same way that YHWH had earlier "sold" the sinning Israelites into the hand of Jabin. Not only, then, will Barak gain no credit for a victory that will be YHWH's alone, neither will he be allowed to defeat the enemy general; that part of the struggle will go to a mysterious woman.

And just who is this woman? Barak and we should certainly assume that the woman is none other than Deborah herself. She is the only woman thus far introduced to us, and she plainly is the most significant figure in the story. However, the fact that Deborah calls her "a woman," rather than making a direct reference to herself, holds open the possibility that some as yet unnamed woman will serve as victor over Sisera.

With the last part of vs. 9, the first real action of the story begins. "Deborah arose (the first time in the story that she is said to have moved from her sitting position) and went with Barak to Kedesh." She had promised the faltering leader that she would go with him, and she fulfills her promise by accompanying him to the place of battle. Once there, Barak proceeds to follow the commands of Deborah, at least at the beginning. He summons the tribes to Kedesh, "and there went up at his heels ten thousand men." When the divine oracle was given, Barak was told first to "gather at Mount Tabor" and then to take ten thousand men. The only indication that Barak has gone to Tabor is found in the verb "go up." The fact that we are not told the actual whereabouts of the Israelite forces until Sisera is told makes us wonder whether indeed Barak is capable of leading the army in the way it is supposed to go. And the narrator adds to our uncertainty in the matter by reminding us that "Deborah went up with him." Barak is far from an independent agent in this affair, and the narrator goes out of his way to continue to remind the reader of that fact.

When we leave the Israelites, led by a frail man and a female legal expert, we are beset with questions. How can this strange duo hope to defeat the forces of Sisera? Though we are assured by the pattern, illustrated by the stories of the book of Judges, that it will happen, the means of its accomplishment are far from clear. Will Barak be able to maintain his courage to accomplish his God-given task, even though he knows that no glory will be his, either in the general victory or in the specific defeat of the enemy leader? Just who is the mysterious woman who has been designated by God to defeat Sisera, and how can any woman defeat a general armed with nine hundred iron chariots?[6] Our simple story, an illustration of the victory of God over the enemies of Israel, has become in fact a complex tale, replete with possibilities and gaps in meaning that the reader is urged to close with further careful reading.

Judges 4:11–16

> (11) *Now Heber the Kenite had separated himself from the Kenites, the descendents of Hobab, the father-in-law of Moses. He had pitched his tent near the oak of Zaanannim which is in Kedesh. (12) Sisera was told that Barak, son of Abinoam, had gone up Mount Tabor. (13) So Sisera summoned all his chariots, nine hundred iron chariots, and all the people with him from Harosheth of the Gentiles to the stream Kishon. (14) Then Deborah said to Barak, "Arise, because this is the day in which YHWH will give Sisera into your hand! Does not YHWH go forth before you?" So Barak went down from Mount Tabor with ten thousand men at his heels. (15) And YHWH routed Sisera and all his chariots and all the army at the edge of the sword before Barak. And Sisera went down from his chariot and fled on foot. (16) But Barak pursued after the chariots and the army all the*

6. Ibid., 275.

> *way to Harosheth of the Gentiles. And all the army of Sisera fell at*
> *the edge of the sword; not even one remained.*

Scene three of the story begins with what looks to be a parenthetical note. We can be certain that this vs. 11 begins a new scene due to the grammatical structure of the sentence. It begins with a circumstantial clause, the subject resting in the emphatic first position.[7] Just as in vs. 4, where the sentence begins, "Now Deborah . . . ," so here in vs. 11 we read "Now Heber . . ." Though it would be possible to read quite smoothly from vs. 10 to vs. 12, avoiding vs. 11 altogether, the impact of vs. 11 at this point is important for several reasons. First, not only does it announce a change of scene grammatically, it shifts the reader's interest from the movements of Deborah and Barak toward the response of Sisera by picturing a man who is a kind of middle term between two warring forces. As we watch Heber move his tents far from his Kenite homeland to settle right near Kedesh, Barak's base of operations, we can picture him poised directly in the line of fire.

The reader might have several thoughts about the surprising appearance of this wandering Kenite. How unfortunate that the poor man has wandered onto the field of battle just prior to a great conflict! However, we know from other references to the Kenites that they are apparently smiths; that is, they make their living by the forging of weapons and tools. What better place for a smith to be than the site of a battle! But the second reason for the appearance of Heber now presents itself; he is a descendant of Hobab, the father-in-law of the great and fabled Moses. Surely a relation of Moses can be expected to side with the Israelites in the coming conflict, if he must choose a side. What role he is to play is far from clear at this point.

A third relation to the surrounding story appears. Deborah was sitting under a famous tree, dispensing judgment, before she announced the prophetic oracle that called Barak into action. Now we are told that Heber pitched his tent near another tree, apparently well enough known to have a name, oak of Zaanannim. In this way the narrator closely ties Heber to Deborah and perhaps to her cause. The reference to Kedesh as the place of Heber's encampment links him to Barak as well.

One final implication can be drawn from the location of this sentence here. The portrait we have seen of the man, Barak, has been less than flattering, while Deborah, the woman, has been the major figure, directing the action through word and deed. Furthermore, she has just warned Barak

7. Murray, "Narrative Structure and Technique in the Deborah-Barak Story," 162.

that the path he is taking as apparent leader of the forces of Israel will bring no glory to him; rather a woman will receive the glory. As another *man* is introduced, the reader might well suspect that this man may not be a character who will play a significant role in the tale.[8]

Finally, in vs. 12, Sisera and we are told where the Israelites have gone; they have "gone up" on Mount Tabor. Like Barak before him in vs. 10, Sisera "summons all his chariots, 900 iron chariots, and all the people with him from Harosheth of the Gentiles to the stream Kishon." As the Canaanite war machine reaches the stream Kishon that the story implies runs at the base of Mount Tabor, Deborah, the prophet, speaks again to Barak. "Arise!" She first issues a command to Barak precisely as she did in vs. 6, and we by this time ought not to be surprised that she needs to tell Barak what to do. Deborah was the first to "arise" in vs. 9; she now commands Barak to join her. He is again the follower, no real leader at all. "This is the day in which YHWH will give Sisera into your hand!" This language of course returns us to vs. 7, the first prophetic call to Barak. There, as well as here, Deborah promises clearly that Sisera will be "given" into Barak's "hand." However, both we and Barak know that in between these two prophetic speeches, Deborah has said something quite different. She warned Barak in vs. 9 that "into a woman's hand" will Sisera "be sold." Which call are Barak and we to believe? Is Deborah here in vs. 14 inciting Barak to action with a false promise? If so, it will not be the last time in the story that a woman issues a false promise to a man.

The last part of her call to Barak is deliciously ambiguous.[9] "Does not YHWH go forth before you?" she cries. To a military leader, charged by a prophet of God to take action against the enemies of that God and promised that the enemy general will be given into his hand, this final cry could only sound like the prophet's assurance that God indeed is leading the divine hero into battle. Thus, the force of the preposition "before" would be "in front of" in a physical sense. However, if this is another of Deborah's warnings to Barak not to expect any glory from the coming engagement, the force of the preposition might be "in front of" in a temporal sense. In other words, one might translate, "But YHWH has already gone before you; i.e., you are too late!" Given Barak's immediate actions, we can be certain that

---

8. Ibid., 179–80 for other possible reasons for the placement of vs. 11.

9. See Sternberg, *The Poetics of Biblical Narrative*, 276–77, for a similar notion that he develops rather differently than I do.

he has heard the former meaning, but the reader ought to be by this time in this story more suspicious. This same ambiguity will recur very soon.

"So Barak went down from Mount Tabor with 10,000 men at his heels." Deborah's call has worked beautifully; Barak now leads his force into battle with the waiting Canaanites. But the very next verb indicates that YHWH was there first! "So YHWH routed Sisera and *all* his chariots and *all* his army at the edge of the sword before Barak." The verb translated "routed" occurs at some very memorable and significant places in the Hebrew Bible. At Exod 14:24, YHWH "looked down on the army of the Egyptians, and routed the army of the Egyptians." The victory over Egypt is the result of God's fiery glance; no human agency plays any role in Egypt's defeat. So also in Exod 23:27, God promises the people of Israel that the people who are living in the land of promise will be "blotted out" before the Israelites, because God will "rout" them with the result that all of their enemies will "turn their back to you." Similarly, YHWH "routed" the Gibeonites which enabled the Israelites to achieve a great slaughter (Josh 10:10). And just as the Philistines were poised to destroy the Israelites as they were being led in worship by the prophet Samuel, "YHWH routed" them (1 Sam 7:10).

In each of these cases, YHWH is alone in victory. Even in the Joshua story, where the Israelites are described as killing many of the enemy themselves, without YHWH's prior "routing," Israel would have been annihilated. So here in Judges 4, YHWH has preceded Barak *both* physically and temporally completely to "rout" Sisera, along with all of his chariots and all of his army. What then is left for Barak? The answer to that question depends again on how one reads the force of the preposition "before." It could imply that the enemy was routed by YHWH *by means of* the swords of Barak and his soldiers. In this understanding, we would see another example like that of Joshua 10. However, it could also imply that YHWH, by means of a mysterious divine sword, routed Sisera "in front of" Barak, that is, right before his eyes. Or, there is one other possibility. If the preposition has temporal force, then it could mean that YHWH routed Sisera before Barak even arrived on the scene. If the latter reading is assumed to be possible, then vs. 16 becomes high farce, as we will see in a moment.

But first the narrator has a bit of fun with Sisera. Barak swept down (*yarad*) Mount Tabor with ten thousand men at his heels. Now Sisera "went down" (*yarad*) from his chariot, and fled "on his heels." The great enemy general, far from "going down with the ship," has fled ignominiously away, and the author painfully compares his "going down" from his chariot in disgrace to Barak's "going down" from Tabor to supposed victory, as well as his solo flight from the battle "on his heels" to Barak's leadership of ten thousand "at his heels." We were warned of Sisera earlier, when he was described as a "sitting" general. Now he is characterized as a coward as well. Thus, *both* generals will have been branded as cowards, and in one possible reading, Barak will now also be seen as a fool.

"So Barak pursued after the chariots and the army all the way to Harosheth of the Gentiles." We were just told in vs. 15 that YHWH had routed all the chariots and all the army, and that the general had fled away from the battle alone. Thus, Barak apparently is pursuing empty chariots and no army at all! And his pursuit ends at Harosheth of the Gentiles, the staging area for Sisera's army. But we were told earlier in vs. 13 that *all* of the men of that place had gone out to fight with Sisera, those same men who were just completely routed by YHWH. Hence, Barak's pursuit of empty chariots and no army ends at a deserted city! There is indeed to be *no* glory for Barak, and we can only chuckle as the general and his men rush up to the city, having overtaken the empty chariots, only to be met by a profound silence from the equally empty town. And, of course, Sisera, the fleeing general, promised to Barak by Deborah, has disappeared.

The last sentence of vs. 16 need not be read that Barak killed "all the army of Sisera." The sentence is quite general in its claim that "there fell all the army of Sisera at the edge of the sword; not even one remained." The narrator here may only be summarizing the results of the action of YHWH's routing. The entire story may possibly leave nothing for Barak at all; he comes up, all too literally, quite empty-handed. But Deborah had warned him and us, after all.

We should perhaps take brief stock of where we are in the story. Our theme for the reading is "things are seldom what they seem." The reading, thus far, has been illustrative of that theme. Three male characters have been introduced. Two have been shown to be cowards, while one has not been delineated for us to date. The one character who has demonstrated initiative and real power and leadership has been Deborah, a female magistrate whom we first saw sitting under her palm tree, dispensing justice. Yet, this Deborah has not been above a half-truth to get the cowardly Barak to do what God has called him to do. Barak, as a man and a supposed leader of men, would have been expected to be the hero of the tale. He is at best anti-hero, as we have seen, acting only when commanded, and when acting arriving too late to make a real difference. The great enemy, Sisera, has proved to be a coward, escaping from the battle with the Israelites alone and on foot. He was of course several times identified to us as the owner of nine hundred iron chariots. The fact that we last saw him hopping out of his chariot and fleeing on foot indicates that all of those chariots finally meant very little to our deeper understanding of this man. In short, the narrator has led us a merry chase, introducing to us characters and expectations for them, and then systematically dashing those expectations to the ground.

At least four anomalies remain. First, who *is* the mysterious woman into whose hand Sisera is supposed to fall? Or was all of that a red herring, dished up by Deborah to Barak to prevent him from vaunting himself as the real victor in the battle against the Canaanites? Second, what will become of the coward, Sisera? If we can believe Deborah, and that is by no means certain, he will fall into a woman's hand. Third, will Barak ever gain some measure of glory, or is he doomed always to be too little and too late? Fourth, what is the role of Heber the Kenite, the relative of Moses, who moved into the field of battle? These questions, and perhaps others as well, urge the reader on in the story to discover possible ways of finding answers.

Judges 4:17–2[10]

> (17) Sisera fled on his heels to the tent of Jael, wife of Heber, the Kenite, because there was peace between Jabin, king of Hazor, and

10. I cannot resist sharing with my readers a limerick from a collection of limericks by D. R. Bensen:

> A patriot lady named Jael
> Drew her courage, though feeling quite frail,
> From deep in her viscera,
> Afflicting proud Sisera,
> With terminal migraine by nail.

At two points I think Bensen has misread the text. I offer my corrected version.

> There was a young lady named Jael,
> Who drew courage, not being a male,
> From deep in her viscera,
> Afflicting proud Sisera,
> With terminal migraine by nail.

There is no evidence in the text that Jael was a patriot, and even less indication that she felt frail. Quite the opposite is the case, as we shall see. What is more significant is that she is not a male, and hence is this story is probably not a coward! Still, Bensen's work is delightful, and I commend it to you.

> *the family of Heber, the Kenite. (18) Jael went out to meet Sisera,*
> *and said to him, "Turn aside, my lord, turn aside to me. Do not be*
> *afraid!" So he turned aside to her into her tent. She covered him with*
> *a rug. (19) And he said to her, "Give me please a little water to drink,*
> *because I am thirsty." So she opened a skin of milk and gave him a*
> *drink. Then she covered him. (20) Then he said to her, "Stand at the*
> *door of the tent. If any man comes and asks you, 'Is there any man*
> *here?' you say, "No one."' (21) So Jael, wife of Heber, took a tent peg,*
> *and put a mallet in her hand. She came to him quietly. She drove the*
> *peg into his skull, so that it stuck in the ground, while he was fast*
> *asleep, exhausted. Thus he died. (22) Here came Barak, pursuing*
> *Sisera, and Jael went out to meet him. She said to him, "Move! Let*
> *me show you the man whom you are seeking." He came to her, and*
> *there lay the fallen Sisera, dead with a peg in his skull!*

The previous scene ended with the flat statement that no one remained from the army of Sisera, but, as we were already told in vs. 15, Sisera himself had fled from the battle "on foot." Now, again, as if our narrator does not want us to miss the point, he reiterates that "Sisera had fled on foot" (or literally "on his feet"). His vaunted chariots, his security blanket, are no more. He is alone, on foot, and the only survivor of a complete catastrophe for the Canaanites.

And where does the coward end up? At the tent of "Jael, wife of Heber the Kenite." Like a bolt from the blue, the narrator introduces to us a brand new character, a woman, the wife of Heber the Kenite. Immediately, our mind wanders back to the introduction of Deborah, the wife of Lappidoth. Now we see for the first time the role of Heber; he is husband of a woman, and that is all. Like Lappidoth, he appears only in name, and like Deborah, Jael will play a vital and active role in the denouement of the story. Thus again are men in the story reduced to ciphers in relation to the women.

Could Jael be the woman of whom Deborah spoke? And because her introduction is reminiscent of Deborah's, will she play a similar role in the story? While we ponder these questions, the narrator hurries on to inject an important and ominous fact. Sisera has come to this tent for one very clear reason: "there was peace between Jabin, king of Hazor, and the family of Heber the Kenite." Sisera will be safe in the tent of Jael, because he is protected under the hallowed and ancient tradition of hospitality. It is this tradition that caused Lot, the nephew of Abraham, to offer his virgin daughters to the lusty mob in Sodom in the place of the strangers who had sought protection under his roof (Gen 19:1–23). As grotesque as his offer might appear to us, it validates the terrible demands that hospitality makes on those who strive to live by its rules. A similar story is found in Judg 19:15–21.

By all expectations, Sisera can expect a warm and cordial welcome in the tent of a woman whose family has a pledge of peace with the subjects of Jabin. And her welcome is far more than cordial. She "comes forth" out of the tent in order to "meet Sisera," and says to him, "Turn aside, my lord, turn aside to me. Do not be afraid." With disarming assonance, Jael urges Sisera with a repeated sibilant word that sounds something like his own name. The Hebrew reader/listener would hear, "*surah, surah*, Sisera." She closes her entreaty with "do not be afraid," a phrase filled with irony, considering that she has spoken it to a coward, so filled with fear that he has abandoned his army to the rout of YHWH.[11] Soggin speaks of the woman's weakness that cannot "prevent the enemy general from entering her tent."[12] Given the portrait of Deborah that the narrator has given us, and the pictures of the two men, Barak and Sisera, any talk of the "weakness" of Jael could only be said to be premature. Indeed, the repeated and reassuring speech with which she meets the fleeing man should rather be seen as part of her attempt to lure him to his doom. Succeeding events in this part of the drama make that reading of her actions certain.

And he responds precisely to her entreaty and "turns aside" into her tent. Immediately she covers him with . . . something. The word is used only here in the Hebrew Bible and is usually translated "rug." That will do, but it is only a guess.[13] We can assume that she performs this action, because she is trying to hide him. The picture of the trembling and terrified general, sweating profusely under a woman's "rug," adds to the ridiculous image of the would-be hero. No wonder his first words to Jael are a request for a drink. His request is a polite one. "Please give me a little water, because I am thirsty." In response, Jael opens a skin of milk and gives him a drink. Whether her goal is to exceed his request with a greater gift or to use the warm milk (or buttermilk or yogurt—any of these products could be meant here) for some kind of soporific, bringing on a drowsiness that would further her murderous intent, can only be decided within the confines of the whole text.[14] However, at least one thing can certainly be said at this point.

11. Murray, "Narrative Structure and Technique in the Deborah-Barak Story," 183.

12. Soggin, *Judges*, 78.

13. For a host of possibilities of translation, see Burney, *The Book of Judges*, 92–93.

14. Both Burney, *The Book of Judges*, 93, and Boling, *Judges*, 97–98, ascribe to the

Once again, expectations have been dashed. The clear request is for water; the clear answer is milk.

The last word of vs. 19 is a bit troublesome. "And she covered him." We might naturally think that she wraps him up again in the rug. That is the implication that Soggin draws when he "translates" "and she covered him again."[15] Yet, the text says nothing about "again." Is it not possible that she covered him herself with her own body? This behavior of seduction would follow directly from the wooing words chosen by Jael to get Sisera into her tent in the first place. If this is a possible implication, there would then be some lapse of time between vss. 19 and 20. After offering both milk and herself to the frightened general, he would begin to calm enough to plan what he should do now. In fact, with his speech in vs. 20, the general begins to sound much more like a general again. His polite speech has been replaced by a word of command. "Stand at the door of the tent," he begins. Like a general ordering his troops, Sisera addresses Jael with a masculine imperative verbal form. Though many scholars see this as some kind of spelling error, it could be the narrator's way of suggesting the increasing ease of Sisera.[16]

As he continues his commands to Jael, his speech is filled with irony, although completely unintentional on his part. The irony is sharply pointed at Sisera himself. "If any man comes and asks you, 'Is there any man here?' you say, 'No one.'" Sisera is obviously terrified still of the coming of any *man*. If he knew what we know about the men and the women in this story, he would be much more afraid of the seductive woman with whom he is alone in the tent. And there is still another irony here. The narrator told us in vs. 16 that "not even one remained" after the destruction of the Canaanites by the rout of YHWH. Sisera's command to Jael that she respond to a question about the presence of anyone in the tent with the negative particle in Hebrew "no one" or "nothing," suggests all too well that Sisera is in reality no one, and that soon he will be in fact no one, when the devious Jael kills him in his sleep.

Sisera ceases his commands. The narrative shifts our gaze to Jael, who up to now has wooed Sisera into her tent and has treated him with superb

---

theory that the milk was intended to help Sisera sleep. Boling, in a memorable phrase, says, "She duped him and she doped him." Sternberg, *The Poetics of Biblical Narrative*, 282, sees the offer of milk as part of Jael's "solicitude for the fugitive," part of her act intended to lead to murder.

15. Soggin, *Judges*, 62 and Sternberg, *The Poetics of Biblical Narrative*, 282.

16. Murray, "Narrative Structure and Technique in the Deborah-Barak Story," 183n.

hospitality as befits the alliance that exists between Jabin and her husband, Heber. But now we watch in horror as "Jael, wife of Heber, took a tent peg, and placed her mallet in her hand, came to him quietly, and drove the peg into his skull so that it stuck in the ground." We have again been duped by the story as surely as Sisera has been duped by Jael! The supposed hospitality of Jael was all a charade; every action she performed for Sisera was only designed to bring him to his doom, a grisly death at the hand of a clever woman. Her call to him to join her in the tent, her calming word to him that he need have no fear, even perhaps the use of her own body, her pretense that she would stand guard at the tent door, watching for any man who might come to harm the general, all have been done to arrange the murder. The shock of this unforgettable act is all the greater in that we are almost totally unprepared for its occurrence. We of course remember the words of Deborah that "YHWH will sell Sisera into the hand of a woman." The word "hand" was highlighted three times earlier, once in the prophecy just named and twice to Barak, as Deborah promised that into *his* hand Sisera would fall. But the woman's hand has indeed triumphed over Sisera, that hand that grasped the mallet and drove the tent peg into the sleeping general's head. The very unspecific phrase "into one's hand" has assumed a horrible specificity with Jael's treacherous killing.

And the deed was performed, "while he was fast asleep, exhausted."[17] To portray the general asleep is to increase the reader's revulsion at the act. And the word the narrator chooses to describe Sisera's last sleep is an unusual one, occurring a very few times in the Hebrew Bible. In all of its uses (save once in Prov 10:5), there is some direct supernatural agency involved. Jonah's sleep in the hold of the ship occurs in the midst of a divinely arranged storm at sea (Jonah 1:5). In Dan 8:18 and 10:9, the prophet falls into a "deep sleep" on his face to the ground when he hears a heavenly voice. In Ps 76:5, the psalmist hymns the power of God at whose rebuke "all the men of war sank into sleep."

Also, the noun that is based on this same verbal root, while rare, is notable for its supernatural connections. At Gen 2:21, YHWH God brings a "deep sleep" on the soil creature, from which is made the man and the woman. In Job 4:13, Eliphaz, one of Job's "friends," describes a chilling vision he had one night, after a "deep sleep" had fallen on him. Elihu, a latecomer to the debate in the book of Job, is so impressed by Eliphaz's

17. The text is difficult here. For detailed discussion, see Grossfeld, "A Critical Note on Judges 4:21," 348–51, and Nicholson, "The Problem of tsanah," 259–65.

words that he borrows them literally and uses them himself in his attacks on the sufferer (Job 33:15). In one of Isaiah's assaults against Jerusalem (here symbolically called Ariel), he claims that YHWH has "poured out on the prophets the spirit of a deep sleep" (Isa 29:10). Finally, in 1 Sam 26:12, David is enabled to steal Saul's spear and water jug out from under the king's very nose because "a deep sleep from YHWH had fallen on them."

These obvious supernatural relationships in the use of this word in all of its forms makes the reader suspicious that Sisera's sleep is not only the natural result of physical exhaustion due to a long run from the battle and/or perhaps a sexual tryst with Jael. The prophet Deborah, speaking the word of YHWH, had assured us that Sisera would fall into the hand of a woman. By using this particular word for "sleep," the narrator subtly suggests that God remains operative in the consummation of the divine will. The narrator closes the appalling scene with the unnecessary, but chilling word, "Thus he died." Sisera has in fact, and more literally than we ever imagined, been felled by the hand of a woman.

Despite some interesting historical attempts to suggest a treaty between Heber and Israel, along with the one between Heber and Jabin mentioned specifically in the text,[18] the fact remains that in this story as we read it, the author gives us no clue at all why Jael murdered Sisera in direct defiance both of hospitality laws and the treaty between her family and the people of Jabin. We can only see that she is the woman predicted by Deborah who was destined to best Sisera. And for the storyteller, it is crucial that no explanation be given beyond that one for her behavior. His theme is "things are seldom what they seem." The murderous Jael shockingly and hauntingly caps the narrator's interest in that theme in this particular telling of the story.

And finally, Barak arrives on the scene, at last "pursuing Sisera." In vs. 16, after the rout of YHWH, Barak pursued, "the chariots and the army," while Sisera fled on foot. Poor Barak has gone after empty chariots and an army already routed and has pursued them all the way to an empty city. At last, he gets on the right track, but the word that just precedes his arrival, "thus he died," tells the reader that once again Barak is too late; there will be no glory for him here either. We should note, too, that the narrator uses a familiar device in vs. 22 to indicate a shift in the point of view of the scene. The Hebrew *hinneh*, often translated "behold," is a marker for a change in

18. Fensham, "Did a Treaty between the Israelites and the Kenites Exist?," 51–54. Both Boling and Soggin approve the results of Fensham's analysis.

perspective. First, the word moves us from within the tent to the outside, allowing us to witness the arrival of Barak, and to witness Jael's quick movement outside to see Barak and to take control of the scene. The second use of *hinneh* again shifts the point of view, this time from Jael to Barak. When he enters the tent, on command from Jael, the text reads literally "Behold Sisera fallen dead." We see the grim scene just as Barak sees it.[19]

"And Jael went out to meet him, and said to him." Jael, the narrator tells us, acted toward Barak precisely as she acted toward Sisera. Because we do not know any other motivation for Jael's murder of Sisera than the prophecy of Deborah, we hold our breath for a moment, wondering if the clever Jael is about to entice still another foolish and trusting man. But Jael does not turn on her feminine charm this time. She commands Barak, and her first word is "Move!" It is exactly the same first word given to Barak by Deborah in vs. 6 when she first called Barak to do the will of YHWH. Barak is destined to be commanded to action exclusively by women. "I will show you the man whom you are seeking," she cried. Barak comes to her and "there was Sisera, fallen dead, with a peg in his skull."[20]

Death at the hands of a woman was most ignominious in the ancient world. For example, when the evil Abimelech is crushed by a millstone, dropped from a tower by a woman, he demands that his armor-bearer kill him with his sword, "lest men say of me, 'A woman killed him'" (Judges 9:54).

Barak is not only the first witness to the murder of Sisera by Jael, he is completely silent in the face of it. Sisera had warned Jael to beware any man who asked after his presence in the tent, but before Barak can frame any question or make any comment, Jael has taken control of the scene. Thus, physically, temporally, and verbally, Barak is too late to be any sort of hero. His only speech in the entire story is found at vs. 8, and it is now to be seen as revelatory of his character. "If you go with me, I will go. But if you will not go with me, I will not go." This whine to Deborah is more than simple reluctance. It is an announcement to the reader just what sort of man Barak is; he can do nothing on his own, and anything that he is finally able to do leads only to emptiness.

And Sisera also spoke in such a way as to reveal his character to us. His command to Jael to answer any questions about his presence in her tent

19. Berlin, *Poetics and Interpretation of Biblical Narrative*, 63.

20. See Soggin, *Judges*, 67 and Burney, *The Book of Judges*, 93, for discussion of the tools as uniquely women's instruments.

with the one Hebrew word translated "no one," says in fact who and what he is—no one. We found him sitting (vs. 2), we observed him "fleeing" (vss. 15 and 17), and we leave him "fallen dead," a tent peg embedded in his skull. At the end, he, along with his army and his vaunted chariots, simply do not exist. One might say with Murray that Barak and Sisera are "united in a tragic fate: ignominious subjection to the effective power of a woman."[21]

This fact may further be demonstrated by noting that both Deborah's and Jael's speeches are rife with imperative verb forms, and their commands are invariably followed by the men to whom they are given. Barak utters no word of direct command, while the only spoken command given by Sisera to Jael is certainly obeyed; but the very next thing she does is to murder the commander in his sleep! Expectations are dashed; things are seldom what they seem. Here one finds the thrust of this narrative.

Judges 4:23–24

> *(23) So on that day, God subdued Jabin, the king of Canaan, before the children of Israel. (24) And the hand of the children of Israel went harder and harder against Jabin king of Canaan until they cut off Jabin king of Canaan.*

It is quite obvious that the final two verses of the narrative form the editorial frame that began in vss. 1–3. However, the origins of the material are far less interesting to this reading than the effect of the material on the text as we have it. And I think it can be well demonstrated just how appropriate to the story this particular ending is. I shall assume that the narrator has taken this framing material, and has adapted it for his special use for this narrative.

Several important effects of this formulaic ending may be noted.

1. The narrator returns us to Jabin, the so-called king of Canaan. It is easily demonstrated that there never was a "king of Canaan."[22] But, as I have said all through this reading, the factual history that may or may not lie behind the story is of less value for understanding the story than a careful examination of the "facts" of the story world as the text provides them. In the world of the story, Jabin is called either king of Canaan or, one time, "king

---

21. Murray, "Narrative Structure and Technique in the Deborah-Barak Story," 173.

22. Boling, *Judges,* 94.

of Hazor" (vs. 17). Jabin plays no active role in the story at all, even though he is regularly mentioned (vss. 2, 7, 17, 23, 24). Because it was into the "hand of Jabin" that Israel was sold by YHWH, Jabin is apparently used as a symbol for the current enemy of Israel, the Canaanites. We have seen that this great king does precisely nothing in the story, and we have witnessed that his general, the mighty Sisera, *becomes* himself precisely nothing, as he "prophetically" announces in vs. 20. Jabin does nothing, and his general comes to nothing. Thus does the author effectively denigrate the enemies of Israel. Also, Jabin ends up just as his general does; the children of Israel "cut him off." In effect, they destroy him completely. Sisera apparently speaks for his king as well as himself in vs. 20.

2. Note that the ambiguity of the preposition "before" recurs in vs. 23. "God subdued Jabin before Israel." How does the narrator mean this "before"? Certainly, God subdued Jabin "in front of," or in "the presence of" Israel. Perhaps God subdued Jabin, "in the face of" Israel; that is Israel had a direct hand in the subduing. However, we have seen time and again that Barak, at least, played no role at all in any subduing. Of course, the women, Deborah and Jael, did certainly have a large role to play. If we confine our gaze to the women, the preposition could have that force. Then, too, God subdued Jabin "before" Israel did; that is, God acted before Israel could. This is also true, especially when we remember vs. 15 and God's rout of the Canaanites. It is best to say that all three of these possible meanings may be included in the force of the word, and by using the word here again, the narrator nicely summarizes the ambiguities of just who are the real actors in the drama.

3. "So the hand of the children of Israel pressed harder and harder against Jabin." It is surely not coincidental that the word that has occurred so frequently and so importantly appears at the end of the story—the word "hand." God first sold Sisera into the "hand" of Jabin. Deborah then promised Barak that God would give Sisera and his forces into his "hand." Then, however, she warned him that God would sell Sisera into the "hand" of a woman. Yet, she reiterated her promise (falsely?) to Barak that God would after all give Sisera into his "hand." But, in fact, the woman Jael, with the instrument of death in her "hand," dispatched Sisera. Now, the "hand" of the Israelites is said to go harder and harder against Jabin. Even though God is not mentioned in vs. 24, it would be a serious mistake to assume that the Israelites are now independently applying the pressure of their own "hand" against Jabin, apart from God's direction. This is so for two reasons.

First, the five other uses of the word "hand" have been clearly engineered by God, either directly or slightly less directly through the agency of the prophet Deborah or the woman Jael. We should not suddenly assume that God has ceased control of the "hand" of the people. Second, a familiar verb is twice used in this final verse, the verb *halak*, "to go." It is this verb, we will remember, that Barak used four times in his refusal to act independently when called prophetically to do so (vs. 8). After witnessing the actions of Barak, and listening to his only speech of vs. 8, we should not think that the children of Israel have suddenly become the sole agents of their "hand." The narrator warns us, by the use of that leitmotif from Barak's speech, that God will still be desperately needed to aid an ever-faltering Israel.

Murray concludes his reading of Judges 4 with the following comments:

> The narrator is not concerned to give a report of any kind; nor is he primarily concerned with history as such: his concern is to narrate a story which appeared to him to comment with telling irony on the roles of two men and two women, and thus on the relationship of men and women in general.[23]

My own reading of the story has confirmed this conclusion of Murray's. However, I do not think that he goes quite far enough in delineating what is most basically at stake for this narrator as he tells this story. I find Robert Polzin closer to the basic thrust of the narrative, although his statement refers to the entire book of Judges; and the ways in which he arrives at his judgment took a very different path than the one we have just traversed. Still, his conclusions about the whole book of Judges are stated in the midst of his discussion of this story. "The Book of Judges is a major turning point in the narrative (he means the long story from Deuteronomy to Kings) because it self-consciously reveals the weaknesses and limitations of all ideologies, however necessary and unavoidable they may be."[24] Thus, as our reading has attempted to demonstrate, the goal of this narrative is the subversion of expectations, in Polzin's terms, to "reveal the weaknesses and limitations of all ideologies."

It is thus not only the ideology of "weak woman" and "strong man" that is pilloried in the story, although that certainly happens. The expectations of all traditional hierarchies are called into question. Three pairs of two persons are presented in the tale. In actuality, the first, and perhaps most

23. Murray, "Narrative Structure and Technique in the Deborah-Barak Story," 185.

24. Polzin, *Moses and the Deuteronomist*, 162.

prominent pair, is really a trio. Deborah is connected to two men. She is "wife of Lappidoth," but her husband means nothing either to her or to the story. Even his name, with its feminine Hebrew ending, adds to the feminization of the entrance of Deborah, as our discussion of vs. 4 attempted to indicate. More important is her relationship to Barak, the would-be hero of Israel. She commands, while he tries to obey. Yet, he is able to do nothing at all; her warning that he would achieve no glory is exactly fulfilled. He plays no role in the victory over Sisera and the Canaanites, and is too late to have any hand in the personal demise of the general. Against all expectations, Deborah, woman and legal expert, is the instigator and sustainer of the human part of the struggle against the Canaanites. Barak is thoroughly secondary to her in every way.

The second pair is Jabin and Sisera. Given the preceding story of the defeat of Eglon, a king, the reader could have expected that Jabin, king of Canaan, would play a major role in this story as well. He does not. His expected role is usurped by his oppressive general, Sisera, who is introduced to us as powerful and cruel, having oppressed Israel for twenty years. Yet, when the general acts, he is shown to be a coward, whose final act in life is to be tricked and murdered by a woman. Sisera acts in the expected place of Jabin, but he acts poorly, thus doubly dashing our expectations for him.

The third pair is Heber and Jael. The former is introduced to us in vs. 11, but no mention is made of his wife. Thus, the narrator builds our expectations that Heber, who, as the male head of the clan has made an alliance of some kind with Jabin, will play a major role in the ensuing conflict between Israel and Canaan. He does not. Our expectations are dashed as Jael, the mysterious woman predicted by Deborah, appears as the major figure, pushing her husband into the shadows just as Deborah's decisive actions rendered her husband a cipher.

Perhaps one more subversion of the reader's expectations should be noted. We all know that Deborah is the judge, and we thus expect her to be the heroine of the story. On the surface, one might conclude that she is in fact so portrayed. However, structurally, only Jael interacts with the two important males in the story. Only Jael commands them both to do her bidding, which they both proceed to do. Only Jael's decisive murder of Sisera finally enables Israel's "hand" to press ever harder against Jabin. It could thus be said that Jael is the ultimate heroine of the tale. Perhaps the poetic account of the story was more correct than usually is recognized when it called Jael "most blessed among women" (Judg 5:24).

Nearly every step of the way, whether in terms of grammar or characterization or plot, this narrator is in the business of the subversion of expectations. A story that appeared on the surface to be so straightforward has yielded a rich harvest of the narrator's art with the express purpose of illustrating the title of our reading: things are seldom what they seem.

The story sermon based on this passage will have that basic thrust of the narrative in mind as the story is retold.

You Just Never Know: A Story Sermon on Judges 4

I hardly know where to begin. You asked me to tell you the story of Deborah and Barak and Sisera, and Jael, and I am happy to do that. But you think the story is just like all those other stories in the old book of Judges. You expect to hear a familiar tale of how Israel sinned, how God handed them over to some foreign enemy or other, how God then sent a great hero to save them from their oppression, and how after the hero died, Israel went right back to sinning again. Well, this story sounds sort of like that, but it isn't finally about that at all. So, before I start, I want to warn you to listen carefully, because you are liable to be surprised. You see, in this story things are seldom what they seem. And after all, you just never know. Ready?

Once upon a time, a long time ago and far away, the Israelites were up to their old tricks; they were sinning up a storm. Now don't ask me what they were doing, because I am just too embarrassed to tell you! There are children here, you know. They were acting in these unmentionable ways, because that old hero, Ehud, the guy who had stuck his short sword into the immense belly of that nasty king Fat Calf, had died. Those Israelites were always ready to go off half-cocked when they had no one to keep an eye on them, so true to form God sold their sorry selves into the hands of another enemy king, this time named Jabin. He was king in the town of Hazor, but he thought he was king of all of Canaan. Well, he wasn't, but he was mean enough anyway.

He had this general, Sisera, who was even meaner than he was. And his meanness was backed up with nine hundred iron chariots. Those old Israelites could hardly get any iron at all in those days, so their bronze swords and shields were hardly a match for Sisera's wagons of death, so Sisera had his way with them for twenty years. Boy, did those Israelites need a hero now! God was ready to give them one again, but God had a surprise this time.

You see, there was this female attorney, who was a female prophet, married to a guy with a very feminine name, who herself was called Deborah. I suppose you get the point that she was a woman! A funny sort of hero this time, wouldn't you say? She was well-known in the community of Israel, dispensing justice day after day, sitting under a palm tree called by her own name. But one day, this Deborah stopped her attorney work, and moved into the role of prophet. Next thing you know, she is calling on the Israelite general, Barak, to rouse himself, to muster his troops, ten thousand of them, near Mount Tabor in order to meet that nasty Sisera and his terrible chariots in mortal combat near the stream bed called Kishon. Just to urge him along, she held out the carrot that any self-respecting general would be thrilled to pursue: she assured him that this call was from God and that God had promised that Barak's own hand would win the victory.

I suppose you imagine that General Barak went right out and issued the orders for troops to muster, for swords to be sharpened, for shields to be repaired, for supply wagons to be ordered, and all those other things that generals do to prepare for battle when called upon to do so. If you imagined that, you would be wrong. The General heard Deborah's words all right, and I guess he understood them, but you will never guess what he said to her. "Well, Deborah, if you will go with me to the battle, I will go, but if not, forget it. I will head back to the barracks and call it a day." I can tell you right now that all who heard that liver-livered little comment were flat convinced that Deborah had gotten the wrong man for the job and that God had better rethink the whole thing. I mean, choosing a woman was one thing, but her choice of a coward to lead the troops was something else.

She looked that snake right in his eyes, and said, "OK, I will go with you, but I warn you, Barak. You will get no glory from this fight, because God has it in mind to sell Sisera into the hand of a woman!" Well, nobody knew what to make of that! First she says that God will give Sisera to Barak, as a way to goad him into the battle. And then after he tried to weasel out of it, she shifted gears and said to him that he will get nothing out of it, and moreover, a woman will get the glory! Did she mean herself? If so, why didn't she say so? I tell you it was no way to begin a campaign; there were too many unanswered questions. Why this woman? Why this cowardly general? Who is this other woman, if there is indeed another woman? But they went anyway. I mean, you just never know, do you?

At the scene of the battle another man showed up, Heber. He was there, I guess, because he was a smith, that is, a worker with metal. Battle sites always attracted them. He was also a member of the Kenite clan, who had a history of metal working, going back to the long-ago days of Hobab, great Moses' father-in-law in Midian.

Sisera, upon hearing of the Israelite troop movements, got his chariots together and moved toward Kishon, just as Deborah had promised. And Deborah went back to her prophetic talk to Barak, "Get up! This is the day when God will give Sisera into your hand. The Lord is really going out before you!" I wonder whether old Barak was really confused now! First, she promised victory by his hand, then he was promised he would get nothing but the hand of a woman would prevail, and now he is told again that it is back in his hand! Deborah seemed to playing the general like a drum! Well, it worked, I guess, because Barak finally got his army together and rushed down the mountain to join the battle.

But he had a surprise in store. You see, God had already routed the chariots of Sisera, I mean all nine hundred of them, before Barak was able to get there! It was just like God's rout of those Egyptian warriors at the Sea of Reeds so long ago. The victory was God's alone, and Barak was left with ten thousand troops with nothing to do. Oh, and Sisera, that mean and nasty Canaanite general with his invincible iron chariots? He had high-tailed it off the battle site, rushing on foot as fast as his scared little legs would carry him. Meanwhile, Barak took his army in hot pursuit of the Canaanites. But the problem was that he was chasing a routed army of empty chariots all the way back to the empty city of Harosheth of the Gentiles! Deborah was right; Barak was getting nothing out of this whole thing!

The desperate Sisera ran like a rabbit in whatever direction would take him away from battle, and stumbled, as luck, or something, would have it into the camp of Heber, the smith. Now Heber had a wife—oh, you didn't know that?—and her name was Jael. Now that name means "YHWH (God of Israel) is God." I suppose you could say that if Sisera had studied his Hebrew a bit more carefully, he might have avoided this particular tent and this particular woman, but he didn't. Now Jael was a looker, it was said, and a lively sort of woman, if you get my drift. That is all I am going to say, since there are children here. She kind of sashayed out of the tent and urged the fleeing general to come on in. What she said was, "Sura, sura, Sisera," in her best sibilant tones. Now if you have been studying *your* Hebrew, you will hear right away what that means. "Turn aside, turn aside, Sisera," but it sounds much more fetching in Hebrew, don't you think? Well, he did.

As he hurried into the tent, she hid him under a blanket of some sort, because he was trembling and sweaty from his escape. He asked her for some water, but she gave him some yogurt instead, since that was the right thing to do, hospitality-wise. It is, as you all know, very important to be hospitable, especially to strangers, even if they are cowardly foreign generals. After he drank the soothing yogurt right down, she covered him up. Now I don't know if that means she covered him up again with the blanket or whether she herself covered him, you know . . . well that is all I am going to say. The children, you know. He ordered Jael to stand at the door of the tent and warn him if any man happened to come by. If that occurred, he demanded that she lie and say, "No man is here." Well, in a kind of funny way, there really was no man there, Sisera being a coward and all, something rather less than a man. Whatever, the exhausted general went to sleep, I mean sound asleep.

I hardly know how to tell this next part. It is so surprising, so shocking, so blood-curdling, well . . . Here goes. Jael grabbed onto a tent peg with one hand—you know, one of those large wooden stakes we use to keep the tents anchored into the ground—and with the other hand snatched a mallet we use to drive the stakes in. She walked very quietly over to the sleeping Sisera, placed the tent stake onto his temple, right where the vain was throbbing with the regularity of sleep, and she . . . Well, let's just say he died. That sleep just went on forever.

And just then poor old Barak showed up, once again too little and too late! Jael stepped out of the tent to greet him—wonder if she still had that stake and that mallet in her hands—and invited him into the tent to see what was left of Sisera. Barak went in, and once again realized that this was just not his day! He did not, for a fact, get anything out of this whole event, and God really did give victory into the hand of a woman, I mean quite literally into her mallet-wielding hand. I guess Barak left, but he just disappears from the story.

And what a story it is! You never know, do you? You just thought that God always acted in the usual ways, sending males to do the work, using generals and chariots and swords and battles to effect the divine will. But not always, not always. Both the male generals here are cowards, and the other mentioned men are ciphers. Deborah is the initiating heroine and Jael is the active heroine. When generals are cowards and women show their power, the world's expectations are dashed, and the settled order of society is decidedly unsettled. Open your eyes, my friends. With this God, you just never know.

> I did not comment on the story as it progressed, because, as you can see, it is just told straight through, by an unnamed teller, who uses his first-person power to comment on the story as it was revealed in our detailed reading of the story. He (or she) has the right both to tell the story of the Bible, but also to comment upon it, since the teller is omnipotent; he/she both knows the story and can share his/her understanding of its meaning. It would be a good exercise for you to go back through the sermon and note those places where the teller has injected his/her comments on the story that were gleaned from the reading. I tried to inject those comments fairly regularly in order to keep the telling alive and not thereby allow the story itself to overwhelm the reasons for the telling of it.
>
> This device of a first person/third person teller is a good one, since it allows for immediate telling with comment. This is unlike the role of a character who is in the story, who can only relate the story as a part of it, and hence has limited knowledge. Of course, you could also use a teller who is part of the story, but not a main part. I might here, for example, have selected a soldier from one of the armies as my teller. But, as you can see, he would not be omnipotent, as my unnamed teller is, who knows the whole story and knows what he/she thinks it means.
>
> I find this sort of sermon exhilarating, because it puts parts of my imagination into play that too often lay dormant in my preparation of other kinds of sermons. So now I commend the fun to you!

Is This an Effective Story Sermon?

I do think this sermon on Judges 4 is an effective one. It does provide a measure of biblical context as it relates the tight ideology of the editors of Judges, but says clearly that that ideology is shattered by the remarkable storyteller's attack on the expected realities of God and God's chosen agents. There can be little doubt in the story that the God who calls all hierarchies into question is front and center. There are no easy universalisms of human behavior here. All ontological neatness is challenged directly in the reading and the telling. Those who live lives without simple closure can hear in this sermon the possibility of a new way to live in a world that too often demands closure. The surface ease of the story, God's call and God's victory, is troubled by the undercurrents of the surprise of that call and the surprise of the means for the victory. The sermon does far more than tell the story; it comments on it all along the way, conceptualizing theologically concerning the nature of God and God's actions in the world. The call for change comes in the sermon's demand that the hierarchies created by the human world are not forever fixed, nor are they from God. "My ways are not your ways, says YHWH," and this sermon announces that divine truth in ways that attempt to help us think again about our hierarchical ordering of the world.

Conclusion

MY GOAL IN THIS book has been to present the possibility of a story homiletics, a way to present especially the narratives of the Hebrew Bible in some fresh and memorable ways. I have suggested that this style of preaching is actually old in the histories of synagogue and church and remains, if carefully and sensitively done, a viable means of communicating the great word of the gospel in the twenty-first century. While some would say that such a story approach can only work in a community of those who already have a deep acquaintance with the ancient biblical traditions, I would say that story sermons may be among the more important tools to re-story the church, to provide the old basic materials in a new way in order that communities of faith can once again begin to work on the central issues of their calling, rooted in the substance of that calling from God, as recorded in the Bible's stories.

It is no accident that the African-American church, along with Jewish synagogues, have year after year found their very lives in the story of the Exodus from Egypt. For African-Americans, who were forcibly removed from their ancestral homelands, ferried across the vast waters of the Atlantic packed into leaking ships, and put to back-breaking, soul-numbing labor in a new land, the triumph of God over Israelite oppressors could not fail to speak directly to their hearts, as they yearned for a similar freedom. Similarly, Jewish practice has had at its very heart an annual recital of that same story, since in nearly every age and place, Jews have found themselves trapped in oppressive places, crying out for God's power to free them. And it was the story itself, told and retold, that stood at the base of that cry. At celebrations of Passover in places of mortal danger, the story was recounted. In hidden forests of the south, slaves told that same story, and sang songs based on it, calling on God for a freedom only God could give. This story all church and synagogue goers must know well enough to tell it at times when telling is dangerous and at times when telling is necessary in order to keep the flames of hope alive.

Elie Wiesel, Nobel-prize winning author, holocaust survivor, begins one of his novels, *The Gates of the Forest*, with a justly famous rabbinic story. It can serve as a fitting epitaph for this volume that urges the power of story.

> When the great Rabbi Israel Baal Shem-Tov saw misfortune threatening the Jews, it was his custom to go into a certain part of the forest to meditate. There he would light a fire, say a special prayer, and the miracle would be accomplished and the misfortune averted. Later, when his disciple, the celebrated Magid of Mezritch, had occasion, for the same reason, to intercede with heaven, he would go to the same place in the forest and say: "Master of the Universe, listen! I do not know how to light the fire, but I am still able to say the prayer." And again the miracle would be accomplished. Still later, Rabbi Moshe-Leib of Sasov, in order to save his people once more, would go into the forest and say: "I do not know how to light the fire, I do not know the prayer, but I know the place and this must be sufficient." It was sufficient and the miracle was accomplished. Then it fell to Rabbi Israel of Rizhyn to overcome misfortune. Sitting in his armchair, his head in his hands, he spoke to God: I am unable to light the fire and I do not know the prayer; I cannot even find the place in the forest. All I can do is to tell the story, and this must be sufficient." And it was sufficient.

So tell the stories with energy and imagination, with joy and hopefulness, with smiles and with tears. Weisel also writes, "God made man (and woman), because he loves stories."[1] And I believe that that "he" (and I hasten to add "she") refers both to us humans and to God.

---

1. Both the rabbinic story and the aphorism are found on the unnumbered frontispiece of Weisel's *The Gates of the Forest*.

Bibliography

BIBLIOGRAPHIES ARE IN THE main reports of those books and articles that proved especially important for the composition of a particular book. This particular bibliography is by no means comprehensive; many other books and articles formed the bedrock of the work, but remained firmly in the background of a long time of learning. The listed works are those that were used directly in the formation of this work for this time in the author's life.

READING THE OLD TESTAMENT'S STORIES

Achtemeier, Elizabeth. *Preaching from the Old Testament*. Louisville: Westminster John Knox, 1989.

Alter, Robert. *The Art of Biblical Narrative*. New York: Basic Books, 1981.

———. *The Art of Biblical Poetry*. New York: Basic Books, 1985.

———. *The Five Books of Moses*. New York: Norton, 2004.

———. *The David Story*. New York: Norton, 1999.

Auerbach, Erich. *Mimesis: The Representation of Reality in Western Literature*. Translated by Willard R. Trask. Princeton: Princeton University Press, 1953.

Bailey, Kenneth E. *Poet and Peasant* and *Through Peasant Eyes: A Literary-Cultural Approach to the Parables in Luke*. Combined Edition. Grand Rapids: Eerdmans, 1980.

Bar-Efrat, Shimon. *Narrative Art in the Bible*. JSOT Supplimental Series 70. Sheffield: Almond, 1989.

Berlin, Adele. *Poetics and Interpretation of Biblical Narrative*. Bible and Literature Series 9. Sheffield: Almond, 1983.

The Bible and Culture Collective, *The Postmodern Bible*. New Haven: Yale University Press, 1995.

Booth, Wayne C. *A Rhetoric of Irony*. Chicago: University of Chicago Press, 1974.

———. *The Rhetoric of Fiction*. Chicago: University of Chicago Press, 1961.

Breech, James. *The Silence of Jesus: The Authentic Voice of the Historical Man*. Philadelphia: Fortress, 1983.

Brichto, Herbert Chanan. *Toward a Grammar of Biblical Poetics*. New York: Oxford University Press, 1992.

Burrows, Millar. "The Literary Category of the Book of Jonah." In *Translating and Understanding the Old Testament: Essays in Honor of Herbert Gordon May*, edited by Harry Thomas Frank, 80–107. Nashville: Abingdon, 1970.

Crossan, John Dominic. *Cliffs of Fall: Paradox and Polyvalence in the Parables of Jesus.* New York: Seabury, 1980.

Duke, Paul Simpson. *The Parables: A Preaching Commentary.* Nashville: Abingdon, 2005.

Ellingsen, Mark. *The Integrity of Biblical Narrative.* Minneapolis: Fortress, 1990.

Fokkelman, J. P. *Reading Biblical Narrative.* Louisville: Westminster John Knox, 1999.

Fretheim, Terence E. *The Message of Jonah.* Minneapolis: Ausburg, 1977.

Good, Edwin M. *Irony in the Old Testament.* Philadelphia: Westminster, 1965.

Gros Louis, Kenneth R. R. *Literary Interpretations of Biblical Narratives*, vol 1. Nashville: Abingdon, 1974.

———. *Literary Interpretations of Biblical Narratives*, vol 2. Nashville: Abingdon, 1982.

Gunn, David M. *The Fate of King Saul.* JSOT Supplimental Series 14. Sheffield: University of Sheffield Press, 1980.

Gunn, David M. and Danna Nolan Fewell. *Narrative in the Hebrew Bible.* New York: Oxford University Press, 1993.

Hirsch, Jr., E. D. *Validity in Interpretation.* New Haven: Yale University Press, 1967.

Holbert, John C. "Deliverance Belongs to Yahweh." *JSOT* 21 (1981) 59–81.

———. *Preaching Old Testament: Proclamation & Narrative in the Hebrew Bible.* Nashville: Abingdon, 1991.

Kugel, James L. *The Idea of Biblical Poetry.* New Haven: Yale Universssity Press, 1981.

Lacocque, Andre and Pierre-Emmanuel Lacocque. *Jonah: A Psycho-religious Approach to the Prophet.* Columbia: University of South Carolina, 1990.

Magonet, Jonathan. *Form and Meaning: Studies in Literary Techniques in the Book of Jonah.* Bible and Literature Series 8. Sheffield: Almond, 1983.

Miscall, Peter D. *1 Samuel: A Literary Reading.* Bloomington: Indiana University Press, 1986.

Robertson, David. *The Old Testament and the Literary Critic.* Philadelphia: Fortress, 1977.

Scholes, Robert, and Robert Kellogg. *The Nature of Narrative.* New York: Oxford University Press, 1966.

Scott, Bernard Brandon. *Hear Then the Parable: Commentary on the Parables of Jesus.* Minneapolis: Fortress, 1989.

Skinner, John. *A Critical and Exegetical Commentary on Genesis.* International Critical Commentary. Edinburgh: T & T Clark, 1910.

Sternberg, Meir. *The Poetics of Biblical Narrative.* Bloomington: Indiana University Press, 1985.

TeSelle, Sallie. *Speaking in Parables.* Philadelphia: Fortress, 1975.

Trible, Phyllis. *Rhetorical Criticism: Context, Method, and the Book of Jonah.* Minneapolis, Fortress, 1994.

———. *God and the Rhetoric of Sexuality.* Philadelphia: Fortress, 1978.

Von Rad, Gerhard. *Genesis, Revised Edition.* Westminster: John Knox, 1973.

Via, Dan Otto, Jr. *The Parables: Their Literary and Existential Dimension.* Philadelphia: Fortress, 1967.

Wilder, Amos N. *Early Christian Rhetoric.* Cambridge: Harvard University Press, 1964.

———. *The Bible and the Literary Critic.* Minneapolis: Fortress, 1991.

———. *Jesus' Parables and the War of Myths.* Philadelphia: Fortress, 1982.

Preaching the Old Testament's Stories

Allen, Ronald J. *Patterns of Preaching: A Sermon Sampler*. St. Louis: Chalice, 1998.

Bausch, William J. *Storytelling: Imagination and Faith*. Mystic: Twenty-Third Publications, 1984.

Berndt, Brooks. "The Politics of Narrative." *Homiletic* 29:2 (2004) 1–11.

Boomershine, Thomas E. *Story Journey: An Invitation to the Gospel as Storytelling*. Nashville: Abingdon, 1988.

Brown, David M. *Dramatic Narrative in Preaching*. Valley Forge: Judson, 1981.

Broadus, John A. *On the Preparation and Delivery of Sermons*. 4th ed. San Francisco: Harper & Row, 1979.

Buechner, Frederick. *Telling the Truth: The Gospel as Tragedy, Comedy, and Fairy Tale*. San Francisco: Harper & Row 1977.

Buttrick, David. *Homiletic Moves and Structures*. Philadelphia: Fortress, 1987.

Camery-Hoggatt, Jerry. *Speaking of God: Reading and Preaching the Word of God*. Peabody, MA: Hendrickson, 1995.

Chapman, Raymond. *Godly and Righteous, Peevish and Perverse*. Grand Rapids: Eerdmans, 2002.

Chatfield, Donald F. *Dinner with Jesus and Other Left Handed Story Sermons*. Grand Rapids: Zondervan, 1988.

Cox, James W. *Preaching: A Comprehensive Approach to the Design & Delivery of Sermons*. San Francisco: Harper & Row, 1985.

Craddock, Fred B. *Overhearing the Gospel*. Nashville: Abingdon, 1978.

Davis, H. Grady. *Design for Preaching*. Philadelphia: Fortress, 1958.

Edwards, O. C. *A History of Preaching*. Nashville: Abingdon, 2004.

Eslinger, Richard L. *A New Hearing: Living Options in Homiletic Method*. Nashville: Abingdon, 1987.

———. *Narrative Imagination: Preaching the Worlds that Shape Us*. Minneapolis: Fortress, 1995.

———. *The Web of Preaching: New Options In Homiletic Method*. Nashville: Abingdon, 2002.

Freedman, David Noel. *The Anchor Bible Dictionary*. New York: Doubleday, 1992.

Freeman, Harold. *Variety in Biblical Preaching*. Waco, TX: Word, 1987.

Jensen, Richard A. *Telling the Story: Variety and Imagination in Preaching*. Minneapolis: Augsburg, 1980.

———. *Thinking in Story: Preaching in a Post-Literate Age*. Lima: C.S.S. Publishing, 1993.

Lischer, Richard. "The Limits of Story." *Interpretation* 38 (1984) 26–38.

———. *The End of Words The Language of Reconciliation in a Culture of Violence*. Grand Rapids: Eerdmans, 2005.

Long, Thomas G. *The Witness of Preaching*. Louisville: Westminster/John Knox, 1989.

———. *Preaching and the Literary Forms of the Bible*. Philadelphia: Fortress, 1989.

———. "What Happened to Narrative Preaching?" *Journal for Preachers* 28.4 (2005) 9–14.

Lose, David J. "Narrative and Proclamation in a Postliberal Homiletic." *Homiletic* 23.1 (1998) 1–14.

Lowry, Eugene L. *The Sermon: Dancing the Edge of Mystery*. Nashville: Abingdon, 1997.

———. *The Homiletical Plot The Sermon as Narrative Art Form*. Expanded Edition. Louisville: Westminster John Knox, 2001.

McClure, John S. "Narrative and Preaching: Sorting it All Out." *Journal for Preachers* (1991) 24–29.

Mitchell, Henry H. *Black Preaching: The Recovery of a Powerful Art*. Nashville: Abingdon, 1990.

———. *The Recovery of Preaching*. Nashville: Abingdon, 1977.

Reynolds, David S. "From Doctrine to Narrative: The Rise of Pulpit Storytelling in America." *American Quarterly* (1980) 479–98.

Rose, Lucy Atkinson. *Sharing the Word: Preaching in the Roundtable Church*. Louisville: Westminster John Knox, 1997.

Salmon, Bruce C. *Storytelling in Preaching: A Guide to the Theory and Practice*. Nashville: Broadman, 1988.

Schlafer, David J. *Surviving the Sermon: A Guide to Preaching for Those Who Have to Listen*. Cambridge: Cowley, 1992.

Steimle, Edmund A., et al. *Preaching the Story*. Philadelphia: Fortress, 1980.

Thompson, James W. *Preaching Like Paul: Homiletical Wisdom for Today*. Louisville: Westminster John Knox, 2001.

Williams, Michael E. *A Storyteller's Companion to the Bible*. Vol. 1. Nashville: Abingdon, 1991.

Willimon, William H., and Richard Lischer. *Concise Encyclopedia of Preaching*. Louisville: Westminster John Knox, 1995.

Wilson, Paul Scott. *The Practice of Preaching*. Nashville: Abingdon, 1995.

———. *Preaching and Homiletical Theory*. St. Louis: Chalice, 2004.

Other Texts Cited

Achtemeier, Elizabeth. *The Old Testament and the Proclamation of the Gospel*. Philadelphia: Westminster, 1993.

Allen, Ronald J., and John C. Holbert. *Holy Root, Holy Branches: Christian Preaching and the Old Testament*. Nashville: Abingdon, 1995.

Bensen, D. R. *Biblical Limericks*. New York: Ballantine, 1986.

Boling, Robert G. *Judges*. Anchor Yale Bible Commentaries. Garden City, NY: Doubleday, 1975.

Bond, Ronald B., and David L. Jeffrey. *A Dictionary of Biblical Tradition in English Literature*. Grand Rapids: Eerdmans, 1992.

Botterweck, G. Johannes, and Helmer Ringgren. *Theological Dictionary of the Old Testament*. Grand Rapids: Eerdmans, 1986.

Bright, John. *The Authority of the Old Testament*. Carlisle: Paternoster, 1997.

Broadus, John A. *On the Preparation and Delivery of Sermons*. New York: Harper & Row, 1979.

Brueggemann, Walter. *Genesis*. Interpretation. Atlanta: John Knox, 1982.

Brynmor, F. Price and Eugene A. Nida. *A Translator's Handbook on the Book of Jonah*. London: United Bible Societies, 1978.

Burney, C. F. *The Book of Judges*. London: Rivingtons, 1920.

Campbell, Charles. *Preaching Jesus: New Directions for Homiletics in Hans Frei's Postliberal Theology*. Grand Rapids: Eerdmans Press, 1997.

Crites, Stephen F. "The Narrative Quality of Experience." *AAR* 39 (1971) 291–311.

Davis, Ellen, *Wondrous Depth: Preaching the Old Testament*. Louisville: Westminster John Knox, 2005.

Dudder, F. Homes. *Gregory the Great: His Place in History and Thought*. 2 vols London: Longmans, Green and Co., 1905.

Fensham, F. C. "Did a Treaty Between the Israelites and the Kenites Exist?" *BASOR* 175 (1964) 51–54.

Fox, Everett. *The Five Books of Moses*. New York: Schocken, 1995.

Franklin, Benjamin. *Autobiography*. New York: Holt, 1916

Goldsworthy, Graeme. *Preaching the Whole Bible as Christian Scripture*. Grand Rapids: Eerdmans, 2000.

Gowan, Donald. *Reclaiming the Old Testament for the Christian Pulpit*. Atlanta: John Knox, 1980.

Grossfeld, Bernard. "A Critical Note on Judges 4:21." *ZAW* 85 (1973) 348–51.

Klein, Ralph W. *1 Samuel*. Waco, TX: Word, 1983.

Landes, George. "The Kerygma of the Book of Jonah." *Interpretation* 28 (1967) 3–31.

McCarter, P. Kyle, Jr. *1 Samuel*. Anchor Yale Bible Commentaries. Garden City, NY: Doubleday, 1980.

McClure, John S. *Other-wise Preaching: A Postmodern Ethic for Homiletics*. St. Louis: Chalice, 2001.

Murray, D. F. "Narrative Structure and Technique in the Deborah-Barak Story (Judges IV 4–22." *Supplements to VT* XXX Leiden: Brill, 1979.

Nelson, Richard. *Deuteronomy*. Old Testament Library. Philadelphia: Westminster John Knox, 2007.

Nicholson, E. W. "The Problem of *tsanah*." *ZAW* 89 (1977) 259–65.

Pelikan, Jaraslov and Paul Lehman. *Luther's Works*. American Edition in 55 vols. St. Louis and Philadelphia: Concordia and Fortress, 1955.

Polzin, Robert. *Moses and the Deuteronomist: Deuteronomy, Joshua, Judges*. A Literary Study of the Deuteronomic History, Pt. 1. New York: Seabury, 1980.

Randolph, David. *The Renewal of Preaching*. Philadelphia: Fortress, 1969.

Rice, Charles L. *Imagination and Interpretation: The Preacher and Contemporary Literature*. Philadelphia: Fortress, 1970.

Rose, Lucy Atkinson. *Sharing the Word: Preaching in the Roundtable Church*. Louisville: Westminster John Knox, 1997.

Soggin, J. Alberto. *Judges*. Old Testament Library. Philadelphia: Westminster Press, 1981.

Speiser, Ephraim. *Genesis*. Anchor Yale Bible Commentaries. Garden City, NY: Doubleday & Co., 1964.

Stowe, Harriet Beecher. *My Wife and I*. New York: Riverside, 1967.

Towner, W. Sibley. *Genesis*. Westminster Bible Companion. Louisville: Westminster/John Knox, 2001.

Vawter, Bruce A. *On Genesis: A New Reading*. Garden City, NY: Doubleday, 1977.

Weisel, Elie. *The Gates of the Forest*. New York: Holt, Rinehart and Winston, 1966.

Westermann, Claus. *Genesis 1–11: A Continental Commentary*. Minneapolis: Augsburg, 1984.

———. *Basic Forms of Prophetic Speech*. Philadelphia: Westminster, 1967.

Williams, Jay G. *Understanding the Old Testament*. New York: Barron's, 1972.

Wilson, Paul Scott, *Preaching and Homiletical Theory*. St. Louis: Chalice, 2004.

———. *The Practice of Preaching*. Nashville: Abingdon, 1995.

Bibliography

Wolff, Hans Walter. *Obadiah and Jonah.* Continental Commentaries. Minneapolis: Augsburg, 1986.

Young, Carlton R. *The United Methodist Hymnal.* Nashville: Abingdon, 1989.

Made in the USA
Lexington, KY
22 August 2016